LA SANTA
Muerte

ABOUT THE AUTHOR

Tomás Prower is a graduate of the University of California, Santa Barbara. He holds two degrees: one in global socioeconomics and the other in Latin American and Iberian studies. A natural-born globe trekker, he sought additional education at the Universidad de Chile while working as a translator for their literature department. Due to his fluency in English, French, and Spanish, he was given the opportunity to become a cultural liaison for the French Government in South America between France, the United States, Chile, Peru, and the member states of Mercosur. During this time, he traveled extensively in the Amazon Jungle, learning as much as he could about the region's indigenous peoples.

Upon returning to the United States, Tomás moved to Reno and became the External Relations Director for the American Red Cross in Nevada. Since then, he has returned to Los Angeles where he works as a mortician while pursuing his fascination for the macabre. When he is not dealing with the recently deceased, he studies the magical and religious practices from cultures all over the globe and writes every chance he gets. His world travels continue to provide the spiritual outlook behind his eclectic style of witchcraft and the philosophic subject matter in his writings.

LA SANTA
Muerte

Unearthing the Magic & Mysticism of Death

TOMÁS PROWER

Llewellyn Publications
Woodbury, Minnesota

FIRST EDITION
Eighth Printing, 2023

Cover design: Ellen Lawson
Cover illustration: Sam Guay, additional imagery: iStockphoto.com/25314496/©bennyb
Editing by: Lunaea Weatherstone
Interior photographs by Anthony Louis of Twenty-Deux

Llewellyn Publications is a registered trademark of Llewellyn Worldwide Ltd.

Library of Congress Cataloging-in-Publication Data
Prower, Tomás.
 La Santa Muerte : unearthing the magic & mysticism of death / Tomás
Prower. — First Edition.
  1 online resource.
 Includes bibliographical references and index.
 Description based on print version record and CIP data provided by
publisher; resource not viewed.
  ISBN 978-0-7387-4670-8 () — ISBN 978-0-7387-4551-0 1.
Death—Miscellanea. 2. Death (Personification) 3. Grim Reaper (Symbolic
character) I. Title.
 BF1442.D43
 133.4'3—dc23
      2015021777

Llewellyn Publications
A Division of Llewellyn Worldwide Ltd.
2143 Wooddale Drive
Woodbury, MN 55125-2989
www.llewellyn.com

Printed in the United States of America

Contents

Introduction

Death has always been the single greatest motivating force in all of human history. Whether it be our basic instincts of hunting and gathering to fend off starvation or an ultimatum of war that serves as a rallying cry to unite us for the cause of the greater good, nothing has shaped the history of humankind like death. Moreover, many of humankind's greatest cultural and architectural wonders have been created in honor of death: the pyramids of Egypt, the mausoleum and terra-cotta army of Emperor Qin Shi Huang, the Al-Masjid al-Nabawi, the Taj Mahal, St. Peter's Basilica, Westminster Abbey, and much more. Even if not directly dedicated to death, many of the greatest books, songs, and achievements throughout the ages have been the result of a single person, aware of his or her own inevitable mortality, who wanted to make a mark on the world and leave a legacy by which they would be remembered.

As humans, one of our greatest powers over all other living beings on earth is our foresight, but this evolutionary gift comes at a great cost. Yes, we are the only animals that possess advanced logical reasoning skills and can envision far beyond our current reality, but we are also the only ones that know that we are destined to die. While many people, unable to cope with this predetermined fate, paralyze themselves with fear and anxiety, a growing number of people see it as an ultimate source of power.

These people are the devotees of the Spirit of Death herself, La Santa Muerte. Rather than shy away from thoughts of our impending mortality, those who are devoted to Death utilize this uncomfortable foresight, like the greats of history, to make a difference in the world here and now. Thinking "we have forever" might be more cheerful, but in no way does it compare to the motivational power of "we're only here temporarily."

Understandably, the modern veneration of Death (the Spirit of Death with a capital "D," not the physical act of death with a lowercase "d") is a type of faith that is still mostly underground and in the shadows of society. This is because death makes people uncomfortable, especially in the Western world. With medical breakthroughs and stronger environmental laws, infant mortality rates are at an all-time low while the average lifespan continues to rise, thus making death all the more unfamiliar. And even when a death does occur, we have an entire funeral industry to take care of all things postmortem so we never have to interact with death or see it on a daily basis. In the not too distant past, it would have been very difficult to find someone who wasn't well familiar with death and their own mortality, but nowadays, the first time many of us confront the reality of our own death is at the DMV when we have to check that box deciding whether or not to be an organ donor.

Death has become so unfamiliar to us that it is seen as almost unnatural, when it is the most natural thing in the world. Not too long ago, I was also a "death denier." I had graduated from the University of California, Santa Barbara with a degree in global socioeconomics and another degree specializing in Latin American studies. My life focus was on *living* people and how they interacted with other *living* people. Even when I lived in Mexico, Chile, Argentina, and the Amazon jungle, Westernization was everywhere. Death was hardly ever present to inconvenience the lives of the living, let alone openly venerated by a group of devotees. It wasn't until I returned to Los Angeles that I came face to face with the mystery school of La Santa Muerte ... on a dare, no less.

One of my best friends had been looking for new and exciting things to do while hanging out in the heavily Latino-populated gateway cities of L.A. He mentioned a place that was rumored to hold midnight Masses by candlelight around a giant statue of the Grim Reaper. Growing up with a love for the macabre, nurtured by movies like *The Addams Family* and *Beetlejuice*, I was instantly fascinated, and he dared me to go in and talk to one of "them," a devotee of Death. Admittedly, I was a bit scared, especially by the Grim Reaper statue that went to the ceiling and took up a good sixth of the building, but my anthropological curiosity was stronger. That subsequent conversation with a priestess of Santa Muerte lasted only a couple of minutes, but a fire had been lit within me to learn more. I wanted to be like them, able to talk openly about death without fear and using its mysteries to live a more connected, magical life here and now during my living years. Thus began my initiatory journey into the mystery school of La Santa Muerte.

This book is the accumulation of everything I have learned since then about La Santa Muerte, her unique brand of death magic, and the growing number of people who use her dark philosophy as a credo for life. The morbid and magical information found within these pages is the result of not only objective academic research and interactions with modern devotees, but also of firsthand experience as a devotee myself and practitioner of cross-cultural religious and spellcrafting traditions.

The book is written in a three-part format designed to be approachable to novice practitioners of magic, veteran spellcasters, students of academia, and those just curious about this macabre veneration of Death and its philosophies for the living.

Part I introduces you to the cross-cultural sociology of how humans have interacted with death and the historical origins of how people first came to venerate La Santa Muerte.

Part II dives into an overview of the mechanics involved in death magic, giving a general tutorial of the magical side of La Santa Muerte, including what tools we use in spellcasting, how we use them, why we use them, and the scientific psychobiological effects they have on us.

Part III contains actual spells from the Santa Muerte tradition, arranged in a step-by-step format that is easy to follow, covering everything from money, love, and healing to protection, lust, and legal magic, and more.

Until now, the history and magic of La Santa Muerte have been kept buried underground, shrouded in a black veil of esoteric Latino mysticism. With their spellcrafting tradition condemned as "infernal," those who dare to seek out Death as an ally have disguised it as an eccentric form of Roman Catholicism to hide its darker secrets from the judgmental public. A veneration of the macabre that unabashedly counts the LGBT community, feminists, prostitutes, thieves, drug smugglers, prisoners, police, and armed services members among its most devout. You are about to learn the unearthed wisdom of Death that has for so long been predominately passed down in Spanish language oral traditions.

So come and face your fears head-on. To deny death is to deny one of the greatest unchanging truths of life. It is a truth that, once accepted, will lead to a greater understanding of life. Much like the innumerable funerary rituals throughout the world, the philosophy of La Santa Muerte is intended for the living. It is not a manual on how to die, but rather, how to enjoy life because it won't last forever. We are here on earth to be human, not gods. And the human experience involves death, a lesson not to be feared, only understood. Now is your chance to learn the lessons of death without having to die. Let your old life and preconceived notions of death pass away. Your new, magical life is about to begin.

PART I

History and Mythology

1

The Patron Saint of Sinners

"The fear of death is worse than death."
~ROBERT BURTON, *THE ANATOMY OF MELANCHOLY*

What does Death look like to you? I don't mean your actual, physical death with a lowercase "d." I mean Death with a capital "D," the Spirit of Death itself ... or rather, herself. You see, to me and millions of people all over North and South America, Death is a woman. Not just any woman. She is a skeletal figure who wears a black, hooded cloak and carries a scythe. Yes, our image of Death is the Grim Reaper, or better yet, the Grim Reapress (a title coined by Dr. Chesnut in his book *Devoted to Death*).[1]

If you're like most people, this frightening embodiment of Death is probably something you wouldn't want to dwell upon, much less venerate, and yet in the U.S. alone there are hundreds of thousands of people who not only dedicate their lives to her magic and philosophy but also see her as a comforting mother figure. And this number is growing exponentially. But why? When there are so many religions and deity figures in the world, why do countless people choose this Día de los Muertos (Day of

---

1. Chesnut, Andrew R. *Devoted to Death: Santa Muerte, the Skeleton Saint*. New York: Oxford University Press, 2012.

the Dead) embodiment of Death as their patron deity and supreme source of both inner peace and personal empowerment?

Very rarely is someone a devotee of La Santa Muerte from birth. Most of us come from other faiths which, for one reason or another, were not able to provide us with the answers we are searching for. Many of us come from faiths that outright and unabashedly condemned us, saying that due to our professions, past mistakes, or sexual identity/orientation, we are not welcome into their good graces. Some of us, desperate for a miracle, turned to La Santa Muerte as a last resort and witnessed her special brand of magic firsthand, ever after becoming staunch believers. And still others have come due to curiosity about the mystery school of La Santa Muerte, only to discover that her worldview and spiritual philosophy resonate with their souls. No matter the origins of our relationship with La Santa Muerte, we are all devotees because we have communed with her and worked with her magic well enough to know that she is very real and very willing to help us if we call upon her.

When I was a child, I never would have guessed that I'd be writing a history on La Santa Muerte, let alone a book of spells whose efficacy I have experienced personally. With an Irish father and a Mexican mother, I grew up a good Catholic boy. In fact, I even attended Catholic school all my life until college. I learned about Jesus and the Bible, I received Holy Communion every Sunday, I confessed my sins to a priest, and I believed that to worship anything other than a single, masculine God was utterly blasphemous. Little did I know at the time that my childhood world of holy mysteries, incense, saints, and ceremony was preparing me quite well for a future steeped in magic.

Like many of La Santa Muerte's devotees, I was drawn to her through a sense of not belonging. I was always a sensitive kid who was too feminine to fit in with the boys, too masculine to fit in with the girls, and too smart for my own good. Like anyone, I just wanted to be accepted. So, from outside the crowd, I studied human behavior, psychology, pop culture, and everything I could to figure out what everyone else seemed to just inherently know: how to fit in. And the more I learned, the more I realized that it was all an illusion. *No one* knew what to do to fit in, so everyone just pretended to act like everyone else in the hopes that they'd be accepted, giving up personal interests and self-expression for comfortable conformity.

This realization changed my life forever. If fitting in meant having to sacrifice who I truly was and confine myself into this box of constantly worrying what other people think of me, it just wasn't worth it. If I hadn't learned that lesson, I would never have found the fortitude necessary to be an open devotee of La Santa Muerte. Because, let's be honest, practicing a form of witchcraft that invokes the aid of the Spirit of Death will attract a lot of negative attention. The more I lived my own life, the more other people began to think highly of me—ironically, though, the less I cared about what other people thought of me.

Sure, I didn't care if human people didn't like me, but having the One True God not liking me was something else entirely. Growing up Catholic, the concept of original sin, wherein humanity's natural state is that of wickedness and sinfulness, just seemed wrong. So did the notion that God is some ever-disapproving parent who could become eternally angered over the smallest thing. To me, anger is such a petty human emotion for anyone to have, let alone Almighty God. I began to question all that I had just passively accepted to be true about the nature of the Divine. If I was created with such a damning flaw as original sin, then maybe God isn't actually all-powerful. If I was purposely created with that flaw, then God must not be a loving deity. If God is all-powerful and loving, then why was I created to be damned? And if God is somehow neither all-powerful nor loving, then why worship him and call him God at all?

These questions are not unique to me. Every devotee in the mystery school of La Santa Muerte has asked these same questions, and there are as many answers as there are devotees. The vast majority of us have been labeled "bad" by society and by organized religions, so we had to look inward for our answers. My answer, after much soul searching, resulted in the acceptance of God as an all-powerful and loving deity (though not the only deity) and that it was his self-proclaimed interpreters here on earth who were twisting his words into something ugly, hateful, and untrue. If you ask any other devotee of La Santa Muerte, they will proudly tell you that they also believe in an all-powerful and loving deity beyond La Santa Muerte. For most, that deity is the masculine, solitary God of Christianity. For others, that deity is actually a pantheon of multiple all-powerful and (in their own way) loving deities. And some of us even adhere to a nebulous deity that is ultimately an ineffable and intangible energy beyond human comprehension, such as the Tao. To believe in La Santa Muerte and adopt her as a patron saint/ deity, we do not have to abandon our prior religion; we only have to bring her into our current religion and be willing to learn the eclectic secrets of her mystery school.

But still, the question remains: why choose to dedicate your time, energy, and life to La Santa Muerte and her mystery school when there are so many other deities and philosophies of life to follow? What makes her, the Spirit of Death, so attractive, especially when death is something so naturally abhorrent to us as living beings?

Santa Muerte Philosophy 101

I admit that when I first heard of La Santa Muerte through word-of-mouth gossip from a close friend who was also on the spiritual path, I was terrified. Dark magic was not something for me. Being a good person, light magic seemed more appropriate. I studied the esoterics of more popular faiths and philosophies, including Islam, Judaism, Buddhism, Taoism, and Wicca, while staying far away from anything that smelled of Christianity. It wasn't until I met the ancient/alternative Christianity philosopher B. Dave Walters that I discovered the mysticism and magic of ancient Christianity as it was before it became distorted as an organized institution. He encouraged me to seek out and study the dark side of magic as a natural companion to the light side. In Hermeticism, this is called the Law of Polarity, meaning that everything has an equivalent opposite, and by studying one end of the pole, you can better understand the other end. Without an up, how can there be a down? How can you appreciate health if you haven't experienced sickness? How could good exist without labeling something else as bad?

How is it possible to truly understand the light if you cannot truly understand the darkness? Thus, if I wanted to understand the mystery of life, I had to first understand the mystery of death.

Truth be told, when I first began exploring the ways of modern Death worshippers, I was expecting to see a bunch of somber Goths who wore all black, read Edgar Allan Poe, and obsessively watched Tim Burton movies. I was laughably naïve about the cult, and, like most people, I had an incorrect assumption about the modern devotees of La Santa Muerte. Yes, we do evoke the Spirit of Death and cast spells, but we look just like anyone else. And, in truth, we *are* just like anyone else, except we have a different philosophic outlook on life.

Essentially, we believe that the world is good. We believe that the divine energy (God, the universe, the Tao, etc.) is perfect, and since that divine energy is in everything, everything is perfect. Everything is also perfectly connected to and depends on everything else in a symbiotic relationship for harmony and survival. The problems of life result from a self-disassociation with everything else, the belief that you are separate from all other things. This sense of separation leads to constant judgments and comparisons as being either better or worse than all other things. If you believe that you are better than something, it often leads to the self-justification of harmful deeds. This can be exemplified by some people's belief that they (mankind/males) are more important than all other forms of life, and so they treat animals, the environment, and females as objects only to be utilized for their own enjoyment. Conversely, if you believe that you are worse than something, it *also* often leads to the self-justification of harmful deeds. This can be exemplified by some people's belief that having less money than other people makes them less important or worthy than those other people, and so they do anything to obtain more money and thus become "better" via robbing, cheating, or killing.

By believing that we are all equally connected in the web of life, harming others becomes much less appealing since the destruction of a single strand ultimately affects the whole and threatens the stability of the entire web. A more philosophical concept of this belief is popularly known in dharmic religions as karma. Everything you do will eventually come back to you. If you do good deeds, then good things will happen to you. If you do harmful deeds, then harm will happen to you. Thus, a devotee of La Santa Muerte and a practitioner of her magic would, at the very least on a selfish level, not want to cause harm to another because it would result in harm ultimately coming to themselves. Although not all devotees explicitly call it karma, this ethic of cosmic reciprocity is a main tenet of working with La Santa Muerte and understanding how to utilize her magic.

This overarching idea of treating others as equals might seem like a utopian ideal of a young New Age religion, but in truth, it is a guiding ethic in all religions, most commonly known as the Golden Rule. Some examples are:

Buddhism

"Treat not others in ways that you would find hurtful."
—Udanavarga 5.18 [2]

Christianity

"So whatever you wish that men would do to you, do so to them."
—Matthew 7:12 (Revised Standard Version Catholic Edition) [3]

Confucianism

"Try your best to treat others as you would wish to be treated yourself, and you will find that this is the shortest way to benevolence."
—Mencius VII.A.4 [4]

Hinduism

"This is the sum of duty: do not do to others what would cause pain if done to you."
—Mahabharata 5:1517 [5]

---

2. http://www.buddhanet.net/

3. https://www.biblegateway.com/

4. http://nothingistic.org/

5. http://www.sacred-texts.com/

Islam

"None of you truly believes until you wish for others what you wish for yourself."

—Hadith 13 [6]

Jainism

"One should treat all creatures in the world as one would like to be treated."

—Mahavira Sutrakritanga 1.11.33 [7]

Judaism

"What is hateful to you, do not do to your neighbor. This is the whole of the Torah; all the rest is commentary."

—Talmud, Shabbat 31a [8]

Taoism

"Regard your neighbor's gain as your own gain; and regard your neighbor's loss as your own loss."

—T'ai Shang Kan Yin P'ien 213–218 [9]

Wicca

"An it harm none, do what ye will."

—The Wiccan Rede [10]

Yoruba African Traditional Religions

"One going to take a pointed stick to pinch a baby bird should first try it on himself to feel how it hurts."

—Yoruba Proverb [11]

---

6. http://40hadithnawawi.com

7. http://www.sacred-texts.com/

8. http://www.sacred-texts.com/

9. http://www.sacred-texts.com/

10. http://www.wicca-spirituality.com/

11. http://www.unification.net/ws/theme015.htm

Zoroastrianism

"Do not do unto others whatever is injurious to yourself."
—Shayast-na-Shayast 13.29 [12]

AN ATTRACTIVE DEATH

With this underlying similarity among all spiritual philosophies, why would one specifically choose the veneration and magic of La Santa Muerte? Every devotee's specific reasoning is unique, but in general, there are two main, overarching reasons why people are attracted to the devotion of La Santa Muerte.

The first is the fact that La Santa Muerte is a nonjudgmental deity in every sense of the word. Most other deities, whether from a monotheistic or polytheistic pantheon, are in some ways judgmental in the sense that they reward those who have their favor and punish those who fall out of their favor. The god of monotheistic religions is known for rewarding the righteous with eternal paradise and punishing the wicked with eternal torment, while the gods of polytheistic religions are notorious for the blessings they bestow on those who respect their dominion and the anguish they cause for those who disrespect their dominion.

La Santa Muerte gives no such preferential treatment to anyone. In a sense, she can be most likened to the Tao since she is neither good nor bad and yet both. She interacts with humanity without a set agenda or expectation of behavior in mind. Whether you are a devoted follower of her mystery school or an opponent who crusades against her and her "evil" cult, La Santa Muerte does not care. She will treat both of you equally, without favor or disdain.

The basis for this supreme neutrality of La Santa Muerte can be found in the fact that Death treats everyone equally. It doesn't matter if you are rich or poor, man or woman, young or old, good or bad. Death comes to all, and she will take the life of a king just as readily as she will take the life of a peasant. This is why so many people find refuge in their devotion to La Santa Muerte despite not receiving her preferential

---

12. http://www.sacred-texts.com/

favor for doing so. She doesn't judge you in any way whatsoever. In particular, this is why an overwhelming number of her devotees are people who are not accepted by mainstream society. Most frequently, these outcast devotees are gay people, self-empowered women, and people with criminal records.

Gay people often come to her as a result of continuously being judged as immoral by society and many organized religions. To finally find a belief system (though not the only belief system) where your patron deity will never judge you for your sexual orientation or identity is comforting.

Self-empowered women are similarly judged in a negative way by a patriarchal society and numerous gender-biased organized religions for not being passive and submissive. To finally find a feminine deity who does not see gender and allows anyone to become priests and priestesses in her mystery school is refreshing.

People with criminal records are also constantly judged and labeled as evil in a society that allows no room for mistakes and where one mishap with the law will follow you forever, preventing future employment, promotions, and success in life. Thus, criminals come to La Santa Muerte knowing that she does not judge them by their past sins, nor will she judge them if they "fall off the wagon" and sin again.

But this welcoming and comforting attitude is not exclusive to La Santa Muerte. Her devotees are also dedicatedly just as nonjudgmental. Granted, we are all human and sometimes fall short of our patron deity's perfect level of neutrality, but to attain a state of never judging others and treating everyone equally (just like Death) is our ideal for which we strive. So not only are gays, self-empowered women, and people with criminal records welcomed and seen as equals in the eyes of La Santa Muerte, but they are also welcomed and seen as equals in the eyes of her devotees. Deep down, we all know that none of us is perfect, and so we live by the credo "do not judge somebody just because they sin differently than you."

The other main, overarching reason people are drawn to the mystery school of La Santa Muerte and remain devoted to her for the rest of their lives is the fact that she is the de facto saint of desperation.

Commonly, you will hear testimonies from people actively engaged in her mystery school that say they were very hesitant and unwilling to turn to La Santa Muerte for help. Fearing her cult as something evil, they prayed to other gods and saints for divine intercession, only to have their prayers unanswered or unfulfilled.

Similarly, those who engage in spellwork experience a similar non-manifestation of their spells when working with particular deities even though they performed the spell correctly and in perfect love and perfect trust. Feeling rebuffed by their traditional god or pantheon of deities, they experiment with the prayers to and magic of La Santa Muerte, and universally, their prayers are answered and their spells are manifested. In fact, her devotional prayers and spells are so effective that Catholic devotees of La Santa Muerte in need of a miracle have overwhelmingly begun to seek her divine intercession over that of St. Jude, the Vatican-approved patron saint of lost causes and desperate situations.

The basis of La Santa Muerte's supreme efficacy in answering prayers and manifesting spells goes back to her neutrality. Oftentimes, especially in desperate situations, we want something so badly that we cannot see how *not* having it is benefitting us. As humans, we can't see into the future or predict all the long-term effects of certain events, but the Divine (God, the universe, the Tao) can. Sometimes what we so desperately want is not for our greater good, and so an unanswered prayer or a spell that doesn't manifest is quite often a blessing in disguise. Examples of this are endless. Imagine praying to be hired for a job for which you have just been interviewed, only to not be selected, but by being forced to continue searching for a new job, you are hired elsewhere with a higher salary and more job satisfaction, or maybe you meet the love of your life through this different job. None of that would have happened if your prayer had originally been answered. Likewise, you may have also dodged an unseen bullet by not being hired, such as a severely hostile and crippling work environment or a fatal car accident on your way to the first day on the job.

The Divine, regardless of what you call it or how you conceptualize it, is always looking after your greater good. With La Santa Muerte, however, this is not the case. Because of her supreme neutrality, she will answer your prayers and manifest your spells regardless of whether it will ultimately cause you harm or whether something better would have happened if your petition had remained unanswered. In a sense, one can argue that La Santa Muerte is no more efficacious in her miracles than any other saint or deity, but because working with her lacks the safety guard of only materializing things that will be for your greater good, the number of testimonials to her indiscriminate miracle working is tremendously high, especially since most people don't recognize the miracle of unanswered prayers.

This also explains why La Santa Muerte is often associated and seen with the most dangerous and ill-meaning people in society. Her neutrality dictates that prayers and spells done with the intention of knowingly and purposely harming others will be answered just as readily as those done for benevolent intentions. It is not uncommon for assassins to pray to La Santa Muerte to guide their bullet into the heart of their victim, nor is it uncommon for shrines to be built in her honor on the U.S.-Mexican border by drug traffickers to ensure the safe delivery of their cargo and protection from the law.

While those cases are extreme, it is more likely that morally ambiguous devotees will call upon La Santa Muerte to facilitate a crime of necessity. Prostitutes and thieves are among those most devout to her since—although they would prefer to not break the law—their socioeconomic circumstances provide them with no other way to survive. They find solace in knowing that La Santa Muerte will not only not *judge* them for what they are about to do, she will also *help* ensure a profitable night and their safe protection.

The supreme neutrality of La Santa Muerte, whether she is answering prayers that are not for our greater good or manifesting the spells of those who intentionally seek to harm others or commit a crime of necessity, is a big reason why she has such a bad rap with those not familiar with her mystery school. But it just comes with the territory. A deified personification of Death who looks like the Grim Reaper; welcomes gay people, strong-willed women, and criminals; and grants miracles that could harm you or someone you know is undoubtedly going to be a lightning rod for controversy. Her devotion and mystery school have been condemned by the Vatican and several Protestant branches of Christianity. And it also doesn't help her public image that the news media is obsessed with presenting her in a light that is negative and frightening, in accordance with the old adage "if it bleeds, it leads."

But does La Santa Muerte care? Not at all. Throughout time, Death has been praised and maligned by human societies all over the world, and yet she has remained an ever-constant presence with us, continuing the same work no matter our opinion of her. She holds no grudges and no opinion of you, and to those who are willing to learn the secrets of her mystery school, she will be a powerful ally for the rest of your life and whatever awaits you after that.

So, I invite you to bury your preconceived notions, beliefs, and assumptions about who or what La Santa Muerte is. Read this book and the magic contained within with a nonjudgmental mind and open heart. If what you read does not resonate with you, take this information as nothing more than an academic study into a unique and growing spiritual philosophy. But if on some level within your soul the information in this book speaks to you, intrigues you, or calls to you, let this book be your initiatory experience into the community and mystery school of La Santa Muerte, wherein you will learn the magic of life through the exploration and understanding of Death herself.

2
Let's Talk About Death

"At the end of the game, the king and the pawn go back into the same box."
~ITALIAN PROVERB

It is no accident that you are reading this book. Everything happens for a reason, and that reason is ultimately *you*. There's a saying, often attributed to Carl Jung, the founder of analytical psychology: "Until you make the unconscious conscious, it will direct your life, and you will call it fate." This is a startling concept to many. The idea that we are the cause of all our successes and all our failures frightens people. It is much more comforting to believe that our successes derive from our hard work while our failures derive from circumstance or even from external obstacles. It takes great courage to own up to everything we do, but once we truly realize that both success and failure are the result of our thoughts and actions, we become the master of both success and failure.

As a devotee in the mystery school of La Santa Muerte, you must become such a master. You must wholeheartedly believe that you have the power to co-create miracles with this deity of Death. Magic, after all, is simply the knowing manipulation of natural energies to create an intended result. In truth, we are manipulating energy all the time, but because we have become so accustomed to it, we don't call it "magic," reserving that word only for things that we don't understand how to intentionally manifest.

Think of an airplane; think how magical this mode of transportation would have seemed to people for the majority of human history! But because we see it every day and understand that it has to do with the generally accepted laws of physics, air travel has lost its sense of magic. The miracle of flight is nothing more than the knowing manipulation of wind, velocity, reshaped metals, and fuel propulsion energies to create the intended result of air travel. To harness the power of flight, we must understand physics, and to harness the power of death magic, we must understand La Santa Muerte.

Once we truly know her and understand her, only then can we better understand how to work with her magic in this world. In order to have a proper understanding of La Santa Muerte, though, we must first understand death.

GENESIS OF DEATH

Officially, death has been around for as long as life has been around. Death and life are cooperative partners who are dependent upon each other. And since humans can be categorized under living things, death has existed side by side with us through all stages of our evolution.

Technically speaking, though, we only have been aware of our modern concept of death since Paleolithic times approximately 300,000 years ago. Neanderthals were the first human species to bury their dead. Before this, the cadavers of deceased members of the human tribe were just left in the same location and position in which the person had died. But this new practice of burying the dead served as a then-perceived hygienic benefit to human civilization wherein the toxic miasma released as a byproduct of putrefaction was relegated underground. Although modern microbiology has debunked this myth of decomposing bodies being toxic (known as "miasma theory"), an interesting thing of note is that the Neanderthals of the Paleolithic era were wandering hunter-gatherers. The disease-causing implications of leaving an organic body to putrefy and decompose above ground aren't enough of an argument to justify the time and energy involved to ritualistically bury the deceased. They could just move on to healthier locations and put that time and energy into endeavors more productive for the living members of the tribe. Thus, burials must have been done for other reasons.

While we can't know with certainty why our Paleolithic ancestors buried their dead, anthropologists have generally accepted that it was for religious reasons, pointing to artifacts buried with the deceased that signify a belief in an afterlife. Whether the artifacts and burial were motivated by generous concern for the well-being of the deceased in the afterlife or by the selfish concern for the well-being of the living—to not be haunted by the deceased due to a lack of respect for their remains—some kind of continuation after physical death was believed to be real. From this perspective, one can assume that our very first conceptualized notion of death was not one of finality but rather one of transition.

This idea of "death as a transition" stayed with humanity all the way to the modern age. In popular magic, this aspect of death can be seen in the Rider-Waite-Smith tarot deck in the thirteenth card of the major arcana: the Death card. This card shows Death as a skeleton who wears a suit of black armor, holds a black flag emblazoned with a white rose, and rides a white horse. At the horse's hooves are a young child, a grieving maiden, a member of the clergy, and the cadaver of a king lying face up with his crown irreverently tossed beside him. While there are many ways to interpret this illustration, in very broad strokes it reflects Death's neutrality and indiscrimination (killing royalty, children, women, and holy men all equally), while the white rose (often called the Mystic Rose) symbolizes life or rebirth. In addition to this depiction and symbology of Death having many similarities with the figure of La Santa Muerte, the overarching message of the Death card is one of transition. In a tarot reading, drawing the Death card rarely signifies actual death, but rather the end of something that ultimately leads to a change through sudden transition.

Such focus on transition, specifically a transition into an afterlife, proved to be a main focus of human civilization's earliest religions. One of the most well-known of these is the complex and multifaceted poly-theistic religion of ancient Egypt. The ancient Egyptians' preparations for the afterlife are one of the most enduring aspects of their culture in modern times. They believed that everyone had a soul that was comprised of two parts: a *ka* and a *ba*. Both being ethereal, the *ka* is closer to the popular Christian concept of a soul wherein it is the life energy that leaves our body upon death, although since it was nourished during life through food and drink, it needed to continue receiving offerings of food and drink even after death. The *ba* on the other hand is very attached to the body, and the only way it could be released to join the *ka* and thus form the *akh* was through a proper funeral. Since the actual physical body continued after death to be the nourishing energy necessary for the *ba* to survive, it was imperative to preserve the body from decay through mummification. Originally, it was believed that only a pharaoh possessed a *ba*, but as time went on, it became common acceptance that everyone had a *ba*.

The reunion of the *ka* and the *ba*, however, had many afterlife challenges set in place to determine whether the soul was worthy enough to be reunited into the *akh*. The final challenge was known as the "weighing of the heart," wherein the heart (thought by the ancient Egyptians to be the center of thought, memory, and emotion) was weighed against an ostrich feather that represented Ma'at, the goddess of truth and justice. All of a person's wrongdoings would stay in the heart, making it heavy, while a pure heart would be free of burden and therefore light. If the heart was lighter than the feather of Ma'at, the *ka* and *ba* could be reunited into the *akh*, but if the heart was heavier than the feather of Ma'at, the heart would be immediately eaten by a chimeric beast that sat in waiting at the base of the gigantic scales.

This practice bears a strong resemblance to the Christian concept of the Last Judgment, wherein, after death, a soul is judged whether it is worthy of the Kingdom of Heaven based on the quantity and severity of the person's sins committed on earth. Modern devotees of La Santa Muerte regard the scales as one of her main tools with which she judges the quality of one's soul in relation to one's goodness while alive and also as a symbol of divine justice. It is important to remember, however, that although La Santa Muerte has the charge of judging the quality of one's soul, she is still ever neutral and nonjudgmental. Officially, it is the mechanics of the nonsentient scales that determine a soul's goodness. Consequently the judgment is controlled purely by one's actions while alive. La Santa Muerte merely acts as the enforcer of the judgment whose ruling we created while on earth.

Despite this idea of death as a transition and not a finite ending, death was still a frightening thing. Since ancient times, we have tried to devise ways to prolong life and keep healthy. This fear of death is often misunderstood to be a fear of the act of dying. In actuality, what we all fear is the unknown, specifically the unknown of what happens to us after our physical death.

The truth is that none of us actually knows for certain what happens to us after our physical death—the only ones who do know are dead. Each of us, however, has something of a personalized idea of what will become of us, and some of us even believe wholeheartedly that we know what happens after death. But a belief (even a very strong belief) is not the same as actually knowing. Whether we are judged and sent to realms of perpetual bliss or torment, reincarnated on this earth in another form, or simply disappear into an endless void of nothingness, they are all equally valid possibilities because the correct answer is unknown to us.

If we explore further into this fear of the unknown, we come to a startlingly honest discovery. The truth is that we don't really fear the unknown; we fear our negative assumption of the unknown. By definition the unknown is not known to us, and as such there is a 25 percent chance that it is bad, 25 percent chance that it is good, 25 percent chance that it is both, and a 25 percent chance that it is neither. The probabilities as to the positive/negative outcome of what happens to us after death are no different because it is unknown.

If we absolutely knew with 100 percent certainty that something purely wonderful and joyful will happen to us after death, there would be no reason to fear death. It has become known, and the known is a positive outcome. We might be sad to leave our loved ones, but we would not actually *fear* death. Likewise, if we knew with 100 percent certainty that something purely horrifying and torturous will happen to us after death, we still wouldn't *fear* death because it has become known, and the known is a negative outcome. We would dread and have much anxiety about our life after death, but we wouldn't *fear* the act itself.

While both of those hypothetical examples are great for explaining the rationale for our fear of the unknown after death, they are not much consolation for us here and now. As mentioned earlier, none of us actually knows with 100 percent certainty what happens to us after death, and so there will always be a lingering unknown and doubt in our rational minds. But that has not stopped the human race from trying to learn what would happen to us after death and attempt to gain ourselves an advantage in the afterlife. To do this, many mystery schools were developed in the ancient world that dealt with this unknown and the many other unknowns in life.

Mystery Schools of the Classical Age

Two of the most famous mystery schools that focused on death and the afterlife were the Eleusinian Mysteries and the Orphic Mysteries of the Greco-Roman era. Of course, as their names suggest, much of the intimate details of these mystery schools remain, well...a mystery. Secrecy was of the utmost importance, only initiates were allowed to know the sacred knowledge, and even then, there were gradations and levels of initiates who were allowed to know more than others.

From what we know now, the Eleusinian Mysteries centered around the Greek myth of Demeter and Persephone. A basic summary of this myth is that the young goddess Persephone was taken to the underworld by Hades, the god of death and the underworld. In some versions she is sexually abducted, while in other versions she went willingly, but in either case, she was taken to the underworld. Her mother, Demeter (goddess of fertility and agriculture), was so angry and distraught by her daughter's disappearance that she stopped tending to her divine duties of assisting with agriculture. Humans began to see their crops wither, and they prayed to Zeus (the king of the gods) to do something to save them from starvation. Zeus eventually did intercede and forced Hades to return Persephone to her mother, but while in captivity, Persephone had eaten seeds of an underworld pomegranate. Eating underworld food meant she was technically bound forever to the underworld, but Demeter was adamant in refusing to allow the crops to grow so long as her daughter was with Hades.

Striking a compromise, Zeus declared that Persephone would return to her mother, but she would also have to spend one month a year in the underworld for every pomegranate seed she had eaten. Thus this myth served the purpose of explaining Persephone's position as Queen of the Underworld and the changing of the seasons: summer being the vibrancy of Demeter with her daughter, autumn being the sadness of Demeter knowing her daughter would soon be returning to the underworld, winter being the sorrowful time of Demeter separated from her daughter, and spring being the joyous time of Demeter's reunion with her daughter.

The Eleusinian mystery school focused heavily upon this myth and believed it to contain the secret of eternal life. Initiates into this mystery school believed that just as Persephone was taken to the underworld and then was able to return to the world of the living, they, too, could transcend death. Such transcendence was secured by the initiate elevating him or herself to the level of a god and attaining immortality. Because of the secrecy involved, the exact teachings and knowledge of the Eleusinian mystery school and how they professed to become immortal are still not fully known.

The other death-based mystery school of note was the Orphic Mysteries. Best described as a combination of modern Hindu, Buddhist, and Christian philosophy within the framework of fourth century BCE Greek culture, the Orphic mystery school developed its own unique method of transcending death based on the underworld-transcending myths of Orpheus, Persephone, and especially the birth of Dionysus.

While there are multiple and varied stories of Dionysus' birth, the basic commonalities are that Dionysus was a son of Zeus born as the result of an extramarital affair with a mortal. Hera, the wife of Zeus and goddess of the family and marriage, is angered by this and sets in motion a scheme to murder the illegitimate child. Dionysus is ultimately killed but not before a piece of him is saved and sewn into the thigh of Zeus, from which Dionysus goes through another gestation period and is reborn.

Initiates of the Orphic Mysteries take this myth to show that the death of a physical body does not necessarily mean the death of an individual. According to them, the human soul is immortal and goes through many reincarnations after death. Life in any incarnation, however, was ultimately one of discomfort in the sense that we hunger, thirst, feel pain, and are forced to labor all our lives. The Orphic mystery school claimed that there was a way out of this reincarnation cycle via asceticism, knowing how to navigate and properly commune in the underworld between reincarnations, and secret rites that remain unknown to this day.

These ancient mystery schools are worth noting because they can be seen as early equivalents to our modern mystery school of La Santa Muerte. While not having the same objectives of transcending death or breaking the cycle of reincarnation, the various devotees of La Santa Muerte, like the devotees of the Eleusinian and Orphic Mysteries, are a minority that is united by a philosophy on death that is seen as transgressive to the religious philosophy of the contemporary majority. Though the mystery school of La Santa Muerte may seem like a twentieth-century phenomenon, research into these and other mystery schools of the ancient world show that such death cults have been around since the beginnings of human civilization.

To be clear, though, it is important to differentiate a mystery school from a religion. Essentially, a religion is a social, organized belief system that attempts to explain the relationship between humankind, the world, and the Divine. A mystery school is a supplemental philosophy that gives more explanation of a certain aspect of the aforementioned relationship. A mystery school is not a religion unto itself because, although it has a very distinct view on a certain aspect of life, it is only an elaboration upon the religion. In both the Eleusinian and Orphic mystery schools, initiates held unique and transgressive philosophies that elaborated upon the aspect of death and the afterlife in the already established and commonly accepted religion of ancient Greece and Rome. Similarly, the mystery school of La Santa Muerte holds a unique reverence and philosophy about Death and her interactive role with humanity that elaborates upon the religion of their choosing.

A good analogy would be likening mystery schools to sunglasses and religions to the landscape around us. Landscapes can vary wildly from urban to suburban to rural and everything in between. These different landscapes compel us to interact with each other and the world differently even though the basic necessities of survival are universal. The landscapes have been long established and are slow to change (if at all), but if we don a pair of sunglasses, we begin to see things differently. The landscape hasn't changed, but our perception of it has.

Though our daily lives are still lived in accordance with our landscape, the tint of our sunglasses allows us to better see certain details to which we were previously blinded. And we can take these sunglasses to different landscapes, allowing us to tint these different places in the same way to emphasize the same details. The mystery school of Santa Muerte helps us to better see the details of transition, change, and impermanence in any religion to which we currently adhere. Of course, Santa Muerte is just one of many mystery schools out there, akin to how black is just one color that sunglasses could be tinted. Changing the color doesn't change what we see, but it changes *how* we see it.

This is why, contrary to popular belief, you do not need to be a Christian to become a devotee in the mystery school of La Santa Muerte. Just as there are Christians who believe in reincarnation, and Buddhists who believe in a singular, masculine deity, so too are there people of various faiths who believe in the power and magic of La Santa Muerte. The reason why much of the modern devotion to and magic of La Santa Muerte is associated with Christianity and Roman Catholicism in particular is that the majority of devotees come from and live in a Catholic landscape. Thus, the current majority will often do things in a Catholic way, whether through habit or necessity, but their devotion to La Santa Muerte tints how they see what they are doing. And unless you have the same tint to your vision, you may both be looking at the same thing as a devotee, but you are each seeing something very different.

Remember, La Santa Muerte is nonjudgmental, and she comes to everyone regardless of their religious adherence. So long as you come to her with an open mind and an open heart, the philosophy and co-creational magic of La Santa Muerte are adaptable to any faith.

Preferably, an eclectic and well-rounded knowledge of comparative religion is ideal for any devotee in the mystery school of La Santa Muerte because all knowledge ultimately leads to self-knowledge. Specifically, knowledge of how various cultures view Death can best help in understanding the various ways humanity has interacted with her. To best understand how the majority (though not all) of modern devotees of the Santa Muerte Mysteries interact with her, it is important to have some knowledge of the Aztec view of death, the main pagan religion from which our modern Santa Muerte developed.

DEATH IN THE NEW WORLD

Religion permeated every aspect of Aztec society. It was a polytheistic religion wherein different members of society would adopt different patron gods or goddesses based on that deity's dominion and sphere of influence while still recognizing the divinity and authority of all other deities in their pantheon, especially the chief deity Huitzilopochtli, god of the sun and war. In their view of the cosmos, the world was divided into the heavens, the earth, and the underworld Mictlán, which were each further divided into more layers. Upon death, the afterlife destination was dependent upon one's cause of death, but in general there were three main afterlife locales.

If a person had experienced a hero's death (in battle, as a sacrifice, or while giving birth), their soul would transform into a hummingbird and accompany Huitzilopochtli and the sun. If a person had experienced a water-related death (drowning, waterborne diseases, lightning from a rainstorm, etc.), their soul would enter a verdant paradise known as Tlalocán. And if a person had experienced a natural death (the majority of people), their soul would go to the underworld of Mictlán.

In modern times, Mictlán is seen as one of the origins of La Santa Muerte's neutrality toward the living. It did not matter if you were a wealthy noble in an Aztec court or a foreign slave owned by that noble, everyone went to the same Mictlán equally. There was no dichotic division between one heaven for the righteous and one hell for the wicked. The only earthly action that determined one's afterlife was one's cause of death.

Regardless of who you were on earth, if you died a natural death, you would not immediately be sent to Mictlán. The Aztec underworld consisted of nine progressive levels, and Mictlán was the last level. Getting there meant enduring a four-year afterlife journey of traveling through the eight other levels of the underworld where various forms of pain and torture awaited. After arriving at Mictlán, the soul would finally be allowed to rest in peace and remain in a pleasant underworld.

One of the strongest connections of the Aztec philosophy of death and the Santa Muerte mystery school philosophy of death is the concept that life is dependent upon death. Such was the case of Aztec society's infamous obsession with sacrifice, in particular human sacrifice. While sacrifices were performed for a variety of reasons, one of the main reasons for human sacrifices was due to their belief in being indebted to the gods. In broad strokes, Aztec legends tell of how the gods had sacrificed themselves so that humankind could live, since everything on earth that sustains life grew from the blood and severed body parts of the self-sacrificed gods. In turn, humanity had to continuously offer blood sacrifices to ensure the continuity of life, particularly the daily rejuvenation of the sun. Thus, in Aztec mythology, death is the forebearer and prerequisite of life, not the other way around. We don't die because we live; we live because we die.

These two important concepts—the neutrality of death and death preceding life, both fundamental to the mystery school of La Santa

Muerte—are not only derived from Aztec religion but also from the Santa Muerte Mysteries' other foundational faith system: Roman Catholicism, in particular Spanish Roman Catholicism.

Around the same time as the Aztec empire, the various factions of Christian Spain had united under King Ferdinand and Queen Isabella and successfully conquered the Muslim caliphate, thus regaining control of the entire Iberian Peninsula in Europe. But prior to this, medieval Spain had been ravaged by the bubonic plague, famine, ceaseless wars against the Muslim "invaders," and the insidious witch hunts of the Spanish Inquisition. Death was, therefore, an omnipresent possibility and an everyday reality to all people.

For Roman Catholicism in general, though, the afterlife was supposed to be constantly in the back of the minds of the faithful. The religion's main focus is upon how to enter the Kingdom of Heaven and avoid the fires of Hell, and the way to go about this is by being a good, kind, and loving person in this life. Conversely, by being a wicked, hateful, and sinning person, we would be barred from entering Heaven and be condemned to Hell. Of course, the Roman Catholic Church of medieval Spain had a much more far-reaching and unforgiving definition of sin. In comparison, the modern Roman Catholic Church post–Second Vatican Council, while by no means a liberal and all-accepting institution, is much less severe, damning, and Hell-focused as it was back in the fifteenth century.

This meant that while many of the opportunities to live life to the fullest were still off limits to a medieval Spaniard, the Catholic Church was able to placate the faithful with the promise that our *real* life would begin in Heaven, after our mortal death. Thus the credo of "suffer in this world, live in the next" was born, wherein our physical life is just a testing ground to see if we deserve the reward of Heaven or the punishment of Hell.

The omnipresent possibility of sudden death, however, is the part most relevant to our modern philosophy of the Santa Muerte Mysteries. To those living in medieval Spain, this threat was real and posed a daily concern. A person back then *always* remembered that they could very well die tomorrow, and thus the actions of each day were paramount. Nowadays, although still a possibility, the chance of sudden and unexpected death is nowhere near as high.

Our industrialized world provides every opportunity for one to keep in good health, and scientific breakthroughs are constantly being made in medicine, surgery, and rehabilitation, thus making sickness and physical injuries much more survivable and even preventable. Because of this, the vast majority of people do not worry about death in the way our ancestors once did, now relegating it as a concern only for the elderly. The assumption that we are going to wake up tomorrow makes our actions of today seem less important since we'll always have tomorrow to start again or correct any mistakes. The people of medieval Spain did not think that way, and neither do the modern devotees of La Santa Muerte.

While most of us don't actually think we will die tomorrow, we devotees in the mystery school of La Santa Muerte try to always keep in mind that this is only an assumption and that no one knows how long they have here on earth. Through this bit of Roman Catholic philosophy, we try to make each day count and not put off for tomorrow what we can do today, especially since we know that through the co-creational magic of La Santa Muerte, there is very little that we cannot do on any given day.

In further chapters of this book, you will learn how to do this magic. But it is important to remember that the magic of the Santa Muerte Mysteries is a magic of co-creation with La Santa Muerte. Now that you have a general knowledge of the history of death and some of the main parallels of La Santa Muerte's ancient roots, only one more lesson is necessary before you should actually begin practicing magic: you must learn the history of La Santa Muerte herself.

3

Her Story

"Death is not extinguishing the light;
it is only putting out the lamp because the dawn has come."
~RABINDRANATH TAGORE

You won't find the history of La Santa Muerte in any textbook. Being a predominately clandestine mystery school, the devotees of La Santa Muerte have preferred to keep this particular avatar of Death a secret known only to them and other initiates. Of course, just because a history is hidden doesn't mean it doesn't exist. In the case of our modern image of the scythe-wielding La Santa Muerte as a skeletal Grim Reapress, her genesis can be found in the syncretism of Mesoamerican religion and Spain's colonial presence in the New World.

After the fall of the Aztec empire, Catholic Spain had secured Mesoamerica firmly under its sphere of influence, and they wanted to dominate these new peoples and lands in the name of God, gold, and glory. The religious aspect of God was heavily emphasized as an excuse to justify the extraction of gold and glory. Additionally, with the fervor of the Spanish Inquisition and not too long ago having expulsed the Muslim caliphate from the Iberian Peninsula, religious fervor was at an all-time high, and missionaries were sent *en legion* to convert the natives of the New World to the one true faith of Roman Catholicism.

The natives were difficult to convert at first, but once the missionaries made the decision to purposely blend the native religion with that of Catholicism, the number of converts began to rise dramatically. Rather than try to explain to the natives why their pagan religion was inherently evil and incorrect by pointing out the two faith's differences, the missionaries changed tactics by focusing on the similarities of both faiths, and from this common ground, the more oppositional aspects of Catholicism could be better understood and explained.

The best example of this syncretism in our world today is the famous Mexican image of the Virgin Mary: Our Lady of Guadalupe. According to Catholic legends, an avatar of the Virgin Mary appeared to a native convert named Juan Diego on the hill of Tepeyac. None of the established members of the clergy believed that this illiterate native had seen the Blessed Mother and so they dismissed him. It wasn't until the miraculous intercession by the Virgin of imprinting her likeness onto Juan Diego's cloak and manifesting roses that were not native to Mexico that the clergy finally believed Juan Diego and built a church to the Mother of God on the hill of her apparitions. The likeness that appeared on Juan Diego's cloak is the same image we have today of Our Lady of Guadalupe wearing a star-spangled blue-green mantle and standing atop a crescent moon with sun-rays radiating from behind her.

Prior to the building of this church, however, the hill of Tepeyac was the site of the native worship of Tonantzin: a Gaia-esque deity representing Mother Earth. When missionaries built a church on that very same sacred hill, the transition of Mother Earth to Mother Mary was not too difficult. During Spanish rule, many natives even continued to address and refer to the Virgin Mary as "Tonantzin," but to the missionaries at the time, the name used wasn't so important as long as they were coming into the Catholic fold.

Whether Our Lady of Guadalupe was an actual Marian apparition or just a syncretistic device to convert the natives depends on one's own belief. Having a degree in global and Latin American and Iberian studies as well as personally witnessing the co-creational magic of miracles, I firmly believe that both interpretations are equally valid. And like Our

Lady of Guadalupe, it is this same syncretistic ambiguity that brought about our modern image of La Santa Muerte.

LATIN DEATH

For Spanish Catholics of the fifteenth and sixteenth centuries, there was no deity of death, and so to represent this intangible and unseen natural force, artists of the time took license and depicted this invisible entity as a skeleton wielding a scythe. This is the same image popularized throughout medieval Europe in the famous "Danse Macabre" paintings during the time of the bubonic plague. The Spanish name given to this personification of Death was La Parca, the singularized form of the Latin word Parcae.

In Latin mythology, the Parcae were the Roman equivalent of the Fates of ancient Greece. Both the Parcae and the Fates were personified as three women of different generations who wove the tapestry of fate and held in their hands the thread of life for every person. A young girl spun the raw material into a person's thread of life, symbolizing youth and transformation; a middle-aged woman controlled and wove the thread into the tapestry of fate, symbolizing the self-management of one's life as an adult; and an elderly crone cut the thread of life with a pair of scissors, symbolizing old age and death. This generational triad is familiar in Wiccan lore as the Maiden-Mother-Crone triumvirate.

In the Roman version, the elderly crone was called Morta, from which the Latin word *mors* (death) originated. Thus the root prefix for English words involving death/finality was created, such as mortician, morgue, mortuary, mortal, and moratorium. In Spanish, the word for death, *muerte*, is also derived from the Latin name of this elderly deity in charge of ending human life. The title La Parca came into vogue for Spanish artists as a way to differentiate between the physical act of death (with a lowercase "d") and the artistic personification of the Spirit of Death (with a capital "D").

And because the words *Parca* and *muerte* are feminine (all Latin-based languages, including Spanish, have gendered words primarily based on spelling), the feminine article of *la* is used when talking about either La Parca or La Santa Muerte. Thus, in medieval and Renaissance Spain, the nebulous concept of Death was addressed and personified as a woman. This is also why the word *santa* is used in reference to La Santa Muerte. In Spanish, *santa* is the feminized version of the masculine word *san/santo* (saint), whose own etymological origins mean "holy."

For this reason, the title of La Santa Muerte translates to Saint Death, or more accurately Holy Death. While *santa* means both saint and holy, the word *holy* is technically a more correct interpretation in the context of La Santa Muerte since a saint is a human who achieved divine status through the performance of miracles and strong faith. La Santa Muerte, being the essence of death, was never human and never canonized into sainthood by any faith. As a devotee in the mystery school of La Santa Muerte, the use of Saint Death instead of Holy Death will not have any effect upon your co-creational magic with her, but for the more linguistically inclined, it's worth knowing this nuanced difference in the etymology behind her title.

The Spanish missionaries to the New World imported this depiction of a feminine Death in the image of La Parca to Mesoamerica and were able to create another syncretistic connection through the similarities of some deities in Aztec society. In particular, La Parca held similarities with the goddesses Mictecacíhuatl and Coatlicue. Mictecacíhuatl was the goddess of the Aztec underworld of Mictlán who watched over the remains of the deceased and was celebrated through memorial festivals of the dead, from which Mexico's Día de los Muertos (Day of the Dead) celebration originated. Mictecacíhuatl was depicted as being fleshless and skeletal with an unhinged jawbone opened wide, an image similar to that of the Spanish invaders' image of La Parca.

Coatlicue, on the other hand, was the Aztec goddess of fertility, life, death, and rebirth. She was also known as the Mother of the Gods who was killed and dismembered by her children due to their offense at her mysterious pregnancy with their newest sibling-to-be: Huitzilopochtli, god of the sun and war. Being a goddess who experienced death, she can empathize with the mortality of humans in the same way as Persephone and Dionysus of Greek myths. According to legends, she is the supreme mother figure whose womb is a portal of life and death, keeping in line with the Santa Muerte Mysteries' belief that we are all brought into this world through a woman and we will all leave this world through a woman (the female personification of Death).

By taking the life, death, and rebirth attributes of the motherly Coatlicue, mixing them with the physical appearance and mysticism of Mictecacíhuatl and the Spanish La Parca, the modern concept and image of La Santa Muerte was born. However, the very first record of La Santa Muerte wasn't written down until the eighteenth century. According to the logs of the Spanish clergy in Mexico, they claimed to have witnessed the natives talking to skeletal figurines and threatening to harm the figurines if they did not perform miracles for them. Most striking of all was that the natives addressed these figurines as "Santa Muerte." [13]

Other than these documented instances, the devotion to La Santa Muerte remained clandestine, with her traditions, prayers, and spells passed down orally. As with any reemerging belief system that relies on oral history to connect itself with its origins, there results much diversity. Like playing a game of "Telephone," some of the information gets lost or distorted along the way. Fortunately, an exact lineage of tradition is not necessary in the mystery school of La Santa Muerte. The Santa Muerte Mysteries are intensely personal experiences, and when you co-create magic with Death herself, it will only be you and her working together. Others may help you as moral support, but ultimately it is *you* who must work with her directly. As long as you can make a personal connection with her, your magic will be efficacious.

When one is devoted to Death, it just makes sense to keep that part of your life private since it is a given fact that most of your peers will either be frightened by you or think you're morbid or psychotic—or more likely both. Taking into account how conservative and unforgiving most of history has been to those who have had "fringe" beliefs, it is completely

---

13. Chesnut, *Devoted to Death.*

understandable why the devotion to La Santa Muerte has been largely underground since its syncretistic origins in colonial Mexico.

ORGANIZED DEATH

Depending on which oral history source you subscribe to, public devotion to La Santa Muerte began either in Mexico City in the 1940s or the Mexican state of Hidalgo in the 1960s. In both cases, the devotees were largely the urban working poor and those on the fringes of Mexican society. These public groups were relatively small, and the group Masses, prayers, and spells were largely directed for the protection of those whose professions put their lives in constant danger, especially those who worked at night. Other than thieves and prostitutes, these night-workers included bartenders, taxi drivers, and mariachi players, all of whom can be counted among La Santa Muerte's most devoted to this very day.

Still, it wasn't until the mid-1990s that it became safe to be a public devotee of La Santa Muerte. A revolution of Santa Muerte acceptance was occurring in Mexico during this time, and like all revolutions, its catalyst was poverty. Mexico's economic crisis of 1994, a result of signing the North American Free Trade Agreement (NAFTA), exponentially increased the number of the working poor, destitute, and people being marginalized by society. The free market policies of NAFTA created a perfect climate of financial inequality where the number of Santa Muerte adherents began to grow, all looking for a way out of the nation's rapidly increasing poverty, all turning to the saint of desperation and last resorts.

In 1998, an onslaught of bad press began to cement La Santa Muerte and her devotees as "evil" in the minds of Mexico's middle and upper classes. Her image and what little was known about her filled the front pages of sensationalist newspapers all across the country on a massive scale, and whatever was left unknown, the media took liberties and invented sensational rumors to help sell papers. The cause for all this publicity was the arrest of the infamous Mexican kidnapper and murderer Daniel Arizmendi López, known as El Mochaorejas (The Ear Chopper), and the discovery of his personal shrine to La Santa Muerte. These police discoveries of devotional shrines being tended by the nation's bloodiest and most grisly murderers would soon become a recurring theme.

Despite La Santa Muerte now being stigmatized as "evil" by the nation's middle and upper classes, a large percentage of Mexico's population was made up of the working poor, and as the number of working poor continued to increase in Mexico, so too did the number of devotees of La Santa Muerte. With this numbers advantage, adherents to her mystery school began to organize and make progressive headway in the legal-political realm. In 2000, the Iglesia Santa Católica Apostólica Tradicional Mex-USA (ISCAT Mex-USA) became an officially recognized church and legally protected religious faith in Mexico. Of course, in petitioning the government for such recognition, the church kept images of and references to La Santa Muerte at a minimum, instead presenting itself as a new branch of mainstream Christianity as the name, the Traditional Holy Catholic Apostolic Church Mex-USA, suggests.

Headed by the self-proclaimed "bishop" David Romo, the ISCAT Mex-USA is very similar to the Roman Catholic Church except with a devotion to La Santa Muerte and a vastly more liberal stance on social issues. As a general reference, the chart below shows some of the main ideological/social differences between the Roman Catholic Church and the ISCAT Mex-USA.

	Roman Catholic Church	Iglesia Santa Católica Apostólica Tradicional Mex-USA
Currently recognized by and registered with the Mexican government:	Yes	No
Approximate number of believers in Mexico:	97 million	2 million public (5 million including private)
Principal religious figures:	Jesus, the Virgin of Guadalupe	Jesus, La Santa Muerte
Leader of the Church:	The Pope	None (officially)

Mandated celibacy of the clergy:	Yes	No
Promotion of familial monogamy:	Yes	Yes
Permission of premarital sex:	No	Yes
Position on contraception:	Only permits natural contraceptive methods within matrimony (the "rhythm method")	Permits all types of contraception, including the "morning-after pill"
Permission of induced abortion:	Under no circumstances whatsoever	Only in cases of rape
Acceptance of homosexuality:	No	Yes
Acceptance of same-sex marriage:	No	Yes
Acceptance of the ordination of female clergy:	No	No
Acceptance of the seven sacraments:	Yes	Yes
Acceptance of the seven Ecumenical Councils:	Yes	Yes
Acceptance of the Nicene and Athanasian Creeds:	Yes	Yes
Acceptance of papal infallibility:	Yes	No
Acceptance of the Assumption of Mary	Yes	No
Acceptance of the Immaculate Conception	Yes	No

By no means does the ISCAT Mex-USA represent the beliefs of all devotees of La Santa Muerte. Truth be told, they don't even represent most devotees of La Santa Muerte. The overwhelmingly vast majority of modern devotees does not belong to the ISCAT Mex-USA and still remains largely deregulated and unorganized.

Within Santa Muerte groups throughout Mexico and the United States, you will find temples with female priestesses, devotees who don't recognize the Catholic-heavy beliefs and sacraments of the ISCAT Mex-USA, and even devotees who do believe in the Assumption and Immaculate Conception of the Virgin Mary. Again, devotion to La Santa Muerte is a mystery school whose philosophical lens builds upon and elaborates on the already established landscape of the devotee's religion, and it is not a religion unto itself. The ISCAT Mex-USA is just one Santa Muerte lens within the landscape of the Roman Catholic faith and has organized itself into a religion so as to obtain legal recognition (and all the rights and benefits associated thereof) in the eyes of the Mexican government.

Upon close inspection of the chart above, you may have noticed that the ISCAT Mex-USA is listed as not being legally recognized by the Mexican government. Although it obtained legal recognition in 2003, this was revoked in 2005. The reason was largely political, both figuratively and literally.

THANATOPHOBIA

On December 1, 2000, Vicente Fox became president of Mexico, the first president not to be from the Partido Revolucionario Institucional (PRI) in seventy-one years. From 1929 until 2000, the PRI was the political party that continuously held the presidency and dominated Mexican politics. The economic crisis of Mexico in the 1990s (among many other reasons) damaged the image of the PRI and allowed Vicente Fox, a member of the Partido Acción Nacional (PAN), to become president. While the PRI is a center-right party, the PAN is a far-right party, and President Fox sought to use the PRI's unprecedented loss as a chance to enact massive deregulation policies. Part of this deregulation included decentralizing the government and granting legal recognition to a number of private, nontraditional religious groups. It was during this permissive government atmosphere that the ISCAT Mex-USA was granted its legal status as a fully recognized church.

The PAN, however, was far more subservient to the Roman Catholic Church than the PRI had ever been. With most of his party's voting base being conservative Catholics, President Fox had the precarious position of being ever mindful to not upset the Catholic Church. When he granted various nontraditional religious groups legal recognition in Mexico, the Catholic bishops of the nation got together and formally expressed their outrage at the president and his perceived socially liberal policies, as well as going on record to speak of the evils of these newly recognized "religions."

Taking personal offense at this, the founder and head of the ISCAT Mex-USA, David Romo, filed a lawsuit against the high-ranking Catholic Bishop Martín Rágabo for defamation of character of the ISCAT Mex-USA (at that time a legally recognized "person" in the eyes of Mexican law). According to Romo, he was harassed and threatened by the Catholic Church to drop the lawsuit, but he refused. Instead, he organized a large political march of devotees in Mexico City. The Catholic Church went on the offensive and claimed that devotion to La Santa Muerte was "satanic." When the devotees came to David Romo's political march with statues of La Santa Muerte in hand, the middle- and upper-class public was horrified to see such a massive group of people comprised of outcasts and criminals with figurines of the Grim Reaper marching through the streets in an organized manner. This public march confirmed in the public's mind the legitimacy of the Catholic Church's claim that devotion to La Santa Muerte was evil, being a real threat to the religious status quo. With both the Catholic Church and his conservative voter-base now pressuring him to do something about this "evil" cult that had taken to the streets, President Fox revoked the ISCAT Mex-USA's status as a legally recognized church.

To this day, David Romo continues to advocate for the ISCAT Mex-USA and its readmission into Mexico's group of legally recognized and protected religious institutions. Learning from the bad press, he has made some changes to the ISCAT Mex-USA in an attempt to make it more "approachable" for the general public. He has changed the image of La Santa Muerte into that of a heavenly angel. Rather than a jarring and startling Grim Reaper figure, he has opted to portray La Santa Muerte as an "Angel of Death" with light skin, beautiful hair, feathered wings, and attractive face. In doing this, he hopes to distance the ISCAT Mex-USA from all claims of Satanism and be more accepted by the masses by visually appearing more like Catholicism.

Ironically, this change led to a loss of support for the ISCAT Mex-USA by many within the Santa Muerte community. The skeletal and ominous depiction of La Santa Muerte is what attracted most of the ISCAT Mex-USA members in the first place. So, while his church might now be more acceptable in the eyes of the general public, it has become less reputable in the eyes of the majority of Santa Muerte devotees.

While President Vicente Fox brought the mystery school of La Santa Muerte as an organized institution into the limelight of the Mexican media, it would be his successor, Felipe de Jesús Calderón Hinojosa, who would make her an international sensation to be feared. President Calderón assumed the Mexican presidency on December 1, 2006, and became the second non-PRI chief of state since 1929. Just like his predecessor, Calderón was a member of the conservative PAN, but unlike Vicente Fox, he proved to be much more of the ultraconservative bent.

In an attempt to deal with the nation's notorious drug cartels and trafficking problems, Calderón officially declared war on them both. He militarized the country and utilized the national army to go on the offensive against the cartels, but this only made the cartels more hostile, violent, and proactive, effectively making the country a war zone. The threat of sudden death became an omnipresent reality for ordinary citizens, which, in turn, increased devotion to La Santa Muerte and her mysteries.

Devotion especially increased among the cartel members and various drug traffickers. With more pressure being placed on them and with their profession becoming even more deadly than it already was, they built shrines and altars to La Santa Muerte en masse throughout Mexico and along the U.S.-Mexican border. As the bloodshed spilled over onto U.S. soil and these shrines and altars were discovered, the American public was horrified.

The skeletal image of La Santa Muerte thus entered the American consciousness by being a frightening figure associated with some of the most violent and deadly people in North America. The U.S. news media capitalized on the disturbingly raw image of La Santa Muerte and used her as the symbol of Mexico's drug war and border violence. To the average American citizen who felt indirectly threatened by the Mexican cartels and drug traffickers, it only made sense that such "evil" people would pray to skeletons and be devoted to Death.

It also didn't help that most of these altars on the border in devotion to La Santa Muerte contained spells, prayers, and petitions for the death of all those who opposed the cartels and traffickers, especially police. So not only was the United States' first introduction to La Santa Muerte born from border violence, it was also tinged with elements of "black magic" and supernatural intentions to do harm. It would be the equivalent of someone first learning about Roman Catholicism by witnessing the atrocities of the Crusades and the Spanish Inquisition.

Things escalated dramatically in 2009 when President Calderón ordered the army to go to the U.S.-Mexican border and destroy all shrines, altars, and images that even somewhat depicted the skeletal image of La Santa Muerte. However, many of the altars and shrines to La Santa Muerte were not drug related, instead being created as offerings for safe passage into the U.S. and as offerings of general protection in an area of the world notorious for many kinds of danger. Not only did this indiscriminate eradication of all things Santa Muerte on the border enrage the nonviolent devotees, it also enraged the cartels and drug traffickers, many of whom revere La Santa Muerte as sacred. And if cross-cultural history is anything to go by, the premeditated mass destruction of holy shrines and artifacts by an opposing party doesn't subdue the target group; it makes them more impassioned, dangerous, and entrenched in zealotry.

But it isn't just the cartel members and drug traffickers who are praying and casting spells in devotion to La Santa Muerte; the police and army are also increasingly doing the same. In addition to outcasts and those marginalized by society, devotion to La Santa Muerte can be found strongly in anyone whose profession involves life-threatening danger. The police and armed services members on the opposing side of these drug wars are no exception. Some Mexican units and battalions even have the image of La Santa Muerte as a symbolic patch on their uniforms for both decorative and amulet-like protective purposes. For similar reasons, Mexican prison guards also tend to be as highly devout to La Santa Muerte as their prison populace.[14]

To add yet another divisionary nail into the public's perception of La Santa Muerte, in 2011, the self-proclaimed bishop of the ISCAT Mex-USA, David Romo, was arrested under suspicion of involvement with a notorious kidnapping ring in Mexico. According to the Mexican attorney general, Romo provided bank accounts that facilitated multiple kidnappings in Mexico. Romo claimed he was being framed by his political enemies so they could appear tough on crime via the imprisonment of the most controversial and aggressively outspoken devotee of La Santa Muerte, the de facto symbol of Mexico's drug war.

Regardless of whether or not the allegations were true, David Romo was eventually convicted of robbery, kidnapping, and extortion and given a sentence of sixty-six years in prison as well as a fine of 2,666 days' worth of minimum-wage salary in Mexico. As of yet, few devotees of La Santa Muerte have come to his aid, ever unforgiving of his attempts at commercializing and softening La Santa Muerte for public appeal and financial profit over staying true to the image and philosophies of the Santa Muerte Mysteries. Those few who do still regard him as a leader and are adherents to the ISCAT Mex-USA, however, have been quite vocal online about this "false conviction," stating its equivalency to a declaration of war on their faith.

---

14. Chesnut, *Devoted to Death.*

THANATOPHILIA

But the recent history of La Santa Muerte isn't all doom and gloom; in fact, the world's most famous shrine to her is actively promoting peace and communal unity. Located in the infamously dangerous neighborhood in Mexico City known as Tepito, a public shrine to La Santa Muerte is on display, welcoming all her devotees from inside her protective glass display box. The caregiver of this most popular shrine is often called the Madrina (Godmother) of the Santa Muerte community due to her bold devotion and disregard of what anyone thinks of her and her faith.

On All Saints' Day 2001, Enriqueta Romero (better known by the endearing title Doña Queta) proudly displayed her medium-sized statue of La Santa Muerte outside her home in plain view of the public, becoming the first person in the megalopolis of Mexico City to do so. Prior to this, she had been a clandestine devotee for most of her life, passing her faith on to her children. When one of her sons was incarcerated, he began praying to La Santa Muerte with the petition that he might be granted a quick release from prison. Miraculously, his prayers were answered, and to show his gratitude, he erected an almost life-sized statue of his patron deity inside his mother's home.

At the time, Doña Queta supplemented the family's income as a street vendor selling quesadillas outside her home, and through her open door her customers were able to see the large statue. Rather than taking their business elsewhere, customers began coming in droves and spread the word around town about this quesadilla vendor's large statue of La Santa Muerte. Before long, devotees from all over the heavily populated city began coming to Doña Queta's home—not for her food, but to pay tribute and their respects to this large, semi-public statue of their miraculous deity. In solidarity with all her fellow devotees, the Madrina of the Santa Muerte community moved the large statue outside where it still remains in public view for all to visit for free.[15]

---

15. Chesnut, *Devoted to Death*.

Reflecting the community as a whole, Doña Queta's public shrine in Tepito has continued to see increasing numbers of new devotees to the Santa Muerte Mysteries while at the same time remaining very informal, nondogmatic, and largely unorganized. So long as you come with love and respect for La Santa Muerte and all of her devotees, you are welcome to the shrine. Visitors come from all over the world as a pilgrimage in gratitude for miracles performed on their behalf by the deity of Death, and many come bearing gifts or with the intention of donating money at the shrine, all of which the Madrina uses for the daily maintenance and upkeep involved with managing an international public shrine that receives countless devotees on any given day.

The biggest attraction, however, is the monthly group rosary held at the shrine. On the first day of every month, Doña Queta and a number of devotees gather together to change the clothes of the statue and communally say the rosary. Together, the initiates pray for a common, general petition and for any intentions the individuals carry within their hearts. By the force of numbers, everyone gathered attempts to spiritually augment the power of everyone's prayers as a sort of magical support system by which all those in attendance swear.

On November 1 (All Saints' Day), the anniversary of the shrine's public debut, a large celebration is held in Tepito in front of Doña Queta's home. An average of 5,000 devotees congregate to say prayers, celebrate, eat, drink, listen to music, and dance in honor of Death. Because of this, and the already established association with death that November 1 has in the Catholic religion and other faiths, this has become the de facto feast day of La Santa Muerte as unofficially recognized by her followers all over the world.

Since the establishment of the world's most famous and visited shrine to La Santa Muerte in 2001, countless others have been established. The growing number of devotees and the liberalizing attitudes of new generations toward spirituality and multiculturalism have made the public veneration of Death much less of a taboo, though not without stigma. Because of her origins in Mexico, most of the shrines, temples, churches, and places of communal worship to La Santa Muerte are located in Mexico and in cities worldwide that have heavy Mexican populations. But that does not mean those are the only places to find a community of devotees. In fact, because of the pervasiveness of her mystery school, even smaller, more rural places with negligible numbers of Latinos can be locales of devotion to La Santa Muerte, albeit more clandestine.

Additionally, with the miracle of modern technology, so long as you have an electronic device with Internet connection, you can join any of the countless online communities dedicated in La Santa Muerte regardless of your physical location. There are websites filled with spells, Facebook pages with endless testimonials of her miraculous powers, YouTube channels with songs dedicated to her honor, and even actual Santa Muerte Masses that are streamed live for anyone to see and join. For more advanced devotees who have an understanding of spellwork, there are numerous online sites where one can buy magic supplies, enchanted jewelry, iconic clothing, and even pre-made spells and have them shipped anywhere in the world. As a reference, I will post at the end of this book many of the more popular temples, websites, and Santa Muerte magic stores so that you may explore them online and/or in person.

As the devotional community grows and becomes more courageous in vocalizing their faith, so, too, will more stories of the mystery school's past be revealed. Truth be told, though, most initiates into the mystery school of La Santa Muerte don't know even these little excerpts of the community's history, and many more are quite frankly uninterested. Part of this is because many new initiates are only interested in being able to perform magic and not in the history of such magic being performed. This is emphasized by the fact that people often only come to La Santa Muerte in times of dire necessity, when they need a miracle ASAP and don't have the time to do an in-depth study of her history.

The other part is the fact that one does not need to know the history of La Santa Muerte in order to co-create magic with her. Given the fact that there does not currently exist an unbroken and absolutely verifiable historical chain on the subject of La Santa Muerte from her genesis to modern times, and the fact that we can still co-create magic with her, it seems logical that knowing her history is both unnecessary and ultimately futile.

While this is true, devotees of the mystery school of La Santa Muerte do not learn her fractured history for the end goal of obtaining more power, but rather as a sign of respect to the deity of Death. Since her magic is ultimately co-creational, advanced initiates in the Santa Muerte Mysteries will come to see Death as both a trusted partner and a beloved friend, not as a subservient medium. And as with anyone close to us, we wish to know more about them not because of what that knowledge can do for us but because of what we can do for them with that knowledge.

Thus concludes this chapter and part I of this manual. From this stage forward, you will begin working and co-creating magic with Death. Part II will focus upon the tools of the trade and the inner mindset to facilitate the conjuring of magic, as well as a powerful meditation on how to meet La Santa Muerte herself. But before you journey on to your next level of learning, I would suggest spending a week in contemplation of the knowledge you have gained in part I of this book. Anyone familiar with cramming for school exams will remember firsthand that absorbing a lot of information really quickly is only effective in the short term to regurgitate the information, but just as quickly as you learned it, the information is forgotten. True, lasting knowledge comes from learning small portions at a time and applying them on a daily basis.

If you are unsure as to whether or not La Santa Muerte and her mystery school is right for you, then by all means read this entire book all the way through, and then if you are convinced or still innately curious about working with her particular brand of magic, you can always come back and reread the book more slowly and thoroughly. There is no wrong way to become a devotee. The guidelines provided by this book are just a structured way to introduce you to the Santa Muerte Mysteries—a way I wish I had had when starting my journey into her mystery school. But by no means is this the only way to be or become a devotee.

Nevertheless, if you choose the path of lasting knowledge, I suggest spending the next seven days in contemplation of death. This is not to say that you should obsess and grieve over loved ones who have died, but rather that you should cultivate an awareness of death, seeing the cycle of new beginnings as a result of endings and how this cycle permeates all things. Don't worry about not knowing all the secrets of Death or about not having met her in meditation yet. Simply observe the everyday world around you with new eyes, and let yourself sink into the acceptance of the mystery. For reasons that will become clear to you later, these seven days of the awareness of Death and her partnership with life will allow you to work magic on a level like you have never experienced before, regardless of your prior familiarity with magic. Enjoy this week of contemplation, and I will see you again in seven days to discuss with you the next level of your learning.

PART II

Tools of the Trade:

Death's Magical Correspondences

4
The Look of Death

*"It is difficult to accept death in this society because it is unfamiliar.
In spite of the fact that it happens all the time, we never see it."*
~ELISABETH KÜBLER-ROSS

Welcome back to your initiation into the mystery school of La Santa Muerte. While the first level was focused on the acquisition of knowledge about the Santa Muerte Mysteries from an outside perspective, this second level will focus on the acquisition of knowledge about the Santa Muerte Mysteries from an inside perspective. I will reveal the codified and cryptic symbology used in evoking the Spirit of Death as well as an explanation of the tools and various ways to go about co-creating magic with her. By the end of part II, you should have a strong enough understanding of the secret language and etiquette used in communing with Holy Death so that in part III you will be able to read between the lines and see both the forest and the trees when it comes to actual spellwork.

But for now, let's talk about the experiences you've had over the past week in the mindful contemplation of death. Contrary to popular belief, there is no right or wrong way to envision Death, let alone penetrate into the sanctity of her mysteries. We each have different strengths, backgrounds, and ways of looking at the world, and all of these differences will undoubtedly create different experiences when trying to understand death. If you skipped the week of contemplation assignment, I highly recommend spending at least fifteen minutes now mulling over the concept of death. Go ahead; put the book down, set your alarm to go off in fifteen minutes, and then come back to this paragraph. Trust me, it'll make the rest of your second-level learning much easier.

So, now that you've thought about the mysteries of Death and how she is interconnected with life, write it down. It doesn't have to be spelled correctly, or formatted perfectly, or even be very long. Just write down your current understanding of the mysteries of Death, and write it as if you are trying to explain it to a child or a classroom of elementary school students.

A lot of people scoff at this task, seeing it as a waste of time when they could be learning how to do spellwork, but little do they know that this exercise is the most basic form of magic there is. The act of writing contains much power. It is an ability that, for most of human history, the powers-that-be have tried to keep to themselves, relegating the masses to remain ignorant with no way of sharing ideas or organizing thoughts. This overlooked concept of organizing our thoughts is the most basic exercise in developing and strengthening our magic muscles. They don't call it a "spell" for nothing. Originally, the magic practitioner would *spell* into words their desired will for the universe to manifest. After placing the magical intention onto parchment, the practitioner would then use the parchment as a physical embodiment of their intangible desires, which they could further enhance with ceremonial spells.

From a more practical and scientific point of view, the act of writing down one's thoughts allows a person to concentrate and focus their mind on a single idea. The alignment of the conscious mind and the subconscious mind is a necessary component of all spellwork, and writing down our thoughts allows us to immediately align these two minds.

The act of writing has the extra benefit of allowing us to review and process our thoughts. Going back to correct, clarify, and erase the written word is much easier than trying to correct, clarify, and erase something we said verbally. There are countless testimonials to the therapeutic and cathartic powers of writing something down, but for our purposes, we will focus on its ability to align the conscious and subconscious minds.

To do the next exercise, you will need a piece of paper and a writing utensil. It is preferable not to type this because the physical act of writing is what best aligns the two minds. There is no time limit. Write as much as you need to explain your thoughts on the mysteries of Death (as far as you currently understand them), but make sure that you have enough paper to prevent breaking concentration by going to find more.

Exercise 1: Alignment Writing

1. Find a comfortable place free of distractions where you can be alone.

2. Spend a minute or two remembering your experience over the past week in mindful contemplation of death and its polarity with life, reviewing with special attention anything that seemed significant or unusual.

3. Begin writing. Do not worry about the normal rules of writing or being perfect. Spell words as best you can. Feel free to use slang and expletives.

4. Write as if you are trying to explain your understanding of the Spirit of Death and her role in the world to a child, avoiding complicated jargon and "big" words that are not a part of your normal vocabulary.

5. Continue writing whatever comes to mind. Do not stop to analyze your thought process, review what you've already written, or plan what you will write next.

6. Keep writing until you feel you have sufficiently explained what you currently know. It doesn't matter if it takes one page or several, but be honest with yourself and stop when you feel satisfied.

7. When finished, do something to take your mind off the exercise. Occupy yourself for at least an hour, and then come back.

8. Read what you have written, preferably out loud. Do you feel that it adequately represents your thoughts on Death and her role in life? If not, make the necessary changes to it until it becomes a written mirror of your thoughts.

9. Read the completed writing out loud. Then place it somewhere out of sight and read it again after you have completed this book and performed your first Santa Muerte magic spell.

In part III, we will go over more advanced ways devotees of La Santa Muerte align the conscious and subconscious minds for the purposes of spellwork, but Exercise 1 is necessary to better comprehend these more advanced techniques. You can't run until you learn to walk, and if you somehow manage to run before being able to walk, then a painful fall is imminent. The same is true with spellwork, and especially so with Santa Muerte spellwork.

Now that you've completed your first exercise, let's focus on the actual image of La Santa Muerte and break down the magical symbology associated with her.

Names of La Santa Muerte

We'll start with her name. Just like the Virgin Mary, there is a copious number of titles and endearing nicknames given to La Santa Muerte. They are all interchangeable and equally valid. I will list, in alphabetical order, the most commonly used and recognizable names within the mystery school of La Santa Muerte, but it is important to clarify that not all of her alternate names and titles are respected by the community at large.

The act of giving something (anything) a name is done to separate and label it so as to better identify it and address it specifically. A nickname, however, is an additional label given to someone or something to personalize it in relation to the name giver. By this, I mean it creates a special bond and level of familiarity through the use of a name that can only be used by a chosen few.

For example, I have a cousin whose first name is Nicole. People who are unfamiliar with her address her as Nicole, but to her friends and family, she is Nikki. Addressing her as Nikki shows that one has a closeness with her and a genuine level of friendly familiarity. If I were to suddenly address her as Nicole, it would be a bit jarring and probably imply that I am about to have a serious talk with her. Conversely, if a stranger were to approach my cousin and address her as Nikki, it would also be jarring by coming across as a tad presumptuous.

We all know people with similar nicknames, and the same can be true with the little pet names we give our lovers. After all, if someone approached you and called you "honey" or "sweetie" completely out of the blue, it would probably be a bit awkward if not sleazy, but if your lover called you that, it would be cute and romantic.

Everyone sees and relates to La Santa Muerte differently based on their own personal preferences and personal psyche. Some of her nicknames are blatantly derogatory, but to that devotee, it is meant as a term of endearment and a sign of their close bond (in the same way that you can call your sibling or friend rude names, but if anyone else were to call them that, it would be extremely offensive). To some people, being able to use such vulgarities with La Santa Muerte is just natural because they see her as a member of the family or a very close friend. But not all devotees have that level of playfulness with her, preferring instead to keep things formal. Some even stay strictly hierarchical with their terminology, addressing her only with honorific titles.

With the names below, say each one out loud, and see which ones seem most natural to you. As you develop a stronger relationship with La Santa Muerte and your familiarity with her grows, you may be inclined to start using another name for her. The important thing to keep in mind, however, is to use tact when talking about her with other people. If you prefer to use the more offensive titles, be aware that it might come across as extremely disrespectful in the presence of some devotees. When in doubt, always use the neutral title of Santa Muerte.

Note: The articles "the" and "la" are only used when talking *about* La Santa Muerte in the third person. When talking *to* La Santa Muerte in the second person, don't use these articles. (For example, "I ask help from La Santa Muerte," versus "Help me, Santa Muerte.")

- **La Cabrona** (*lit. She-Goat, fig. Bitch*): This name is in reference to her darker side and to her notoriety for helping devotees manifest spells that could ultimately be harmful to them and others. The name Cabrona has also been attributed to her indifference toward humanity's reverence to her as well as her cold-hearted resolve in taking someone's life when it's their time to go. Although popular, this tongue-in-cheek title is more often used by men than women.

- **La Dama Poderosa** (*The Powerful Lady*): This name is one of the two most honorific titles given to La Santa Muerte. It references the efficacy and abilities of La Santa Muerte in all aspects of life while also showing awareness of her femininity. While "Señora" and "Dama" both mean "Lady" in Spanish, "Dama" carries with it a nuance of regality and deserved respect, while "Señora" is more of a semiformal prefix used when politely addressing a woman older than you or in business situations (akin to the English "Miss/Mrs."). A popular title, devotees tend to reserve its usage for when they are asking for something that is extremely dire.

- **La Flaca** (*The Skinny Lady*): This name is in reference to her thin physique. In a society where being thin is a prerequisite to being sexy and beautiful, devotees use this term to simultaneously address La Santa Muerte and compliment her. Granted, her skeletal physique can be more accurately seen as anorexic than just "thin," those who address her by this title don't mean it literally. They are aware that Death is beyond any notion of vanity and that her actual proportions are an exaggeration of thin, but its usage is simply meant as a way of complimenting her, in a manner that they feel many ladies would like to be complimented. This is one of the most (if not *the* most) frequently used titles within spellwork, when addressing her directly, and when talking about her. It is often given the feminine Spanish diminutive suffix "-ita" meaning "little," thus altering it to La Flaquita.

- **La Huesuda** (*The Boney Lady*): This name is in reference to her skeletal physique. It is most often used in a playful manner when talking *about* La Santa Muerte and less often when talking *to* her directly. Not the most popular of names, it is more common to see this title in writing than to hear it being spoken out loud.

- **La Madrina** or **La Nina** (*The Godmother*): This name is in reference to the role of a godmother in cultures that are predominately Roman Catholic. A Latino godparent is tasked with becoming the legal guardian of the godchild should the biological parents die or not be able to fulfill their duties. For our ancestors, when life was more dangerous and medicine was not as advanced, being orphaned was a much more likely possibility than it is now, and so godparents became the common backup solution to this unfortunate issue in Latino society. A godparent was also the main religious teacher in a child's life; the parents would focus on the child's physical and mental development, while the godparents would focus fully on the development of the child's soul. This is a very popular title used by many devotees. In particular, this name is most popular among people disowned by their biological parents, and so they adopt La Santa Muerte as their godmother to take care of them and nurture their spiritual growth.

- **La Niña** (*The Girl*): This name is in reference to her femininity. It also carries with it a nuance of agelessness, which Death most certainly has. This term is rarely used in spellwork or when addressing her directly, but it is one of the most common titles used by devotees when talking about La Santa Muerte. It is wise to have already identified yourself as a devotee of La Santa Muerte before using this term, though, or the other person will assume you are referring to some other "girl."

- **La Niña Blanca** (*The White Girl*): This name is in reference to both her white bones and the color symbology of white for rebirth and magic. It is important to note that there is no racial implication in the title. In the same vein, the title White Lady (La Señora Blanca) is also used, although not as often as White Girl. In fact, White Girl is a very common title used by all kinds of devotees, second only to La Flaca in common usage.

- **La Niña Santa** (*The Holy Girl*): This name is in reference to her divinity and femininity. It is a unique name in that it mixes both the reverent (holy) with the casual (girl). Rarely is this title used in spellwork or when addressing her directly, but it is often used in conversation with other devotees when talking about her.

- **La Santísima Muerte** (*The Most Holy Death*): This name is the other of the two most honorific titles given to La Santa Muerte. In Spanish, the suffix "-ísimo" (masculine) or "-ísima" (feminine) is added to denote someone or something as "the most" or "top-ranking." Like Powerful Lady, this is a popular title but almost exclusively reserved for spells of dire necessity.

- **La Señora de las Sombras** (*The Lady of the Shadows*): This name is in reference to her dark magic and the association between shadows and the unknown qualities of death. It also references death's eternal yet unseen presence in life as if it was lurking in the shadows. This is one of the most uncommon names to hear, but it is a popular choice among devotees who come from a Wiccan background and/or have had prior experience in working with dark magic.

- **La Señora Negra** (*The Black Lady*): This name is in reference to both her trademark black cloak and the symbology of the color black in regard to death and magic. Again, it is important to note that there is no racial implication in the title of Black Lady. La Santa Muerte is almost never pictured with skin, and therefore has no racial affiliation, which is appropriate for the Spirit of Death. It is one of the least used names as devotees often prefer a name that relates to her physique as opposed to her clothing or dominion. Those who do use this name are most often found among the more magically inclined devotees.

- **Santa Sebastiana** (*St. Sebastienne*): This name is in reference to her association with the Catholic St. Sebastian who was a martyr during the era of the Roman Empire's persecution of Christians. If the name is not familiar, the image of St. Sebastian's execution almost certainly is; he is often depicted tied to a tree with multiple arrows sticking out of him. He is the patron saint of (among other things) a holy death. In heavily Catholic Mexico, devotees often use this feminized name of St. Sebastian as a code word for La Santa Muerte to avoid unwanted attention and stigma. Overtly, this is the preferred name by devotees from a strong Catholic background, assassins (due to St. Sebastian's patronage of sharpshooters), and military personnel (due to St. Sebastian's patronage of soldiers).

While these alternate names and titles for La Santa Muerte are the most popular and recognizable ones, they are by no means the only ones. It is not uncommon for devotees to bestow upon her a nickname that is unique and only makes sense to them. Again, the point of a nickname is to create an endearing bond between people and denote familiarity. If any name does not feel right or resonate well with you, don't use it. And if you'd prefer to make one up, by all means go ahead and do so. But be sure that this new name is not completely random. For spellwork, it is important that the name you choose to call the Spirit of Death makes logical and immediate sense. As mentioned above, Santa Sebastiana was selected, out of all other saint names, because of the known and commonly understood association of St. Sebastian with "holy death."

I am often asked if just addressing her as Death is appropriate. And while it is appropriate, considering that La Santa Muerte *is* the Spirit of Death, it's not a name I recommend using to do spellwork or even to commonly address her. Usually, it's the more rebellious, young, and edgy devotees who are drawn to this name due to the shock value and sense of power it bestows, but let me tell you, that gets old very quickly. The more you use a name, the more you become acquainted and familiarized with it, and thus the less shocking it becomes. Overuse of the word "Death" can make a person jaded to it, and Death is not a name to which one should become jaded.

Additionally, the use of the name Death in spellwork can be very dangerous. For reasons we will explore in part III, it is necessary to be very precise with one's words when casting a spell. Frequent usage of the word "Death" can blur the lines between Death with a capital "D" (the Spirit of Death) and death with a lowercase "d" (the act of dying). It's best to keep a psychological separation between the two, and the less one uses that word, the more precise they'll have to be when electing to say it, as opposed to it casually rolling off the tongue as with other familiar words. So while all names are acceptable, not all are advisable.

With that said, there are certain things about La Santa Muerte that are "unchangeable." I put that word in quotes because there is no official theology that makes these things unalterable, *but* it remains a universal understanding among devotees that they must be left as they are. These fixed things I speak of are her symbology, the way in which we depict her mentally and artistically. In the mystery school of La Santa Muerte, these are as close as we will get to a universal constant within the community. And because her symbols act as a universal constant, they unite the community on a common ground that transcends language and nationality. Various devotees might use different types of spellworks and names, but we all recognize the same symbology of La Santa Muerte.

SYMBOLOGY OF LA SANTA MUERTE

When I say "symbols," I mean the symbols of La Santa Muerte as depicted in artistic representations: paintings, statues, songs, and so on. In the past, the Catholic Church frequently used artwork to teach the Bible to an otherwise illiterate society. Through the use of consistent symbology, the illiterate masses could easily recognize various biblical characters through appearance alone. Some examples include the Virgin Mary and the color blue, Moses and goat horns, and Eve and apples. If we go even further back, we can see symbology in other religious traditions: Zeus and lightning bolts, Ra and the red disk of the sun, Huitzilopochtli and hummingbirds. Having a universal symbology of the Spirit of Death unites us as a community, and it enhances our magic in the sense that we are each evoking and working with the same entity. This is especially true for group devotion and group spells.

Although Death technically doesn't have an appearance, I would not suggest deviating from this universal image of La Santa Muerte by inventing new symbols. There is a reason why she looks the way she does, and these symbolic images speak to our subconscious mind, as most works of art tend to do. As mentioned in part I, David Romo of the IS-CAT Mex-USA changed Death's universally startling image into that of a Renaissance angel. Was this blasphemous? Absolutely not, but it did take away a lot of the symbology associated with Death, symbology that activates the subconscious mind during spellwork. If this sounds confusing now, don't worry; we'll talk about the subconscious mind's role in spellwork in more depth in part III. For now, just familiarize yourself with the symbols of La Santa Muerte that make up her modern imagery.

Boney/Skeletal Physique

She is always, always, always depicted as a skeleton. At the bare minimum, a drawing of a skeleton is accepted as a basic depiction of La Santa Muerte. The symbology behind this is the cross-cultural association of skeletons with death. It is a frightening image mostly because it reminds us of our own mortality and keeps us grounded in the fact that we are looking at our future. The skeleton also symbolizes our equality. There is no skin color, no fancy clothing, no expensive jewelry, just a single common denominator that we all share at our literal core. Technically speaking, the bone morphology of a female skeleton would be most accurate, but this is hardly enforced. Any skeletal depiction within the community in terms of art or spellwork is assumed to be female unless stated otherwise.

Cloak

This is the fundamental article of clothing used in depictions of La Santa Muerte. While statues of her are often dressed in various costumes for different petitions/intentions (nun's habit, bridal gown, handsewn party dresses), all other artistic media show her as wearing a cloak. The color of the cloak can vary as color association is an important aspect of spellwork, but unless it is a rainbow cloak, a single, solid color (never pastels) is exclusively used. In general, black and white are the two main cloak colors when depicting a "neutral" or "universal" Santa Muerte. The cloak itself is almost always one piece of fabric that drapes down floor-length, with a large hood on top, either cinched at the waist with a simple rope or at the neck with a simple fastener. The symbology of the cloak is one of invisibility. In the past, a cloak was often worn for traveling incognito. The cloak represents Death's constant presence among us even though we cannot see her. Magic involving protection and safety often emphasizes her cloak during spellwork.

Halo

The halo is used to reinforce the divinity of La Santa Muerte. It is the same artistic concept found around the heads of saints in Catholic art. Rather than a golden ring halo, La Santa Muerte's is almost always a full, golden disk. This tends to be one of the least used symbols since a devotee of La Santa Muerte, by default, is fully aware subconsciously of her divinity. The use of the halo in art is just meant to add extra emphasis or represent her in a Catholic light.

Hourglass

The hourglass represents La Santa Muerte's dominion over time. The finite amount of sand represents the finite amount of time we have here on earth in this form. The exact number of grains of sand, however, can vary and is never fully known, which reflects the varying num-

ber of years each of us has before we die and the impossibility of knowing our date of death. Because of its mirror symmetry, the hourglass
also symbolizes reincarnation, rebirth, and new beginnings. An hourglass is never used just once—when all of the sand has fallen to the bottom, it is turned upside down, and the cycle begins anew. Similarly, our
death is not a finite ending, but rather the beginning of something new.
However, the level of our new beginning is dependent upon our actions
while in this world, just like, when the hourglass is turned over, the
amount of sand at the top is entirely dependent upon the amount of
sand that has previously fallen to the bottom.

Lamp

The lamp associated with La Santa Muerte is the classic oil lamp à la the
genie's magic lamp from *Aladdin*. Always with a lit flame, the lamp is a
classic cross-cultural symbol for wisdom and guidance. Not only does it
illuminate the darkness (of ignorance), it also guides a person through
the unknown until he or she can reach the light again. This knowledge
and guidance represent Death's omniscient understanding. You can't
fool her, or trick her, or lie to her. A handheld light source (lamp, lan-
tern, torch, etc.) is also recognized to be a symbol of a psychopomp,
one who guides the souls of the dead through the underworld. Regardless of whether you are traveling through hard times or the afterlife, La
Santa Muerte's lamp is a symbolic depiction of her help to guide you
and illuminate your mind to see all possibilities.

Owl

The symbology of La Santa Muerte's owl is threefold. First, owls have a
cross-cultural recognition as symbols of wisdom (most well-known in
Greek myths through Athena's owl). While the lamp represents spiritual
knowledge and seeing the big picture past all illusions, the owl represents
practical, academic knowledge and seeing the details that make up the big
picture. Again, this reflects La Santa Muerte's omniscient understanding
of our world. Second, the owl is a symbol of the night, having excellent
nocturnal vision and being able to thrive in the darkness. In a similar way,

Death is associated with the night and working unseen. Lastly, the owl is an omen of death in Mexican folklore. According to legend, hearing the cry of an owl is a sign that someone is about to die. In fact, the owl was the animal familiar of Mictecacíhuatl, the Aztec goddess of the underworld Mictlán.

Scales

The scales associated with La Santa Muerte are the same ones associated with the zodiac sign of Libra. A cross-cultural symbol of justice and impartiality, her scales are most frequently depicted as being at equal balance and void of any items being weighed. Since Death does not judge a person, the scales are an impartial way of measuring the merits and goodness of a person since, like the "weighing of the heart" in ancient Egyptian mythology, the only thing that determines the outcome of the scales is the actions of that person while on earth. Additionally, the scales symbolize balance. For devotees in the mystery school of La Santa Muerte, balance in all aspects of life is emphasized. The road of excess is to be avoided just as much as the road of self-denial. That does not mean that wealth and luxury are bad, but rather that we should not neglect our personal relationships in the pursuit of our career and success, and vice versa. The more we place on one side of the scale, the more we have to place on the other side to maintain balance, and if that is impossible, then we have to subtract from one side until we reach that equilibrium.

Scythe

Second only to the boney/skeletal physique of La Santa Muerte, the scythe is one of her most well-known and depicted symbols. In practicality, a scythe is an agricultural tool used to harvest crops. In the same vein, La Santa Muerte's scythe is used to harvest souls and end a person's life, much like Roman mythology's Morta who cut the thread of life with her scissors. But again, the ending of one's earthly life is not a finite ending but rather a new beginning, as the harvested crops are not simply discarded but collected and used to create food to nourish humanity. The scythe also relates to the cosmic Law of Reciprocity recognized by devotees in the mystery school of La Santa Muerte wherein we reap what we sow. If we spend much of our time and energy planting crabapples, we shouldn't expect to one day reap Golden Delicious apples. Sometimes the scythe is replaced with another metallic cutting instrument (sword, knife, scissors, etc.), but in spellwork, the symbology of the scythe is almost exclusively used.

World Globe

In many European portraits, monarchs are shown holding a small globe in their hands to represent that king or queen's dominion over the world. Sometimes the globe had a small cross sticking out of the top to further depict the monarch's role as ruling the world through divine right and his or her mission to spread Christianity. In the same way, La Santa Muerte is often shown holding the world in one of her hands to represent Death's dominion over all life on earth. Regardless of borders, nationality, or location, the entire world is firmly in her grasp.

DEITIES OF DEATH

A look back through the ages into the various cultures in human history will also reveal many of these nine symbols were associated with their own deities of death. The symbols may not always be exactly the same, but each era's equivalents correspond almost perfectly. In fact, many of the world mythologies that we humans have developed for the Spirit of Death are quite similar. The magically uninitiated frequently brush this phenomenon aside, relegating it to mere coincidence. However, for a devotee in the mystery school of La Santa Muerte (and to a larger extent all practitioners of magic), there is no such thing as coincidence.

The chances of so many peoples over so many eras of history from so many parts of the world with so many cultural backgrounds having so many similar mythologies about the Spirit of Death is as close to a statistical improbability as one could get, especially taking into account that many of these mythologies were developed before having contact with other cultural groups. Devotees of La Santa Muerte recognize this is because there is only *one* Spirit of Death in our universe. She has many forms, avatars, and appearances, and she appears to different peoples differently based on their cultural understanding of the world and the universe at large. Moreover, Death is but one aspect of the ultimate, ineffable energy that guides the universe and exists in all things.

One of the best explanations I've heard for the various deified depictions of a spiritual energy (in our case, Death) was from a very wise witch named Christopher Penczak with his diamond analogy. A cut and polished diamond is, at its core, one piece of rock. It is impossible to see all sides of the diamond at once, thus making the entirety of the diamond impossible to completely know at any given time. So, in order to understand this beautiful jewel, some people focus on one facet of the diamond. Some people focus on one entire side of the diamond. Some people constantly move all around the diamond. Each of these people will see the diamond differently and will give a different description if you ask them about it. Yet it is still the same diamond, and every depiction will have some similarities and be essentially correct.

In the same way, the ineffable energy of the universe is beyond our human capabilities to know fully and completely at any given time. So, some people view this energy through one facet (a single God). Some people focus on an entire side of multiple facets (multiple gods). Some people try to explore all facets (eclectic spirituality). Essentially, it is the same universal energy, but different cultural perspectives view it differently and sometimes even become so entrenched in their point of view as to declare any other point of view just plain wrong.

The Spirit of Death is no exception to this diamond analogy. To us, she is La Santa Muerte. Does she have other forms depending on how you look at her? Absolutely! The reason we favor the facet of Death as La Santa Muerte is because that point of view works with our subconscious mind to engage in co-creational magic with the Spirit of Death.

No perspective is wrong, and no single perspective is 100 percent the supreme truth. Such truths are beyond human comprehension, but that has never stopped us from trying. And even though we cannot know it all, we *can* know enough. This is explained through the Hermetic Law of Correspondence, sometimes better known by the simplified maxim "As above, so below. As below, so above." In layman's terms, this translates to the cosmic phenomenon that what is true of the whole is also true for its parts, and what is true of the parts is also true of the whole. Thus any *one* depiction of the Spirit of Death contains within it the entire truth of the Spirit of Death.

To supplement your well-rounded knowledge of this Spirit of Death, allow me to present a list of deities of death from cultures around the world. In the brief summaries, try to see if you can recognize any equivalent similarities to the nine symbols of La Santa Muerte. Also be on the lookout for recurring themes and similarities among the deities themselves. Remember, there are many angles from which to look at the diamond, but in the end, it's still the same diamond.

Argentine Mythology

San La Muerte: A folk saint of northeast Argentina whose name best translates to Saint Death (San being the masculine form of Santa). He is the deity closest in appearance to La Santa Muerte and is portrayed as a Grim Reaper figure with a boney / skeletal body, wearing a cloak, and holding a scythe and a globe of the world. The biggest variance is that his cloak tends not to be cinched, thus making his skeletal form more revealing. He is a deity of prisoners, gambling, protection, and luck. Legends of his origin are mixed. Most people say that he is the syncretistic mix of the native spiritualism of the Guaraní peoples of Argentina, Paraguay, and Brazil and the Catholicism of the Jesuit missionaries of the region.[16] To some of his most devout believers, he was once a living Argentine who performed a miracle while dying and spiritually lives on as San La Muerte. His cult following in South America is so large that the Catholic Church has officially declared his veneration as "infernal." [17]

---

16. http:// /www.sanlamuerte.net/

17. Andrew Chesnut, "Vatican Official Denounces Santa Muerte as 'Sinister and Infernal.'" *Huffington Post* (accessed May 7, 2015).

Aztec Mythology

Mictecacíhuatl: Goddess of the underworld of Mictlán, tasked with caring for the bones of the deceased. As mentioned in part I, she provides the final torturous test in the ninth realm of the underworld; upon passing this test, the soul can attain an afterlife of ease. She is depicted as a skeletal figure with an unhinged jawbone.[18]

Celtic Mythology

The Morrigan (Morrigu/Morigan/Morgan): Goddess of war, battle, strife, death, regeneration, and the underworld. She is known as a triple goddess, often being depicted as three women simultaneously. On October 31 (Halloween/Samhain), she is believed to straddle both the physical world and the spiritual world, allowing contact between the land of the living and the land of the dead. She is known to be very ambivalent in her affairs with humans, sometimes helping them and sometimes harming them. Occasionally thought of as a Celtic equivalent to the Norse Valkyries, the Morrigan is more popularly known in modern times through the legends of King Arthur, where she is characterized as Morgan le Fay.[19]

Egyptian Mythology

Osiris: God of regeneration, rebirth, the afterlife, the underworld, and the dead. The cult dedicated to him held a strong interest in the idea of immortality. Legends of Osiris vary, but they all share in common his murder by drowning and later having his corpse dismembered, and his wife, Isis, helping him come back to life either by necromancy or as a reward from other gods for recollecting all of his dismembered body parts from around the world. After his resurrection from the dead, he sired the god Horus and then retired to the underworld again to be its ruler. He is often depicted as having green skin (due to his ability to

---

18. Bodo Spranz, *Los Dioses en los Códices Mexicanos del Grupo Borgia: Una Investigación Iconográfica* (Mexico City: Fondo de Cultura Económica, 2006).

19. Christopher Penczak, *Gay Witchcraft: Empowering the Tribe* (San Francisco: Red Wheel/Weiser, 2003).

send up shoots of vegetation from the underworld, and green being the Egyptian color of rebirth), as well as wearing a crown with ostrich feathers, and holding a crook and a flail (symbols of royalty representing protection and punishment, respectively). Osiris is known for being the overseer of the scales during the famous "weighing of the heart" final judgment of the deceased.

Greek Mythology

Hades: God of the dead and king of the underworld. Despite modern pop culture's depictions of Hades as antagonistic and evil, the ancient Greeks portrayed him more as altruistic and supremely just. It wasn't so much that people disliked him, but rather that they disliked his job, which involved the loss of loved ones and a reminder of their own mortality. The people of the time understood that he didn't choose that job and that he ultimately played a valuable role in maintaining balance in the world. Nevertheless, he was greatly feared, so much so that people often were too scared even to say his name out loud, resorting to euphemisms. One popular euphemism was Plouton, related to the Greek word for "wealth" (and the source for the name of Hades's Roman counterpart, Pluto). It was believed that all subterranean things belonged to his domain, including the riches of precious metals, minerals, and jewels.[20]

Persephone: Goddess of the dead and queen of the underworld. As mentioned in part I, her myths of being abducted by Hades and the subsequent custody battle for her between him and her mother served to explain the phenomenon of the changing of the seasons. Her ability to walk between the physical and spiritual worlds became a main focus in the immortality-seeking Eleusinian Mysteries and a partial focus in the death-transcending Orphic Mysteries.[21]

---

20. Pausanias, *Description de la Grèce*, trans. M. Clavier (Paris: Société Royale Académique des Sciences, 1821).

21. http://www.theoi.com/

Thanatos: The ancient Greek personification of Death. Although Hades, as ruler of the underworld, was often associated with death, he was not Death itself. The actual embodiment of Death was Thanatos, a divinity with the appearance of a young boy (sometimes bearded) and two feathered wings protruding from his back (similar to modern pop culture's image of Cupid). The son of Nyx (goddess of night) and Erebos (god of darkness), he was often depicted in art working to take the deceased to the underworld alongside his twin brother Hypnos (god of sleep). Because of this, Thanatos was often more associated with a gentle death, often in one's sleep, while more violent and grisly deaths were associated with his sisters, the Keres. His symbols include a sword, an upside-down torch (representing a life extinguished), a wreath of poppies (flowers known for their sedative qualities), and a butterfly (a symbol of transformation; the ancient Greek word for butterfly also means, among other things, "soul" and "life").[22]

Hindu Mythology

Kali: Goddess of warriors, thieves, time, change, and destruction. She is associated with darkness and violence as well as the "good fight" against the forces of evil. Frightening in appearance, she is depicted with black or blue skin, multiple arms, disheveled hair, enraged eyes, and wearing a garland of decapitated heads. She is artistically shown as holding a sickle, a sword, a severed human head, and a cup or plate to catch the blood dripping from that severed human head. Still, she is also always depicted as beautiful, thus symbolizing the dichotomy of attraction and fear. Male worshippers are known to cross-dress as Kali and ritualistically cut themselves as a symbol of castration.[23] She is often called to aid in protection magic and magic involving the destruction of barriers and obstacles, whether they be physical, mental, or spiritual.

---

22. http://www.theoi.com/

23. Penczak, *Gay Witchcraft*.

Islamic Mythology

Azrael: The Archangel of Death who divides the spirit from the body and guides the soul to the afterlife. A figure in various religions (most prominently in Islam and Sikhism), he has many different appearances, including being hidden by thousands of wings, being made up entirely of eyes and tongues, a beautiful male with two black angel wings protruding from his back, and a cloaked figure carrying a scythe. He is often associated with divine retribution, tasked with delivering karma (both good and bad) to all peoples. Most of his devotees consider him to be subservient to God, but they are divided on whether he is the actual personification of Death or if he is just a high-ranking angel in charge of the dominion of death. Although not written in scriptures, many folktales tell of his involvement with all of God's prophets by meeting with them and revealing universal truths before they set out on their mission. To many, this is seen as symbolic of wise ones needing to understand death before being able to understand life.[24]

Maori Mythology

Hine-nui-te-po: Goddess of the night, death, and queen of the underworld, often associated with the west and the setting sun. According to legends, she fled to the underworld to hide after traumatically finding out that her husband, Tane, was also her father. Upon discovering that she had run away, Tane heard rumors that she went to the spirit world, and so he went there in search of her. Hine-nui-te-po had become self-empowered during her time alone in the darkness, and she approached Tane at the entrance of the underworld, forbidding him to enter and demanding that he stay away from her for the rest of time. Seen as a protector of incest survivors and those who have been sexually abused, she is often called to aid in protection magic and magic for self-empowerment.[25]

---

24. Brannon M. Wheeler, *Historical Dictionary of Prophets in Islam and Judaism* (Lanham, MD: Scarecrow Press, 2002).

25. B. G. Biggs, *An Encyclopaedia of New Zealand*, 1st ed., s.v. "Maori Myths and Traditions" (Wellington: Government of New Zealand, 1966).

Inuit Mythology

Sedna: Goddess of the sea, animals, hunting, heaven, destiny, life, and death, she is represented as a gynandromorph.[26] There are many myths associated with her, but one of the more well-known ones involves her murder by her father. According to legend, Sedna is sexually uninterested in men and dismissive of all the suitors that her father brings to her. To mock him, she jokingly marries a dog, an act that enrages her father to the point that he tosses her into the sea during a boat ride and subsequently chops off her fingers when she tries to climb back onto the boat.[27] Unable to return to the surface world, she lives in the depths of the ocean with a lesbian lover and controls the life and death of humans by providing or withholding the bounty of the sea (the Inuit people's main food source). Her head priests and priestesses were often gay shamans.[28]

Norse Mythology

Hel: Goddess of an eponymous and frightening land of the dead. Hel is sometimes depicted as a beautiful woman and sometimes as a rotting corpse, but she is always depicted as somber and gloomy. Her skin color is said to be half black and half white. She rules the afterlife destination of those who have not died a hero's death in battle but rather a "regular" death by old age or disease. Norsemen have been known to cut themselves with a weapon upon their deathbed to fool Hel into thinking they had died a hero's death. Her name and her eponymous afterlife of terror were adopted by Germanic-language Christians as "Hell," the place of eternal torment after death.[29, 30]

---

26. Penczak, *Gay Witchcraft*

27. Marijane Osborn, *Romancing the Goddess: Three Middle English Romances about Women* (Champaign: University of Illinois Press, 1998).

28. Penczak, *Gay Witchcraft*.

29. http://www.etymonline.com

30. Snorri Sturlson, *The Prose Edda*, trans. Jesse Byock (New York: Penguin Books, 2006).

Roman Mythology

Morta: A member of the Parcae, the Roman equivalent of the Greek Fates. As mentioned in part I, Morta is the elderly crone who is tasked with cutting a person's thread of life with her scissors in the tapestry of fate. Her name is the Latin precursor for the prefix "mort-," signifying words associated with death.

Shinto Mythology

Izanami-no-Mikoto: Goddess of creation and death. She is the wife of Izanagi-no-Mikoto who together created the islands of Japan through the symbolic act of penetrating a spear into the sea, with each island forming from the drops of water that fell back onto the earth after pulling out the spear. Izanami-no-Mikoto died while giving birth to Kagu-Tsuchi, the personification of fire. Distraught by his wife's death, Izanagi-no-Mikoto traveled to Yomi, the shadowy land of the dead, to rescue her. He found her hiding in the shadows, but before he could see her, she informed him that she had already eaten the food of the underworld and was thus bound to Yomi forever. Undeterred, he lit a torch, only to discover that his beautiful wife was now a maggot-infested rotting corpse. He ran out of Yomi with Izanami-no-Mikoto chasing after him. He was able to successfully escape, and the offended Izanami-no-Mikoto threatened to take the lives of 1,000 of his beloved humans every day—before this humans did not die. Izanagi-no-Mikoto, however, simply replied that he would then have to create 1,500 new humans every day, thus setting in motion the prophetic destiny of the overpopulation of the earth.[31,32]

Sumerian Mythology

Ereshkigal: Goddess of the underworld. Ereshkigal is tasked with being a judge and creating laws for her domain. She is associated with seasonal change, and the autumn and winter half of the year represents her natu-

---

31. Kojiki, *Crónicas de antiguos hechos de Japón*, 2nd ed., trans. Carlos Rubio and Rumi Tami Moratalla (Madrid: Trattora Editorial, 2012).

32. Ian Reader, *Simple Guides: Shinto* (London: Kuperard, 2008).

ral force on the earth. Most notably, she is a key figure in the "descent of the Goddess" myth in which her sister Inanna/Ishtar/Astarte is reborn from the land of the dead. In ancient Egypt, Ereshkigal was petitioned as a "borrowed" deity for spells involving gay love magic.[33]

Vedic Mythology

Yama: God of death. Early legends tell that he was one of the earliest humans, and upon becoming the first human to die, he thus inherited the land of the dead. A multicultural deity, he is mentioned in Buddhism, Hinduism, Sikhism, Zoroastrianism, and Tibetan and East/Southeast Asian folk religions. His domain of the land of the dead, Naraka, is most commonly believed to be only a temporary place for the soul before its reincarnation on earth. Yama does not judge souls, and ultimately it is the quality and quantity of bad karma that is said to affect the length of time the soul spends in Naraka. The true suffering of wicked souls in Naraka, however, is not new tortures being inflicted upon them, but rather their inability to experience joy and oneness with the divine.[34]

Vodou Mythology

Baron Samedi: Loa (spirit) of the dead and magic. He is infamous for being a debaucherous fellow with a penchant for rum, tobacco, and vulgarity. Often depicted as a skeletal figure in a black or purple tuxedo, with a top hat and sunglasses with one of the lenses missing, his image is frequently seen in modern pop culture, most notably in the characters of Baron Samedi in the James Bond film *Live and Let Die*, and Dr. Facilier in the Disney film *The Princess and the Frog*. Outside of pop culture he is frequently depicted by devotees to be a transgendered person, wearing both masculine and feminine clothes, which is often seen (along with his single-lens sunglasses) as being representative of his ability to inhabit the

---

33. Penczak, *Gay Witchcraft*.

34. http://www.sacred-texts.com/

physical world and the spiritual world simultaneously. He is also well-known for being quite lecherous, with a specific appetite for anal sex.[35]

This is by no means an exhaustive list of all the deities of death from all belief systems. It is meant to be just a multicultural handful of representatives from around the world. As you probably noticed, many of these deities—from completely different belief systems in different eras of history at different ends of the earth—have a lot of similarities. Most prominently, themes of impermanence, rebirth, destruction, protection, female empowerment, homosexuality, and walking between the worlds occur frequently. Also, the symbology of skeletons, cutting tools, and illumination have a common recurrence.

Remember, nothing happens by accident. These representations of Death are all different facets and ways of looking at the same diamond. Each view comes with its own rules and magic, but ultimately, all devotees of Death are working with the same spirit.

---

35. Penczak, *Gay Witchcraft*.

5
The Colors of Death

"Death destroys a man: the idea of Death saves him."
~E. M. FORSTER, *HOWARDS END*

Now that you have a multicultural understanding of Death and are familiar with the symbology of La Santa Muerte, it's time to learn about her different dominions of magic. In general terms, a dominion is a genre of magic such as money, love, healing, or protection. To help our subconscious minds connect with the different energies of each dominion, a specific color is assigned to a specific dominion of magic. Within the Santa Muerte community, these colors are called aspects.

Most of the colored aspects rely on the Hermetic Law of Correspondence mentioned in the previous chapter. In the philosophy of Hermeticism, there are a total of seven of these cosmic laws that govern everything in existence. Metaphysical in nature, they are said to date back to the mystery schools of ancient Greece and Egypt.

The role that these seven Hermetic Laws play in regard to the mystery school of La Santa Muerte is of great importance. Essentially, they explain the interconnectedness of the physical world and the spiritual world, and by understanding these ever-present connections, you can understand the fundamental laws of how to work with the energy of both worlds. In the same way the laws of thermodynamics provide the basic, unalienable building blocks to understand and work in the field of physics, likewise do the Hermetic Laws provide the basic, unalienable building blocks to understand and work in the field of energy manipulation, especially in regard to color. Thus, on the fundamental level, in all magical traditions one will find these same seven Hermetic Laws because they are the basic laws of magic itself.

Though fascinating, and essential for all magical work, a complete and detailed explanation of Hermeticism is a subject that could fill volumes of books all on its own. For those who are serious in becoming professional-level experts in Santa Muerte magic, I highly suggest doing individual research into Hermeticism. The most well-known book on the subject is the infamous *Kybalion*, but due to its high level of advanced symbolism and cryptic code writing, it tends not to be very novice friendly.

A more practical and understandable book on the subject (and a personal favorite of mine) is *49 Lost Secrets of Peace, Love, and Money* by the ancient/alternative Christianity philosopher B. Dave Walters. It is a beginner-level e-book that explains the seven Hermetic Laws in such a way that one can take them apart, break them down into manageable bits of information, and see their effects in everyday life. But for now, let's go back and explain a little more about the Hermetic Law of Correspondence in order to understand the inherent magic of colors.

As I mentioned earlier, the Hermetic Law of Correspondence is better known by the maxim "As above, so below. As below, so above." At its simplest core, it explains why there are no coincidences in life. Beyond the larger "coincidences" of meeting certain people at certain times in life and the alignment of the stars with major events on earth, all magical systems most often focus on the smaller "coincidences" of life.

The two most common and basic examples of the Law of Correspondence's presence in magic are the Synchronicity of Colors and the Doctrine of Signatures. All tools used within the magical system of the mystery school of La Santa Muerte utilize one or both of these examples. They are exclusive to no single religion or tradition of magic, and the ways in which they are used by devotees of La Santa Muerte are often similar to the ways they are used by other magical groups throughout the world.

The Synchronicity of Colors basically explains that everything of a certain color has the same or similar magical properties. While a few people believe this to only refer to something's natural color, most magical practitioners have a more liberal view on this synchronicity and extend it to anything that is also artificially colored with paints, dyes, makeup, and so forth. This means that all blue things carry the same or similar magical energy, all red things carry the same or similar magical energy, and so on for all other colors and shades in between. This synchronicity also applies to the unique colors of black and white. Black, being the result of the absence of color due to the absorption of light, has a mix of all magical energies focused inward. White, being the result of the reflection of all visible colors, has a mix of all magical energies focused outward.

While that may all seem far-fetched to the uninitiated, the efficacy of colors to manipulate energy is well documented by the scientific community. Most validation comes from the field of psychology where the use of color has been shown to affect a person's mood: blues and cool colors tend to have a calming effect upon a person while reds and warm colors tend to have an exciting effect. Artists throughout the ages have used this phenomenon to purposely elicit a certain emotional response from their audiences. For example, Picasso's Blue Period works have a more naturally depressing and introspective effect upon the onlooker than works from his Rose Period.

In terms of magic, colors have the same psychological effect, which is essential for uniting the conscious and subconscious minds into a single focus. But the Synchronicity of Colors goes beyond the realm of psychology. Each color also has inherent magical energies.

Take the color green, for example: in Hindu and tantric/yoga traditions, green is often associated with the heart chakra, energetically located mid-chest near the heart. The heart chakra is the center of love, and in all things associated with love, we can find a correspondence to the color green. Green is one of the main color symbols of Aphrodite, the Greek goddess of love. Green is the color of springtime, the season of new romances. Green is the color of emeralds, a stone used in love magic. Green is also the color of love's greatest saboteurs: envy and jealousy. Furthermore, green foods such as leafy vegetables have been proven to lower cholesterol and blood pressure, both of which greatly affect the heart. Green tea is famously praised for its ability to lower the risk of heart disease, more so than black tea, white tea, and herbal teas. Even the color green itself is the result of combining the primary colors blue and yellow, just as the green chlorophyll of plants is primarily the result of blue water and yellow sun. All things green are interconnected through the Law of Correspondence.

Another color with many obvious parallels is red. Used often in sex magic, red is the color of the root chakra, energetically located between the genitals and the anus. The physical act of sex is dependent upon the physiological effects of the blood in the human body, and when exposed to our eyes, blood is a deep red color. Sex also increases body temperature, and besides being naturally associated with heat, red and its shades are also the color of hot and spicy foods such as chili peppers and their derivatives (paprika, sriracha sauce, etc.). The strawberry is considered a sexual food, and red makeup such as lipstick and blush is used to enhance a person's sexual attractiveness. Red cranberries are healthy for the urinary system, which uses the sexual organs for excretion. Most infamously, red has been associated with prostitution in various cultures around the world, creating the term "red-light district" for an area of a city where ladies of the evening can be easily found awaiting johns. All things red are interconnected through the Law of Correspondence.

While innumerable examples and parallels can be given for all colors, the main thing to keep in mind is that everything of the same color shares the same or similar magical properties. The more you work with colors and learn of their magical energies, the more you will see the interconnected Synchronicity of Colors all around you in all things through daily life.

ASPECTS OF LA SANTA MUERTE

La Santa Muerte herself has seven main colors: black, white, red, gold, green, blue, and purple. Sometimes brown is included as an eighth color or as a replacement for one of the other colors, but this tends to be the exception rather than the norm. These seven colors are called aspects in the Santa Muerte community, and in addition to the seven main aspects (plus brown), there are a number of other colors and shades that have popularity within the community, such as copper, silver, orange, amber, yellow, and bone. But the main seven are really the only ones a devotee will ever need to do all magic.

More traditional and conservative devotees of La Santa Muerte only regard three of these as "true" aspects: black, white, and red. To them, all others are superfluous and unnecessary, in much the same way that the three primary colors (red, yellow, blue) are the colors from which all other colors manifest via mixing and blending. While this viewpoint does have logical reasoning, it is, by far, a much less common viewpoint in the community.

Technically, Death is beyond colors, and even the colors visible to the human eye are only a fraction of the totality of colors that could exist in the universe. So, there is no absolutely correct answer to the number of main aspects pertinent to La Santa Muerte, and those who say otherwise either have a very self-limiting view of Death or are trying to convince themselves that they are "more enlightened" devotees because they know the "truth." From my experience in the Santa Muerte Mysteries and exploring the mysticism of Hermeticism and a multitude of world religions, the middle path tends to be the best path, though not the only path. The seven-aspect Santa Muerte provides a good middle ground between the very restrictive three-aspect Santa Muerte and the ultra-liberal infinite-aspect Santa Muerte.

Each of her aspects is usually depicted by the color of her cloak. When not being petitioned or utilized in a spell, La Santa Muerte is shown in her signature black or white cloak. The main consistency is always to leave her bones white, but this is more of an artistic tradition than a rule. For rituals and spellwork, some people will have multiple statues of La Santa Muerte, each wearing a different colored cloak, and some will just have a general skeleton figurine and sew little pieces of cloth onto her. Creativity and ingenuity can be just as effective as purchasing power when it comes to magic. The list below provides all the information on the major aspects of La Santa Muerte.

Black

Black is the default color of La Santa Muerte's cloak. It is used primarily in protection magic and in hexes. Since black is the result of the absorption of light and the absence of color, it is widely associated with death (the absence of life) and witchcraft (whose stereotypical black robes are worn to absorb energies into spellwork). In the Taoist symbol for yin-yang, the yin energy of the universe is symbolized by the black half of the circle, which is often misinterpreted as evil, but is better understood as passivity and receptivity. Thus femininity, intuition, night, soft, cold, wet, and yielding are all categorized under black yin energy. For these reasons, the black aspect of La Santa Muerte is used in protection magic, where the objective is not to project energy, but rather intuitively foresee negative energy and take away its harmful effects and neutralize it, or, if that's not possible, to become invisible to the harmful energy and avoid it altogether. Similarly, it is used in hexes and harmful magic to soften and weaken the intended target and cause them some sort of loss.

White

White is the other default color of La Santa Muerte's cloak. It is unique in that it is not relegated to a single domain of magic and that it can be used in any and all spellwork. Since white is the result of the reflection of all visible colors, it has the magical energies of all colors in it. For this reason, the white aspect of La Santa Muerte is the universal "go-to" color when in doubt of which specific color to use in a spell. White is the only color used in purification rituals. When we purify something we expel and push all the toxins and negative energies away, just as all the colors in the visible spectrum are expelled and pushed away to make something appear white. In the Taoist symbol for yin-yang, the yang energy of the universe is symbolized by the white side of the circle, which is often misinterpreted as good, but is better understood as aggressiveness and projecting. Thus masculinity, logic, day, hard, warm, dry, and giving are all categorized under white yang energy.

Red

Other than the traditional black and white, red has become the most popular alternate color for La Santa Muerte's cloak. This aspect is predominately involved in sex magic, both to impassion a lover and to keep him or her chaste. The synchronicity of red can be found in erotica, blood, and the root chakra, and it is the symbol of basic instincts such as hunger, thirst, sex drive, and survival. In some depictions of the Taoist yin-yang symbol, the white half is substituted by the color red, thereby creating an association between red and the yang traits of masculinity, aggressiveness, warmth, day, and so on. While deep reds are best for sex magic, lighter shades of red (such as pink) can be used for dating magic and romantic quests where sex is not the main focus of the relationship (symbolized by the lessened intensity of the color). Because red is the harshest and most powerful color in the visible spectrum, it is also associated with aggression (as in the term "seeing red") and is used in magic that requires one to aggressively pursue something such as one's dreams. In esoteric stores that sell Santa Muerte merchandise, the paraphernalia of her red aspect is often the highest seller of all seven main colors.[36]

Gold

The gold aspect of La Santa Muerte is a close second in popularity to her red aspect. Gold is the prominent color for money magic. Devotee entrepreneurs will often have a gold-cloaked Santa Muerte figurine in their shops, hidden or in public view, as a charm to attract prosperity. For many people living in the United States, green is often associated with money more so than gold is, because green is the dominant color of U.S. cur-

---

36. Chesnut, *Devoted to Death*.

rency. But since the color of modern currency varies from country to country, green is not universally symbolic of wealth. Throughout time, gold has always been associated with wealth. From expensive and beautiful jewelry of gold metal to the wealth of golden wheat and grains after a bountiful harvest, gold subconsciously symbolizes abundance. Moreover, gold/yellow has a synchronicity with the solar plexus chakra, which is the energy center of personal power; when feeling threatened, we subconsciously tend to cross our arms and protect our solar plexus. Additionally, the amount of self-empowerment one feels can be directly correlated with one's sense of career success and financial security.

Green

The green aspect of La Santa Muerte is used in legal and courtroom magic. In the subconscious, green is associated with nature, which, in turn, is associated with the "natural way of things" and "natural truths." Ideally, the justice system is meant to get to the truth of a dispute between two parties and then deliver a judgment that effectively puts the parties back into their natural states before the dispute occurred. This ideal, however, is not always realized, and so devotees of La Santa Muerte will utilize her green aspect to ensure that the court proceedings play out according to true, natural justice. Ironically, those who know that they are truly guilty tend not to use this green aspect, instead preferring black to evade and become invisible to punishment. The color green also has synchronicity with the heart chakra and is used for love magic. While shades of red are used for sexual and romantic love, green is primarily used for self-love, which truly is the greatest love of all. A final interesting point about her green aspect is that it is also used in healing magic, specifically for autoimmune conditions such as HIV/AIDS, which is a rampant issue in the gay community, a community of people known for having trouble truly loving themselves and accepting who they are.

Blue

The blue aspect of La Santa Muerte is primarily used in wisdom magic. A popular color among students and teachers, spellwork involving the color blue is often utilized with the objective of absorbing and retaining knowledge and then subsequently being able to successfully communicate that information via teaching or performing well on exams. Much like the open sky and the ocean deep, blue is symbolic of mental clarity and the profundity of information in this world. Blue also has a synchronicity with the throat chakra, which is the energy center of communication. The throat is also home to the thyroid, a gland responsible for maturation and growth, two things often correlated with knowledge and wisdom.

Purple

The purple aspect of La Santa Muerte is primarily used in healing magic and transformational magic. While technically every color has its own specific association with healing, purple is the universal color for all healing, whether the ailment is physical, psychological, or spiritual. In most magical systems (including that of La Santa Muerte), there is a common belief that all diseases are essentially psychosomatic, meaning that bodily illness is the result of mental patterns and ways of thinking. Though controversial to nonmagical people, the acceptance of this truth is crucial for success in all healing magic. For a more in-depth and complete understanding of this metaphysical concept, I suggest reading *You Can Heal Your Life* by the profoundly wise author Louise L. Hay. For our purposes here, though, an acceptance that one's thought patterns directly affect one's bodily health is all that is necessary. The color purple has a synchronicity with the third-eye chakra (located on the forehead between the eyebrows), which is the energy center of enlightenment and vision. A correlation is often made between the third-eye chakra, the brain, and the pineal gland, which is the light-sensitive production center of both melatonin (which regulates sleep) and dimethyltryptamine (the human body's only known natural hallucinogen). Interestingly, purple plants often have similar effects upon the human body, such as lavender, which is used to help induce sleep, and grapes, which are fermented and served as an alcoholic beverage to alter one's mind, and whose excess can lead to migraine headaches and sensitivity toward light.

Brown

The color brown is sometimes accepted as an additional main aspect of La Santa Muerte or a replacement for one of the aforementioned aspects, but this varies from person to person. In general, the majority of devotees see brown as an in-between color that is less utilized and less important than the previous colors, yet more utilized and more important than any other alternate or additional color. This is fitting since brown is the aspect of La Santa Muerte most often utilized in necromancy. Subconsciously, brown is frequently seen as a very supportive and foundational color, like the roots of a plant, the trunk of a tree, the wooden frame of a house, and the stability of the earth. In the same vein, our ancestors and the people who inhabited this planet before us have all together formed the foundational basis of our modern society and the world today. To reach out and communicate with the spirits of the dead is to come in contact with our roots as a living being. The color brown is also symbolic of dirt, which forms the middle of the earth between the verdant top and the molten core, and so we use brown in necromantic spells since we are trying to form a bridge between the physical world and the spiritual world. Additionally, autumn has strong associations with brown, and it is the time of the year when plants begin to die en masse and the veil between the worlds becomes its most thin.

Rainbow

No discussion of the aspects of La Santa Muerte is complete without mention of her popular seven-color rainbow depiction adapted from the Seven African Powers candle of Santería. Although the colors and the order in which they appear tend to vary, the generally accepted (and most popular) rainbow aspect of La Santa Muerte is as follows from top to bottom in thick horizontal stripes: silver, copper, gold, red, blue, green, and purple. It is primarily used in a single, all-encompassing spell rather than a single category of spellwork itself. While the use of individual aspects produces a more focused and specific effect, the use of this multicolored rainbow aspect produces a less focused and broader effect. A good analogy would be the use of a hose in projecting water: the more focused the water is, the harder it will hit a specific target, and the less focused the water is, the more softly it will hit multiple targets. Specifically, the seven color correspondences are: silver = luck, copper = breaking of negative energies, gold = abundance/prosperity, red = love/sex, blue = wisdom/connection to spirituality, green = justice, purple = health/transformative thinking. Because it is all-encompassing, her rainbow aspect is often confused as equivalent to her white aspect, but this is not the case. The white aspect (in addition to its own dominion) can be used as a *substitute* for any *one* color, while the rainbow aspect is only used when targeting *all* aspects *simultaneously*.

The Doctrine of Signatures

In addition to the Synchronicity of Colors, the other major example of the Hermetic Law of Correspondence's involvement with Santa Muerte magic is the Doctrine of Signatures. Although in its strictest sense this doctrine only applies to botanical magic due to its origins in ancient herbalism and early medicine, to most devotees, its definition is expanded into the realm of all things organic and inorganic.

Along the lines of the Synchronicity of Colors, the Doctrine of Signatures refers to a thing's shape. If something is shaped similarly to something else, according to this doctrine these two things are energetically connected and correlated. This was first categorized and defined into a system during the eras of ancient Greece and Rome, but humans have been using the Doctrine of Signatures since we were first capable of rational thought. Naturally, it was first used as a way to find medicines due to its simplicity, and although simple, it proved consistently reliable: plants that look like human genitalia can be aphrodisiacs, walnuts look like little brains and are good for the brain, cloves look like little teeth and are good for toothaches, leafy greens have ridges on their leaves that look like the twisting and turning digestive tract and are a good source of fiber.

The visual similarity, however, does not have to look like a part of the human body for it to be medicinally helpful. The practical function of a thing's physical design can signify that, in spellwork, its magical function is the same. For example, take the plants burdock and nettle, which are thistle-like with numerous pointy spines similar to barbed wire that can cut human flesh and leave a lingering sense of burning irritation. Naturally, this evolutionary trait is designed to keep harmful animals away, but interestingly, if ingested as a tea, both burdock and nettle act as a tonic that flushes out toxins. When looked at through the lens of the Doctrine of Signatures, this correlation makes sense since both burdock and nettle are defensive plants that keep out harm from its personal area, thus naturally, when consumed as a tea, they keep out harm from our personal area (the body). In spellwork, burdock and nettle are often used in protection spells to keep harm at a distance.

To the nonmagical community, this and countless other similarities between plant shape and plant medicine are thought of as superstition and explained as mere coincidence. As you are learning, though, there is no such thing as coincidence. Even in modern times, when scientific expeditions set out to places such as the Amazon jungle to find new medicines, they often employ the assistance of local indigenous tribes. The researchers are amazed at how consistent and precise the locals are in using plants to heal themselves despite their lack of familiarity with Western botany, chemistry, and toxicology. Moreover, the researchers are also frequently left in awe over the fact that, although the jungles of the Amazon are home to an array of poisonous plants, the locals never accidentally poison themselves in the search for new medicinal plants. When asked how they can always tell the difference between a helpful plant and a baneful plant, as well as for which specific ailments to use which specific part of the plant, the answer is always the same across various tribes. They "talk" with the plant spirit and/or they "read" the language of the plant expressed through its shape and colors.[37]

---

37. Bradley C. Bennett, "Doctrine of Signatures: An Explanation of Medicinal Plant Discovery or Dissemination of Knowledge?" (*Economic Botany* 61, no. 3 (2007): 246–255).

Even in the herbalism of medieval Europe, the visual logic of the Synchronicity of Colors and Doctrine of Signatures predominated. With mass illiteracy and a severe lack of double-blind scientific experimentation, how could the local healers have known what to use, when to use it, how to use it, and how much of it to use? Any single mistake and they would have undoubtedly lost the community's trust since the death of a person due to medicine given to them was often followed by accusations of harmful witchcraft or deliberate poisoning. Even nowadays, to err in medicine can cost someone their career, as often seen in doctors who make surgical mistakes or pharmacy technicians who make a small imbalance in encapsulating prescriptions. Even if they didn't lose their jobs, no one would ever again trust their skills.

SYMPATHETIC MAGIC

Though there are numerous other examples that could be given for the Synchronicity of Colors and the Doctrine of Signatures, the important thing to keep in mind when working with Santa Muerte magic—and magic in general—is that there are no coincidences in this world. If we look hard enough, we can see patterns in everything, and these patterns repeat themselves in everything else. In Hermeticism, this falls under the Law of Correspondence, since the patterns above repeat themselves in the patterns below, and the patterns below repeat themselves in the patterns above. For magical practitioners who don't subscribe to Hermeticism, the technical terminology for this phenomenon is sympathetic magic.

In almost every magical tradition (Santa Muerte magic included), sympathetic magic is an important and fundamental part of all spellwork. Much like how the indigenous tribes of the Amazon "talk" to and "read" the language of the plants, we must learn how to "talk" to the universe and "read" its responses. But because the universe cannot verbally speak to us or physically write down a response, it uses the patterns, signs, and symbols of sympathetic magic through the Synchronicity of Colors and/or the Doctrine of Signatures. To communicate with the universal forces involved in magic, it is necessary to be able to speak the language, and that language is sympathetic magic.

If this is all new to you, think of sympathetic magic through this example. Imagine that you are in a foreign country where you cannot speak, read, or write the language. You are very hungry and are in need of food, but there is no way to communicate your needs to anyone around you. Thus you are forced to express your desires and receive feedback through symbolism. First, you wave your hand at someone with the palm open, symbolizing that you want their attention. Next, you repeatedly curl your fingers toward yourself, symbolizing that they should approach you. Once they do, you smile to show that you are nonthreatening, and then you express your need. Because you are hungry, you might rub your stomach and follow it by facing your palms toward the sky and shrugging your shoulders, or maybe, instead, you pretend to hold some food and take overly dramatic bites out of it. If they understood, they might draw you a simple map of the closest restaurant or fast food place. Just to make sure you understand, you point to the direction of the restaurant and nod your head up and down. To affirm your assumptions they will repeat the nod, or, to show you that you are incorrect, they will shake their head back and forth and then point in the true direction.

Without speaking a single word, you have successfully communicated with someone by the use of signs and symbols, successfully expressing your desires and understanding their feedback on how to obtain what you want. This is how communicating with the magical energies of the universe works, including the magic of La Santa Muerte.

The most famous pop culture examples of sympathetic magic in action are the notorious voodoo dolls of Afro-Caribbean magical traditions. Through the creation of a doll that looks like someone, that doll becomes energetically connected to the person whom it depicts, and whatever is symbolically done to the doll, the person will symbolically experience. Never are the acts meant to be literal, though. Poking pins into the doll's eyes won't suddenly cause the person to suffer sharp eye pain. Remember, a magical practitioner speaks to the universe through the language of sympathetic magic, and sympathetic magic is never literal. For that previous example, depending on the magical intention, pins in the eyes might symbolize the forcing of that person to see the pain they've caused, or even to help them by symbolizing the granting of sharp eyesight.

The reason the universe does not speak in a literal fashion is because the universe does not speak to our literal, logical mind, but rather it speaks to our intuitive and symbolic subconscious. This is why it is so important to be able to focus both the conscious mind and the subconscious mind together on the same frequency. Already we are accustomed to understanding our logical minds, as doing so is a necessity to function in society, but we have forgotten how to understand our subconscious mind. The only time most of us communicate subconsciously is when we dream, and because our subconscious mind does not function in literalism, it can only express itself and understand new information through symbolism. This is why dreams are often so strange and meaningful yet never direct and logical.

By definition, our subconscious mind is out of our conscious control. Still, it is speaking to us all the time through symbolism. Much like how our eyes are constantly seeing various objects all at once yet we only really notice those objects that we focus on, so too is our subconscious mind constantly receiving information from the world around us, but because most of us don't focus on symbolism, most of us don't notice this information. By learning symbolism, you can become aware of when the subconscious mind is receiving new information, and you can, in turn, program your subconscious mind in the language it understands.

We may not be able to control the subconscious mind, but we can guide it with our conscious minds with training. When both the conscious and subconscious minds are on the same page, sympathetic magic can take place, and the energies of the world can be understood and manipulated according to our will.

A final word on the Law of Correspondence and sympathetic magic. For all of you who are new to magic, this chapter may have been a little intimidating—filled with technical terms, examples, and analogies to better explain concepts that can never be fully understood. It can be challenging. In many ways, you are learning a new language: the language of the universe, the language of magic. And like any new language, perfect fluency seems quite daunting when you are just starting out. Yes, you will make mistakes, you will mistranslate things, you will be at a loss for how to express your desires, and you will make a fool of yourself. But that's all part of the learning process. By first learning the basics, and then building upon them, you will slowly begin to see the patterns of a language, and what seemed to make no sense in the beginning now makes perfect sense. But the only way you can learn a language is through practice and persistence.

Continue reading this book, and immerse yourself further into the language of Santa Muerte magic. Experiment and try things as you go along. If you have the determination and the wisdom to know that mistakes are part of the path, then you'll eventually get to where you want to be in reading the signs of the universe and speaking right back. I believe you have the power to be fluent in this new, magical language. After all, there are no coincidences in life, and the fact that you are reading this book now is a sign that you are ready to learn to co-create magic with La Santa Muerte herself.

6
The Tools of Death

"Despise not death, but welcome it, for nature wills it like all else."
~MARCUS AURELIUS

In the world of magic there are many tools. Some of them are ancient and some are modern, but regardless, their classification as a tool in magic is purely dependent upon their inherent energies (through the Law of Correspondence and sympathetic magic) as well as the intention in the spellwork. While many tools are the same across many magical traditions, certain tools may be used differently in different traditions.

Arguably one of the most striking differences in tools between the mystery school of La Santa Muerte and various other magical traditions is the lack of elemental emphasis. By this, I mean that the elements of earth, air, fire, and water play a less featured role in Santa Muerte spellwork, and, in fact, most devotees don't place any focus on the elements at all.

Most elemental magic in the Santa Muerte tradition comes from devotees with previous magical background, especially witchcraft and Wicca. This is not to say that working with the elements is taboo or ineffective in relation to La Santa Muerte; it is just uncommon and not a prominent feature in the community. The same can be said for directional emphasis wherein an object's directional association and physical location add nuances to a spell. Although uncommon and not a focus of the magical tradition, they can still be used. The idea in the mystery school is that death is beyond direction and all elements can be a tool of death.

Still, in the eyes of outside traditions, La Santa Muerte is most often associated with the elements of earth and water. Deities of femininity and death tend to be associated with the earth because of its ability to create, sustain, and nurture life. Earth is also the element that experiences death most frequently through the changing of the seasons and the finite existence of organic matter. Protection, healing, and prosperity are hallmark traits of earth magic since the earth is strong and stable to provide shelter and barriers, contains the medicine of the natural world, and contains the riches of society buried inside it (precious metals, precious gems, petroleum oil, etc.).

With regard to water, La Santa Muerte's femininity and dual existence in both the spiritual and physical worlds grant her this association. Water is symbolic of emotions and intuition—what is visible on the surface often masks the profundity of what lies below. While both men and women possess logic and intuition, in general, women are blessed with a stronger sense of intuitive wisdom, thus linking them with water. The ability to travel between the worlds is seen as a very water-like characteristic since water has no definite shape, absorbs itself into other materials, and can even travel through a barrier via osmosis. In many mythological traditions, bodies of water often serve as the gateway to the underworld: the River Styx in Greek mythology, stagnant lakes and swamps in Mayan mythology, and the river barrier to the land of the dead in African Ashanti mythology, among others.

In terms of directions, La Santa Muerte is most often portrayed as being in the west. It is the direction of the setting sun and, in many cultures, symbolizes old age and death. Many deities of death are said to reside in the west as well as the spirit worlds and lands of the dead. The west signifies endings and the unknown because Eurocentric views of colonial and territorial expansions in the New World portrayed the west as a wild place, uncharted and largely unexplored. Interestingly, the west is also associated with the element of water, and both earth and water are considered feminine elements, creating a further pattern of synchronicity between them and La Santa Muerte.

Still, the elements of earth and water, and the direction of west will not be a focus of the tools and spells in this book. Their mention here is simply for those who come from magical traditions with an emphasis on elements and directions. For those well versed in these other traditions, feel free to incorporate earth magic, water magic, and westward magic into your spellwork with La Santa Muerte. Although uncommon, they can be just as efficacious if used in accordance with sympathetic magic and intention.

Regarding the tools themselves, let me begin by revealing the most important, fundamental, and indispensable tool necessary for all spellwork…YOU! I know that might sound awfully clichéd, but it's clichéd because it's true. All magical energy is inherently within you. Think back to the Law of Correspondence: if there is a magical energy outside you, then there is that same magical energy *inside* you, and vice versa.

In a certain sense, tools can be likened to props. They themselves are symbols used to help you align your subconscious and conscious minds. Most people cannot do this very easily, and so they employ the use of a physical item to assist them in this mental alignment.

Anyone familiar with theatre and acting is already well aware of this concept. If given the role of a certain character, an actor really needs nothing more than him- or herself. Through the use of costumes and stage props, though, most actors find it much easier to get into the mental state of the character they have to portray. The costume and props are by no means necessary, but they facilitate the acting process tremendously. The same is true of magical tools. They are not necessary, but they make spellwork exponentially easier and more effective.

With that said, however, tools do have inherent power all their own. Yes, you can perform effective magic without tools, but performing that same magic *with* tools can be *more* effective. Just because you possess all the energies of magic within you doesn't mean that you can't add the magical energies of other things to amplify a spell.

Think back to the example in the previous chapter about the ability of burdock and nettle to detoxify the body when consumed as a tea. Can you detoxify your body without drinking burdock and nettle tea? Absolutely! Will it help you and be more effective if you *do* drink burdock and nettle tea? Yes! Additionally, if you were to drink a different herbal tea such as chamomile, would it have the same detoxifying effect on the body? No, it wouldn't. This is because everything in nature has its own energy, its own magic.

Blessing Your Tools

In order to take an item and make it into a tool, it is necessary to awaken its dormant magical energy. Most devotees call this "blessing" a tool, but it goes by other names such as charging, consecrating, cleansing, purifying, etc. When we bless a tool, we align our minds and focus our attention on it. Then we "program" the tool with the specifications of the energies we wish it to share with us. When we use this blessed tool in spellwork, it will know exactly what we expect from it and how it can assist us.

Many people skip this important step in working with their tools, despite it being necessary to awaken the tools' magical properties. No object in this world is two-dimensional in terms of its magical potential. Any single tool can be used for a variety of magical purposes. Take the thistle-like burdock again as an example. Its spines reveal (through the language of sympathetic magic) that it has the magical energy of protection and keeping harm away. However, those same spines also reveal that burdock has the magical energy of attachment and making things cling together. This is because of its reputation for attaching its dried-up burrs to animal fur and human clothing. In fact, the invention of Velcro was inspired by the way burdock firmly attaches itself to clothes, and the design of interlocking fibers of Velcro function in the exact same way as the burdock plant. So, since burdock has the magical energy to repel and attract, how does it know which energy you are expecting of it? By blessing it, you make clear which energies should be awakened and why you are asking to awaken those specific energies.

Most importantly, always remember to make a connection with the tool before using it. It too has spiritual energies and a level of consciousness, though different from our own. On one level, the object you wish to use as a tool may, in actuality, not want to be used as a tool, and if you force it to become a tool, it will resist and work against you. On another level, all workings are more effective when all participating parties have a mutually amicable relationship. Think about any group project you have done. If you work with friends, the entire project tends to be completed more smoothly and enjoyably. If you work with people who dislike each other, the project tends to be more laborious and time consuming.

The same is true of your tools. Before you use it, take the time to get to know it. I'm not suggesting having a chat about how its day went and what it plans to do on the weekend. I'm suggesting doing some research online and if possible observing it in its natural state. Get an overall sense of what it does and does not do, just as you would get a sense of a person's abilities and inabilities when having to work with them in a group project. As with anything in life, show it respect, and it will show respect to you. Make friends with it, and it will help you more frequently and with more energy than it would help a stranger.

The reason most people skip this step is because they think it's silly. Sure, they want to perform magic spells and work with the Spirit of Death, but taking the time to commune with nature—now, *that's* silly. Can you see the selective reasoning at play here? It comes as no surprise that the people who skip this crucial step are the same people who claim that their spells never work or that La Santa Muerte is ignoring their petitions. My belief is that if you are open-minded enough to work with magic, you should be open-minded enough to make friends with the natural energies that make magic possible.

Once you have developed a friendly relationship with an item (or at the very least a working relationship), it is still necessary to ask if it would like to be blessed so as to be used as a tool in spellwork. Just because you are friends doesn't guarantee that it can do everything at all times with you whenever you want. Friendship is a two-way street. You might invite a good friend to the movies, but they might not want to see the movie and decline. It's not that they don't want to do things with you, it's just that they don't want to do that *particular* thing.

In most cases, from my experience, if you've developed a good relationship with a potential magical tool, it will be more than willing to help. To know if it will accept your blessing, simply hold its image in your mind (or touch it if possible and safe) and ask it. You'll intuitively feel the answer, and if it is negative, simply thank the tool and continue on until you find another of the same object that does comply or a completely different type of object with similar magical energies that is willing to be a tool for your spell.

The various tools and their uses will be outlined in detail below. In the Santa Muerte tradition, there are four main tool sets: candles, incense, plants, and minerals. But it is important to note that it is not necessary to become a master of all the tools of magic. Each individual person has his or her own innate talents and weaknesses, interests and disinterests. While going through these tool descriptions, you may find yourself more drawn to one particular tool set than others. Additionally, through experimentation, you may discover that you have a natural talent for some and an intense learning curve for others. This is all very normal. Granted, it is absolutely possible to learn how to become an expert in the wielding of every tool set, but do not be surprised if you find yourself exclusively using only one tool set.

Tool Set I: Candles

Candles are far and away the most popular tool used in Santa Muerte magic. They are easy to learn, easy to use, relatively inexpensive, and phenomenally effective. While there are many types of candles, the use of each type is essentially the same. The candle acts as a vessel into which we infuse our desired petition. As the wax burns away and smoke is released into the atmosphere, the petition is sent out to the universe to manifest itself.

Many religious traditions around the world are familiar with candle magic and use them in a similar way. Catholic churches, in particular, are famous for having numerous rows of candles lit, each candle being a petition to God for the granting of a miracle or an expression of gratitude for miracles already performed. Legends say that the smoke is symbolic of the candle's infused petition rising toward the heavens, effectively acting as a messenger device delivering the needs of humanity to God's ear.

While many devotees of La Santa Muerte take this interpretation literally, the magic of candles (like all magical tools) is really their ability to focus and align the conscious and subconscious minds while adding in the candle's own magical energies to augment the spell's power. The aligning of the two minds is necessary for a spell to manifest, and the longer and more frequently we can align the two minds toward a single intended outcome, the faster it manifests. Because candles are simple to use, many magical practitioners find them to be the easiest tools with which to maintain long periods of such focused alignment.

Candles are also popular because they can be used in conjunction with other tools to create a compound candle. Candles come ready-made in a wide variety of colors. The relative softness of wax makes it easy to carve names, dates, and other intentions into the candle, thus further enhancing the magical intention. They can be sprinkled with herbs, anointed with oils and perfumes, and even placed in different metallic candlesticks, all of which add to the magic.

An example of a compound candle used for love magic would be a pink candle anointed with rose oil and sprinkled with basil, which is placed in a copper candlestick and has hearts carved into the wax along with the ideal traits of the intended lover. Everything added to this candle has correspondences with love from various other tool sets, and upon the lighting of the candle, they will all be activated simultaneously.

In actuality, before lighting the candle, we must bless it and infuse our magical intention into it. An unblessed candle is just like a blank sheet of paper, full of limitless potential but without a specific purpose or duty.

The blessing of a candle is very simple. Hold the candle (unlit) in your hands. Visualize the intended result of your spell. Be as specific as possible and imagine what it would feel like once it has manifested. Really get into the "feeling place" of having received what you desire. The visualization should be so intense that all five senses are fooled into thinking that the spell has already manifested. The goal is to believe you are in possession of what you want, even if it is just for a moment. Then, once your entire body is filled with the sensations of having your spell manifested, release all that energy into the candle. Just as a photograph can forever capture a single happy moment, so too can a candle capture the exact energy that is infused into it.

Now that the candle is blessed and energetically charged with the intention, light it and let it burn. The candle will release that energy into the universe, and it will serve as a reminder of that feeling of having your desire manifested. The more often you stare into the dancing flame and remember the exact feeling you had when you blessed the candle, the faster the spell will manifest upon the complete evaporation of all the wax.

Depending on the type of candle being used, it may be impractical and not possible to have it completely burn after having only been lit once. Fortunately, the candle can be extinguished and relit as many times as necessary for the wax to entirely evaporate without compromising the spell.

And that brings up a major issue with using candles: *be safe!* Just because a candle is blessed and is acting as a tool of benevolent magic doesn't mean that it can't still burn your house down. Always use common sense when dealing with an open flame by never leaving it unattended or in the presence of active animals and young children. If you have to be away from the candle, extinguish it and then relight it when you get back. Also, be aware of any flammable objects nearby, and if you add oils and herbs to the candle, research those substances ahead of time to be sure they will not emit noxious smoke or act as an accelerant for the fire.

Additionally, be mindful of the candlestick. When I was just beginning to utilize candles in spellwork, I initially bought a super-inexpensive glass candlestick because I was trying to be frugal. Well, that proved to be unwise because once the wick had burned down toward the base, the glass candlestick shattered and the candle fell. Fortunately, I did not leave the candle unattended, and so was able to immediately extinguish the candle and sweep up all the glass shards off the tabletop and floor. What I had forgotten to take into account was that the heat of the flame would weaken the glass and cause it to break. So learn from my novice mistake and always be mindful of your candlestick or holder.

Finally, a common misconception about candle magic is that all one has to do is light it and then all the work is over; the wax will burn and our intention will manifest without having to do anything else. However, like all magic, spellwork with candles also needs real-world follow-up to assist in the manifestation, all of which will be explained further in part III.

TOOL SET II: INCENSE

Aside from candles, incense is the other most popularly used tool by religions all over the world. In its broadest definition, incense is any natural material that emits a fragrant smoke upon being burned. Powdered or crystallized herbs and resins are the most common forms of incense available to the general public, and many devotees choose make their own.

The symbolism and mechanics of incense are similar to that of candles. The incense is blessed and charged with an intention, it is lit, and the resulting smoke is representative of the intention rising toward the heavens.

The effects that specific scents have on the human body and human psychology are very real and very powerful. If this were not the case, large shopping centers and amusement parks such as Disneyland would not be spending so much money on ventilating the premises with specific scents to elicit a specific biological and psychological response.[38] In the same way, we can purposefully choose specific scents to align our subconscious with the desired end goal of our spellwork.

Incense is especially popular in the devotion to La Santa Muerte because, around the world, incense is strongly associated with death. At

---

38. Mark David Jones and J. Jeff Kober, *Lead with Your Customer: Transform Culture and Brand into World-Class Excellence* (Alexandria, VA: American Society for Training and Development, 2010).

Catholic funerals, a censer of incense is swung around the casket or urn in a clockwise motion by the priest or his altar servers. The smoke symbolizes the rising of the soul to Heaven, and the ashes left behind are symbolic of the ashes that we will all one day become. On a more practical level, incense was also originally used in funerary rites to mask the smell of the unpreserved, decaying corpse. Thus in the psyche of Catholics (who make up the majority of current Santa Muerte devotees), incense has an ingrained connection with death.

Due to the fact that many incense fragrances are based on floral and herbal scents, I will omit those in the list below, instead leaving them for the section on plants further on in this chapter. The energetic and magical properties of plants transfer over to their scents via incense. For this list, I will describe only those fragrances that are predominantly used as an incense tool and rarely as a plant tool.

Camphor

Camphor is a popular incense in Southeast Asia. Organically, it is extracted from the wood of an evergreen tree native to Indonesia and Taiwan. Energetically, it has cooling properties that allow it to neutralize aggression. For this reason, it is frequently used in spellwork for protection against physical and spiritual aggressors who intend to do harm, as well as for wisdom by calming the mind. In nonmagical uses, it is commonly found in insect repellants, antimicrobial substances, and as a rust preventing agent. Most notably, it is one of the main active ingredients in Vicks VapoRub as well as certain cooling and anti-itch gels. Its use as an important ingredient in embalming fluid grants it associations with death and Santa Muerte magic involving self-preservation and not allowing one's self to be broken down. Due to its toxicity, its utilization as an incense should be done sparingly and in very small amounts.

Copal

Copal is *the* premier incense used in Mesoamerica. Its category as a sacred scent in Aztec and Mayan religions before Columbian colonization is well documented. It has been nicknamed the "New World frankincense" due to its usage in Latin America being similar to the usage of frankincense in the Old World. Organically, it is a resin that looks similar to amber. Energetically, it has sun properties that allow it to enlighten the mind and cast out darkness. Because of this, it was primarily used to purify sacred spaces and temples as well as to facilitate enlightenment in sweat lodge huts. Unique to the mystery school of La Santa Muerte, devotees will often use copal in love magic to "warm the heart" of a lover.

Dragon's Blood

Contrary to the name, dragon's blood is not actually the blood of a dragon. Organically, it is a resin extracted from palm trees native to the Canary Islands, Morocco, and Socotra Island off the Arabian Peninsula. It gets its name from its deep, blood-red color. Energetically, it has fire properties and has been associated with the gods of war from various cultures. In ancient Rome, it was used medicinally for gastrointestinal ailments and as a coagulant to stop bleeding. In spellwork, it is primarily used as an amplifier tool that increases the potency of the spell at large. When utilized for a specific purpose, dragon's blood is often used in love magic and lust magic to rekindle lost passion, manifest opportunities for casual sex, and increase male virility.

Frankincense

Frankincense is one of the most popular incenses used in monotheistic religions. Its use in Roman Catholicism is so widespread that the universally distinguishable "church scent" is actually the scent of frankincense. Its name comes from the Old French term *franc encens*, meaning "true incense." Organically, it is a resin extracted from a genus of tree native to East Africa and the Arabian Peninsula. Frankincense is most popularly known as one of the gifts of the Magi given to the baby Jesus, as told in the Gospel of Matthew. Energetically, it has yang properties and is considered a scent representative of masculinity. Together with myrrh, a plant with feminine energy, it produces a perfect compound of incense. It has been used medicinally by various cultures to treat gastrointestinal ailments as well as arthritis, and in modern scientific studies, promising research is being done on its ability to kill certain forms of cancer, including prostate cancer.[39] The aggressive killing nature of its medicinal properties corresponds well to its masculine properties, and because of these properties, it is most often utilized in spellwork for protection magic and money magic. Specific to the mystery school of La Santa Muerte, frankincense is one of the defining scents of death, stemming from its historical use in funerary rites and to mask the smell of decomposing bodies. Thus it is often utilized as a spell to mask oneself from danger and death.

Myrrh

Along with frankincense, myrrh is the other most popular incense used in monotheistic religions. Organically, it is a resin derived from a genus of thorny bushes and shrubs found in East Africa and the Arabian Peninsula. Myrrh is most popularly known as one of the gifts of the Magi given to the baby Jesus, as told in the Gospel of Matthew. Energetically, it is has yin properties and is considered a scent representative of femininity. In traditional Chinese medicine, it was used to purge the uterus of stagnant blood, and in modern times, promising scientific research is being done showing myrrh's capability of causing the remission of breast cancer.[40] Together with frankincense, it produces a perfect compound of incense. It was also a common offering in ancient Egypt for the deities Isis and Ra, as well as being a main ingredient in mummification. In spellwork, myrrh is utilized in amplifying psychic abilities and intuition. In Islamic herbalism, it was also described as one of the main fumigators for the home to restore the balance of family life.

39. Yingli Chen, Chunlan Zhou, Zhendan Ge, Yufa Liu, Yuming Liu, Weiyi Feng, Sen Li, Guoyou Chen, and Taiming Wei, "Composition and potential anticancer activities of essential oils obtained from myrrh and frankincense," http://www.ncbi.nlm.nih.gov/pmc/articles/PMC3796379/ (accessed May 7, 2015).

40. American Chemical Society, "'Gift of the Magi' Bears Anti-Cancer Agents, Researchers Suggest," ScienceDaily. http://www.sciencedaily.com/releases/2001/12/011205070038.htm (accessed May 7, 2015).

Nag Champa

Nag champa is the premier incense most commonly associated with Hinduism. Organically, it is a compound of sandalwood and plumeria. Its name comes from the Sanskrit words *nag*, meaning "breath/spirit," and *champa*, meaning "plumeria flowers." Energetically, it has air properties and has been associated with mental focus and profundity. For these reasons it is the predominant incense burned in Hindu monasteries and hermitages called ashrams, and it is a leading incense used in modern yoga studios. In spellwork, nag champa is utilized in wisdom magic, meditation, and the enlightenment of spiritual truths.[41]

Patchouli

Patchouli is an infamous incense that gained popularity within the U.S. and European hippie culture of the 1960s and 1970s due to its ability to mask the distinctive scent of marijuana. Because marijuana is a plant sacred to La Santa Muerte, her modern devotees often use patchouli for the same practical purposes in addition to magic. Organically, it is a bushy herb related to the mint family, native to tropical Asia. Energetically, it has "warrior female" properties and has been associated with the yang dot within the yin half of the Taoist yin-yang symbol, thus representing the masculinity within a feminine host. For this reason it is the premier incense used in lesbian love magic.[42] Patchouli has also been historically used along the Silk Road to preserve delicate silks from being eaten by moths due to its unique ability to prevent female moths from mating with male moths and laying eggs.[43] Other than lesbian-themed spellwork, patchouli is commonly used in anti-depression magic that promotes joy and a sense of not taking life too seriously. Because of this, it has been said that this incense attracts fairies and playful spirits.

---

41. http://www.essentialapothecary.com/

42. Christopher Penczak, *The Witch's Heart: The Magick of Perfect Love and Perfect Trust* (Woodbury, MN: Llewellyn, 2011).

43. Deborah Ward, "Patchouli Uses," Nature's Garden. http://www.naturesgardencandles.com/blog/patchouli-uses/ (retrieved May 7, 2015).

Sandalwood

Sandalwood is a very common fragrance used in beauty products, partly because of its universally pleasing scent and partly because of its antimicrobial and pore cleansing attributes. Organically, it is a genus of woody trees native to India, Southeast Asia, Australia, and numerous Pacific Islands. Technically, these trees are root parasites, which means that, in addition to photosynthesis, they tap the roots of other plants to absorb waters and nutrients. This corresponds well with the magical properties of the plant as a whole. Energetically, sandalwood has root properties that allow it to be used in all healing magic. It is often used to get to the root cause of all ailments, in particular psychological ailments. It is popularly used in Japan during meditation (especially Zen meditation) for its ability to get at the root of spiritual truths, and it is also used during tea ceremonies to root one's self in the present moment. In the Sufi tradition of Islam, sandalwood paste is placed on one's grave as a mark of respect and devotion.[44]

TOOL SET III: PLANTS

In recent years, plant tools have seen a rapid surge of popularity among Santa Muerte devotees as more and more people are being initiated into the mystery school from more and more diverse backgrounds. A reason for this is because plant magic seems more "realistic." People, even skeptical people, tend to trust the efficacy of plants, while candles, incense, and minerals are looked upon as too New Age and "airy-fairy" for most people new to magic.

The efficacy of herbs can be backed up by science. In laboratories, various plants have been documented to heal, harm, and have both immediate and long-term effects on the human body and mind. Everything from pharmacopeia-grade drugs to the food we eat has its roots in the plant kingdom. Because the power of plants is known, documented, and witnessed on a daily basis, the use of them in magic is much less of

---

44. Susan Bayly, *Saints, Goddesses and Kings: Muslims and Christians in South Indian Society, 1700–1900* (New York: Cambridge University Press, 2004).

a mental stretch. Plus, because plant magic and incense magic go hand in hand, those with a preference for incense magic will inevitably study the energies of the plant kingdom in order to more appropriately use different herbs, woods, and resins for their spells.

In the Latino community in particular, pseudo-scientific herbalism is accepted by the general public to be valid. Throughout much of Latin America and in cities with large Latino populations, esoteric stores will double as medical centers. These dual-purpose establishments are often called *yerbatería*, meaning "herb store." The proprietor of a yerbatería is called a *yerbatero/yerbatera*, which translates to mean "herb man/woman," but figuratively, they both closely equate to the title "witch doctor" or "medicine man/woman." Alternate names for yerbatero/yerbatera include *yerbero/yerbera* (alternative spelling in some Spanish dialects), *curandero/curandera* (one who cures), and *brujo/bruja* (male/female witch). While technically a yerbatero is one who uses herbs for magic, a curandero is one who uses any/all magical tools specifically to cure, and a brujo is someone who uses any/all magical tools for any/all magic.

Additionally, a yerbatería goes by other names, including *yerbería* (alternative spelling in some Spanish dialects) and *botánica* (botanical store). In general, a botánica carries with it a nuance of being a "magical" store, while yerbaterías and yerberías don't necessarily have an association with magic, though they often do. But the lines between their exact nomenclature are so blurred that all three names are used interchangeably and they are all mutually intelligible by Spanish speakers.

The reason yerbaterías and yerbateros are so popular in Latin American cultures is twofold. On one hand, Latinos tend to have a stronger belief in magic, superstition, and divine miracles. The Roman Catholic Church is arguably the most mystical/magical oriented branch of Christianity (although they will ardently deny this), and hundreds of years of this belief system combined with hundreds of years of Aztec and Mayan magic and mysticism have made the belief in a power greater than ourselves a deeply imbedded fixture within the Latino psyche.

On the other hand, going to a yerbatería is often an act of necessity. In many Latin American countries, the economic gap between the rich and the poor is quite large, and especially in Mexico, the promotion of NAFTA's free-market capitalism has only served to widen this gap even further. Many people don't have the financial luxury to be able to go to a "legitimate" doctor or hospital if they get sick. Additionally, many people cannot afford expensive psychologists if their ailment is emotional or mental in nature. And the purchasing of a cocktail of pharmacy drugs necessary to maintain one's health after a sickness or in old age is just not an economic possibility.

For all these needs, however, there exists another option: the local yerbatería. If the yerbatería is staffed by a curandero (and most are), this medicine man/woman can cure your physical ailments, mental maladies, and spiritual impotency, all for a dramatic fraction of the cost. For a large number of people, it is either this or nothing.

In addition to healing the sick, a yerbatero can create for you a potion or herbal charm to help manifest your desires as well as send out a hex to your enemies. It's a one-stop shop with relatively low prices, and to the poor and desperate such stores are a blessing. That's not to say, of course, that yerbateros are charlatans. In truth, their magic and knowledge of herbs are quite powerful. Granted, they are still human, and like all humans, certain ones may be more competent and reputable than others, and their ethical practices do vary.

But at their core, yerbateros are working with the same magical energies as anyone else, and with dedicated study and practice, anyone can become their own yerbatero. What yerbateros *are* really good for is to help a person believe in the potency and efficacy of a spell. For people new to magic or just not well versed in herbs, there is usually a lack of confidence in one's own abilities in spellwork, and belief and faith in one's own magical abilities are crucial for the efficacy of a spell. It is much easier for novices to simply hire a professional to do the spell for them, and because it was done by a professional, there is no doubt in their minds that it will work. While I fully support yerbateros and have great respect for them and their service, I would like to warn people to not become reliant upon others to manifest spells. Not only will it save you money, but being able to perform your own spell is very self-empowering and spiritually uplifting.

Below, I have made a list of the main herbs used in Santa Muerte magic. While, technically, *every* plant has its own energies and magical properties, to list them all would be just too much. If herbal tools speak to you and resonate with your soul, I highly recommend the book *Cunningham's Encyclopedia of Magical Herbs* by Scott Cunningham, one of the foremost experts in the use of herbal tools in magic. Regardless, the herbs listed in this book will serve all your needs for basic spellwork in the mystery school of La Santa Muerte.

In La Santa Muerte magic, herbal tools are especially valued because they experience life and death more closely to our own than other tools such as minerals and candles. Plants are alive, and to utilize them usually requires their death. In many ways, it is a form of sacrificial magic, animal and human sacrifice not being condoned by the mystery school of La Santa Muerte.

Due to the sacrificial nature of herbal tools, it is absolutely necessary to get the plant's permission before blessing it and using it in spellwork. In my experience, if you come to the plant with sincerity and respect, it will be more than willing to help you, so long as it agrees with the end goal of the spell. You will inherently feel an answer, whether it's affirmative or negative, and when in doubt, move on to another plant of the same or different species. If you make the plant an unwilling sacrifice, not only will it not manifest your spell, but there is also a chance that the spell will backfire. In general, be respectful of plants. They are all connected (as we all are), and so if you have a penchant for littering, carving your name into trees, or other such abuses of the environment, don't expect much sympathy from the plant kingdom should you want or need their help.

When used as a whole vessel, a simple blessing is all that is necessary. When the plant completely wilts, dries, and falls apart, it has done its job. Plants come with their own preprogrammed magical energies, and the selection of certain plants for certain spells is paramount. Be sure to do your own research to know the toxicity and legality of certain plants. The fact that a plant can assist you in magic does not mean that you are protected from its poison or from being arrested and convicted of criminal possession of an illegal substance.

Agave

Agave is a succulent plant native to dry climates of the Americas, primarily found in Mexico. Often confused with a cactus, this plant is most popularly known as the main ingredient of tequila, though its undistilled form has recently come into vogue as a natural sweetener akin to honey. Both the Aztec and Navajo cultures used the agave plant for a myriad of purposes, including food, drink, writing material, furniture, clothing, and rope.[45] Energetically, agave has self-sufficient properties, stemming from its ability to survive with very little water. In magic, it is primarily used in spells to grant self-confidence and be one's own support system. And because of its natural sugars, it is used in love magic to "sweeten a romance."

Aloe Vera

Aloe vera is a succulent plant very familiar to and heavily utilized by Latino cultures. It has thick, fleshy leaves with serrated edges, and inside those leaves is a clear antimicrobial gel used to cool sunburns as well as moisturize and rejuvenate the skin. Its use in medicine and beauty products dates back millennia, and in ancient Egypt, it was given as a burial gift to the pharaohs and nicknamed the "plant of immortality." [46] Energetically, it has motherly energies due to its ability to fiercely protect its leaves that are pregnant with gel and its ability to keep the sun in check (the sun having masculine/father properties). In magic, it is used in protection spells, especially for children, pregnant women, and loved ones. It is also commonly used in spells to bring out one's inner beauty and in love magic where the focus is self-love.

---

45. William H. Prescott, *History of the Conquest of Mexico and the Conquest of Peru* (New York: The Modern Library, 1948).

46. http://nccam.nih.gov/

Apple

Apples have a long history of being associated with wisdom and death. In Norse mythology, golden apples were thought to ward off death by granting immortality. [47] Botanically, the apple comes into fruition in autumn when most plants are dying. In Catholic mythology, the apple is infamous for being the fruit that caused Adam and Eve to be exiled from Eden, but rather than a plant of evil, the apple is a symbol of divine knowledge and wisdom. Energetically, apples have all of the aforementioned properties, and in magic, they are used in spells for wisdom, necromancy, and healing psychosomatic ailments.

Apricot

Apricots have a strong history of being associated with love and wisdom. In Shakespeare's *A Midsummer Night's Dream*, apricot was used as an aphrodisiac, an association of the fruit long held in European lore. In China, the apricot is used as a symbol of education (much like apples are in the Western world), stemming from stories of how Confucius used to teach his students in a grove of apricot trees. [48] Energetically, they have "two-spirit" properties due to their taste having the mixed flavor of peaches (a masculine plant) and plums (a feminine plant). In magic, they are primarily used in love spells, especially for transsexuals and other gender-variant people. [49] They are also used in wisdom spells where the focus is to understand one's own self as well as tap into men's feminine side and women's masculine side.

Avocado

Avocados are a signature plant in Mexican and Central American cuisine, the area of the world where they originated. In the Aztec language of Nahuatl, the word for avocado (*ahuakatl*) is also the word for testicle, due to the fruit resembling a man's testicles. In modern times, avocadoes are

---

47. Rowen Shepherd and Rupert Shepherd, *1000 Symbols: What Shapes Mean in Art and Myth* (London: Thames & Hudson, 2002).

48. http://ctext.org

49. Penczak, *Gay Witchcraft*.

used nutritionally to lower blood cholesterol and as a beauty product for the skin. Energetically, they have masculine properties due to their resemblance to male sex organs. In magic, avocados are used in love and lust spells to attract a man or bring out one's own masculine wiles as well as to increase male virility. They are often used in beauty spells, too, where the focus is on erotic beauty.

Beans

Beans are one of the oldest cultivated plants in human history. They have provided important basic nutrition for peoples around the world; in the New World, they were commonly planted alongside corn and squash due to their symbiotic relationship to help each other grow more sturdy and productive. While there are many varieties of beans, in general they energetically all have helper properties used in spells where the real-world manifestation will inevitably be dependent upon assistance from a group of people. They are also used in friendship magic to make new friends and improve communication between established friends as well as to find common ground between people for mutually beneficial purposes.

Belladonna

Belladonna has a long history of being associated with beauty and death. Its scientific name is *Atropa belladonna*, from the Greek Fate Atropos, who was in charge of cutting a person's thread of life (called Morta in Roman mythology). The Italian name *bella donna* (beautiful lady) is due to its historical use as a cosmetic to increase a woman's pupil size, a biological phenomenon that occurs naturally when a person gazes at something that stimulates them. Belladonna is often nicknamed deadly nightshade due to its high toxicity, which can disrupt the parasympathetic nervous system, causing narcosis, paralysis, and death. Because of this, it has also historically been used as an assassination poison. In European lore, it was one ingredient of a witch's "flying ointment." To onlookers, witches appeared to fly on broomsticks, but in actuality, the belladonna (mixed with an opiate) produced a drug-induced high wherein their spirits were flying. Energetically, it has femme fatale properties, making it popular in lust and protection magic. In lust spells, it is used to enhance one's seductiveness. In protection spells, it is used to metaphorically "assassinate" people from one's life by getting rid of any connections or attachments to toxic people. Due to its use as a "flying ointment," belladonna is often used in spellwork to connect with other dimensions and realms of consciousness.

Berry

While technically the word "berry" includes a wide number of fruits (such as avocados, bananas, and tomatoes), this section is specific to the type of berries known as aggregate fruits (such as raspberries and blackberries) that are the result of several plant ovaries merging together to form one large fruit. Energetically, aggregate berries have motherly properties. In correspondence to the creation/destruction dichotomy of La Santa Muerte, raspberries are used to create while blackberries are used to destroy. In particular, raspberries have been used in female fertility spells, and their leaves when brewed as a tea have been shown to moderate menstruation. Blackberries, on the other hand, represent the defensive and protective side of a mother, being used in spells of protection and to heal injuries, especially psychological trauma.

Burdock

As mentioned in previous examples, burdock is a spiny, thistle-like plant that is used as a tea to detoxify the body and in magic for spells of protection and attraction. Energetically, it has prickly properties that make it ideal in spells for keeping harm and danger away as well as in spells for attracting people, places, things, and events into our life.

Cactus

Cacti are a family of succulent plants that grow in very arid and dry conditions. They are notable for their sharp spines and fleshy stalks engorged with stored water. Energetically, they have guarding properties due to their physical design that prevents animals from getting close to them. In magic, they are primarily used in protection spells to guard against those who wish to do harm. The needlelike spines are used in various craft spells as symbolic proxies for nails. Cacti are also used in chastity spells to ward off unwanted sexual advances and aggression.

Cherry

Cherries are highly sexualized fruit, stemming from their deep-red color, their resemblance to testicles, and the common euphemism of "cherry" to refer to one's virginity. Energetically, they have erotic properties and are commonly used in love and lust spells. For love, they are used to attract passionate romances where lust leads to love. In spells exclusive to lust, they are used to entice a lover to try new things in the bedroom and sexually experiment, in addition to manifesting new sexual partners.

Chili Peppers

Chili peppers are famous for being spicy and high in vitamin C, but contrary to their hot nature, they are often used in magic for chastity spells. This is because, in human biology, the consumption of chili peppers activates the body's sympathetic nervous system to keep the body in homeostasis. The spiciness of chili peppers signals to the brain that the body is too hot and it needs to be cooled down, so the brain activates its natural cooling features such as sweating and the production of endorphins to calm the nerves. Thus, their energetically spicy properties make chili peppers an ideal plant for cooling and calming the enflamed passions of overly promiscuous people. The same attributes are commonly carried over to protection spells where they are meant to cool and calm an aggressor and his or her physical (or spiritual) assaults.

Chocolate

Chocolate is a food product made from cacao beans. Native to Central America, it was used as a drink since pre-Olmec times (circa 1750 BCE). The Aztec and Maya peoples used chocolate for ceremonial purposes as well as an everyday beverage. The cacao plant could not be grown in the Aztecs' highlands empire and had to be imported,[50] thus gaining a status of luxury and expensiveness. This status continued in Europe during the Age of Discovery when it was expensively imported from the New World. Nowadays, chocolate is still associated with luxury and is a well-known aphrodisiac. Energetically, it has celebratory properties due to its use for celebratory holidays and events, rewards, and affirmations of love. In magic, it is used in spells for luxury, prosperity, and erotic love. It is also used in spellwork to express gratitude and thanks for the blessings that are already in one's life. The magical use of chocolate in the Santa Muerte tradition is exclusive to the more natural dark chocolate.

Chrysanthemum

Around the world, chrysanthemums have a strong association with death. In East Asia, white chrysanthemums are symbols of grief, sorrow, lamentation, and loss. In Belgium, France, Southern Europe, and Eastern Europe, chrysanthemums are a symbol of death and are reserved exclusively for offerings to the dead. Spain's use of the chrysanthemum as a grave flower carried over to their colonial empire in the New World where it is still reserved for the same purpose. In modern times, they are a flower emblematic of Día de los Muertos, a Latin American holiday when families visit the cemetery, clean the graves of their ancestors, and offer the deceased a picnic of their favorite food and drink.[51] Energetically, chrysanthemums have "grave" properties, making them an ideal plant for use in necromancy to commune with the dead.

---

50. Terry G. Powis, W. Jeffrey Hurst, María del Carmen Rodríguez, Ortíz C. Ponciano, Michael Blake, David Cheetham, Michael D. Coe, and John G. Hodgson, "Oldest chocolate in the New World." *Antiquity* 81, no. 314 (2007). http://www.antiquity.ac.uk/projgall/powis/ (accessed May 7, 2015).

51. Susan Deary, "The History and Tradition of 'Day of the Dead'," Gomanzanillo. com. http://www.gomanzanillo.com/features/Day of the Dead/ (accessed May 7, 2015).

Cilantro

Cilantro is the Spanish word for coriander. Technically speaking, the English word *cilantro* is used only in reference to the leaves of the coriander plant. Nevertheless, cilantro is a very polarizing plant—people either love it or hate it. Scientists believe that some people's inherent distaste for cilantro is genetic, whereby the taste buds react negatively to the plant causing a severely unsavory reaction.[52] Energetically, cilantro has independent energies due to its ability to be itself regardless of what critics might say. Cilantro does not change itself to appease the masses, but rather, it stays true to itself and allows those who accept it to enjoy it while leaving those who hate it to naturally avoid it. Because of this, cilantro is often used in magic for the self, especially in spells for self-acceptance, self-love, and maintaining grace under fire. It is also used to stop or prevent bullying by giving the victim the courage to no longer tolerate being victimized.

Cinnamon

Cinnamon is a world-renowned spice used to expand the flavor of certain dishes, most commonly desserts. Native to Ethiopia, the Middle East, and South and East Asia, cinnamon has long been prized as a luxury spice fit for royalty and the gods. Most notably, cinnamon is referenced as an erotic scent in the Old Testament of the Bible, specifically in the Book of Proverbs where it is called a perfume of the bedroom, and in the highly sensual Song of Solomon where it is the descriptive fragrance of King Solomon's beloved. In modern times, Realtors commonly use cinnamon cookies to fill a house with a scent that elicits luxury and wealth to help close a sale. Energetically, cinnamon has expansion properties due to its abilities to enhance whatever it is used in. It is most commonly utilized in money magic to expand prosperity and in lust magic to add sensuality (not necessarily eroticism) to a relationship or casual encounter.

---

52. Josh Kurz, "Getting to the Root of the Great Cilantro Divide," NPR. http://www
.npr.org/templates/story/story.php?storyId=98695984 (accessed May 7, 2015).

Coca Leaves

Native to the Andean nations of South America, coca leaves have been used by native peoples for thousands of years, pre-dating the Incan civilization. When consumed, coca has natural compounds that cure the body of altitude sickness while at the same time increasing energy. Coca leaves are the base ingredient for cocaine. The natural coca leaf itself, however, is a far cry from cocaine since cocaine is the result of several chemical alterations to extract the leaves' natural alkaloids, including the use of industrial solvents. Without this synthetic process, the natural alkaloid content of the coca leaf is about 0.50 percent. When consumed, most commonly by chewing the leaves or drinking it as a tea (called Incan tea), coca leaves do not produce the high of cocaine. Energetically, coca leaves have uplifting properties due to their natural ability to cure altitude sickness and uplift the body's physical energy, as well as their ability to produce a stimulating high when used as a drug. In spellwork, coca leaves have long been used by native peoples in South America as an offering to the spirits of the tall mountains, as a tool of divination to possess the knowledge and foresight of the gods, and as an aid to keep the mind energized during long periods of meditation.

Note: Be sure to research the legality of coca leaves where you live. Most countries make no distinction between the naturally occurring leaves and the manmade product of processed cocaine. Only certain companies such as Coca-Cola (whose use of coca leaves as a flavoring agent is evident in its name) are allowed to import the coca plant.[53] If you live in a country where it is illegal to possess coca leaves, the use of classic Coca-Cola can be substituted so long as it is properly blessed before use.

Coffee Beans

Coffee beans are one of the few legal "drugs" that provide people with stimulating energy to go about their day. In many respects, it is a legally tolerated "upper" that is used by societies all over the world in the same

---

53. Clifford D. May, "How Coca-Cola Obtains Its Coca," *New York Times*, July 1, 1988.

way South American societies use coca leaves. Generally consumed as a liquid, coffee has a slightly high acidic level and contains a high dosage of caffeine, which is the agent responsible for its stimulating effects on the body. When consumed improperly or in excess, coffee is infamous for causing addiction, anxiety, headaches, heart complications, and sleep disorders, including nightmares.[54] Because of this, coffee beans energetically have "dark knight" properties wherein they are used in magic to combat our inner demons. Most commonly, coffee is utilized in spellwork to break addictions, and to force us to look at our dark side by breaking any and all illusions we have about ourselves. Such spells are often uncomfortable and terrifying (much like the adverse effects of coffee), but if successful, we emerge stronger than ever and with an awareness of our own divine nature.

Dandelion

Dandelions have a bad reputation as an unwanted weed that grows among more preferred flowers. Because of this, dandelions are synonymous with outsiders and people who don't belong or fit in to regular society. Nevertheless, dandelions have been used in herbal medicine for centuries as a liver detoxifier and bile stimulant to neutralize stomach acid.[55] Energetically, dandelions have lion properties due to their name (from the Old French *dent de lion*, "lion's tooth," for the jagged edges of the leaves resembling the teeth of a lion). In magic, it is often utilized for spells to acquire the self-confidence to be individualistic and stand out from the crowd. Its detoxifying effects on the liver correspond to its ability in spellwork to detoxify our negative thinking about ourselves.

---

54. Sharon Palmer, "Coffee Buzz – Trends and Possible Perks of America's Beloved Beverage," *Today's Dietitian* 11, no. 5 (2009): 26. http://www.todaysdietitian.com/newarchives/050409p26.shtml (accessed May 7, 2015).

55. Katrin Schütz, Reinhold Carle, and Andreas Schieber, "Taraxacum—A review on its phytochemical and pharmacological profile," *Journal of Ethnopharmacology* 107, no. 3 (2006): 313–472

Honeysuckle

Honeysuckle is a genus of shrubs and vines with very fragrant flowers. It has a notorious reputation for being invasive due to its ability to grow very rapidly almost anywhere. For this reason, honeysuckle energetically has quick properties, allowing it to help manifest any spell more quickly. The tradeoff for its ability to expedite the speed of a spell is that it makes the manifestation more ephemeral. An example would be casting a spell to become famous, wherein the use of honeysuckle makes it arrive quickly but only with the result of getting the proverbial "fifteen minutes of fame" rather than anything more lasting. Because of this, honeysuckle is most often used for smaller spells whose effects are not as dire, such as healing magic for small cuts and scrapes, and especially money magic for quick cash of low denominations.

Hyacinth

Hyacinth is the premier tool for gay male love magic (as patchouli is for lesbian love magic). Its name comes from that of a youthful male in ancient Greece who was the mortal lover of Zephyr (the west wind) and Apollo. According to legend, Zephyr and Apollo competed for the beautiful Hyacinth's love, but the boy ended up choosing Apollo as his mate. In jealousy, Zephyr caused a discus thrown by Apollo to go off course and strike Hyacinth's head, killing him. Apollo was so grief-stricken that he took Hyacinth's blood and used it to create a new flower whose petals resembled his lover's curly hair. Energetically, hyacinth has "gentle male" properties and has been associated with the yin dot within the yang half of the Taoist yin-yang symbol, thus representing the femininity within a masculine host. In magic, hyacinth is used in love magic between gay males, as well as for males of all sexual orientations to get in touch with their feminine yin side. The flower has also been used to symbolize rebirth due to its popularity in the Persian New Year celebration, Nowruz, during the spring equinox. This rebirth association of the hyacinth has been utilized by gay males as a magical tool to help come out of the closet and accept one's own homosexuality.

Jasmine

Jasmine is a popular plant whose white petals emit their most intense perfume at night. Its characteristic fragrance is found in products all over the world, and it is one of the few flowers whose scent can be distinctly "tasted" when consumed as a tea. Energetically, jasmine has moon properties due to its nocturnal nature and its bright white petals that resemble the full moon. Jasmine is often used in dreamwork and included in spells designed to manifest prophetic dreams. Because the moon controls the tides, it also has a strong effect on our emotions (since our bodies are about 60 percent water), so spells in which we have strong emotional attachments often utilize jasmine as a tool, whether to enhance an emotional experience (such as love or lust) or to separate us from unhealthy emotional attachments to toxic people and vices.

Lemon

Lemon has a very high vitamin C content, and its extreme acidity has famously been used as a cooking preservative, as a cleansing agent to polish wood and dissolve tarnish and stains, and as an antibacterial liquid. Its natural fragrance is distinctively associated with cleanliness, and in aromatherapy, its scent is used to boost the immune system. Energetically, lemons have cleansing properties. In spellwork, lemons are often used in healing magic, especially for ailments involving the immune system and aging. Its bright yellow color also makes it useful in cleansing the mind to be more optimistic and look on the bright side of life.

Licorice

Licorice is a plant whose flavor is disliked by many, often being called an acquired taste by those who enjoy it. Although it's naturally a brown root, licorice is by and large artificially colored black when sold as a liqueur and candy, so much so that black candy is often naturally assumed to be licorice flavored. When used in large amounts, licorice can be toxic to humans, but scientific research is showing positive results that it may be used to treat cavities[56] and neurodegenerative disorders such as Alzheimer's and Parkinson's.[57] Energetically, licorice has necromantic properties due to people's natural aversion to it as well as its ability to combat the rotting of teeth and the death of nerve cells. In spellwork, it is primarily used in hexes and harmful magic, but it is also often used in healing magic to combat addictions and promote longevity.

Lily

In the Catholic tradition, lilies are often associated with death and resurrection. During the Easter season, they are used to decorate Catholic churches to symbolize the resurrection of Christ. Lilies are also left in cemeteries and mausoleums as a symbol of the soul's resurrection into Heaven. In magic, lilies have transitional properties and are frequently used to break love spells and ease the transitional pain of loss, such as a falling out between friends, dating breakup, divorce, or death of a loved one. Because lilies are unique in having both masculine and feminine parts, they can also be used by gender-variant people to reconcile their own masculine/feminine balance, as well as by preoperative transsexuals to ease the transition between genders.

Lime

Limes are often thought to be similar to lemons, but in addition to being smaller, less sour, and permanently green, they also have a much higher vitamin C content than lemons. In India, limes were used as a tool for exorcisms and driving away evil spirits. Energetically, limes contain cleansing properties, but while lemons are used to cleanse natural

56. Gabriella Gazzani, Maria Daglia, and Adele Papetti, "Food components with anticaries activity," *Current Opinion in Biotechnology* 23, no. 2. (2012): 153–159. http://cafeesaude.com/wp-content/uploads/2012/01/C%C3%A1ries-G-Gazzani-et-al-Current-Opinions-Biotechnology-2011 published-online-ahead-of-print.pdf (accessed May 7, 2015).

57. Ramaswamy Kannappan, Subash Chandra Gupta, Ji Hye Kim, Simone Reuter, and Bharat Bushan Aggarwal, "Neuroprotection by Spice-Derived Nutraceuticals: You Are What You Eat!" *Molecular Neurobiology* 44, no. 2. (2011) 142–159. http://www.ncbi.nlm.nih.gov/pmc/articles/PMC3183139/pdf/nihms307525.pdf (accessed May 7, 2015).

ailments, limes are more often used to cleanse spiritual ailments. Because of their green color, limes are used in love magic as a tool to add zest to a relationship to strengthen it and keep it fresh.

Marijuana

Marijuana is often considered to be *the* plant of Santa Muerte. This is both true and untrue. On the one hand, La Santa Muerte has no "official" plant sacred to her, but on the other hand, many of the people involved in her worship are members of drug cartels as well as independent drug dealers and users. Because marijuana is precious to them and provides as their livelihood, it is common for such devotees to give marijuana to La Santa Muerte as an offering, symbolically giving her a "cut" of the profit for protecting their business. Around the world, marijuana has been used as a drug by countless cultures for thousands of years (the earliest dating back to the Bronze Age). Energetically, every magical tradition grants marijuana varying properties ranging from calming to divinatory, but in the Santa Muerte tradition, it has "necessary evil" properties. It is used in spellwork mainly for protection and money magic, especially where the practitioner will knowingly commit a crime and is seeking a profitable outcome as well as protection from both the law and harm.

Note: Be sure to research the legality of marijuana where you live, since possession of it (even if used for benevolent magic) can result in legal prosecution.

Nettle

Nettle is a common nickname for a number of plants with stinging hairs, but for magical purposes, "nettle" refers to the genus of flowering plants known as *Urtica*. Similar to the thistle-like burdock plant in its detoxifying abilities, nettle tends to be a more subtle plant whose stinging defenses are much smaller and not as easily visible. Nettles also have a long history of being used in medicine, especially for arthritis and ailments of the joints and connective tissue. It has been drunk as an herbal tea and used as a flail to purposely strike the joints, since the stinging hairs provide temporary pain relief and subdue inflammation.[58] Energetically, nettle has grasping properties, allowing it to be used in spellwork to "get a handle on" certain things. It is most often utilized in protection magic to get a handle on what is causing us harm. In healing magic, it is used to get a hold on ailments (especially joint ailments) and deal with them directly as opposed to getting "bent out of shape" or "inflaming" the situation into something worse.

Orange

Like most citrus fruits, oranges are acidic, high in vitamin C content, and associated with cleansing. Its bright orange color and spherical shape grant it correspondence to the belly chakra, which is the home of instincts and intuition. Energetically, it also has cleansing properties, but in contrast to lemons and limes (which cleanse the body and the spirit, respectively), oranges are usually associated with cleansing the mind, clearing away negative, muddled, and harmful thoughts and emotions to better understand our own instincts and intuition. Its physical and biological association with the sun also makes it a good tool to use in money magic and spells to counter depression and sorrow.

Palo Santo

Palo santo is the Spanish name given to three genera of trees native to the Caribbean and South America: *Guaiacum* (aka lignum vitae), *Bulnesia* (aka Argentine lignum vitae), and *Bursera* (Incan lignum vitae). While technically the "best" genus is generally considered to be *Bursera*, it is often difficult to obtain due to South American environmental laws restricting the felling of *Bulnesia* trees and mandating that only "naturally dead" trees can be harvested.[59] Because of this, outside of Latin

---

58. C. Randall, H. Randall, F. Dobbs, C. Hutton, and H. Sanders (June 2000), "Randomized controlled trial of nettle sting for treatment of base-of-thumb pain," *Journal of the Royal Society of Medicine* 93, no. 6 (2000): 305–309. http://jrs.sagepub.com/content/93/6/305.full.pdf (accessed May 7, 2015).

59. Steven D. Farmer, *Earth Magic: Ancient Shamanic Wisdom for Healing Yourself, Others, and the Planet* (Carlsbad, CA: Hay House, 2009).

America, the most common type of palo santo is usually *Guaiacum*. Regardless of genus, though, the name palo santo translates to "holy stick/wood," and its Latin name lignum vitae translates to "wood of life." It was called such names due to its seemingly miraculous cure-all use in herbal medicine. The wood of palo santo, however, is also world renowned for its extreme density, strength, and ability to self-lubricate,[60] making it an elite wood used to create expensive furniture, instruments, ships, and clocks. Energetically, palo santo has restorative properties due to its historical use in herbal medicine and its aforementioned ability to self-lubricate. In spellwork, palo santo is used primarily in healing magic, especially when the ailment is not known or there are multiple ailments working in tandem. Because of its extreme density and strength, it is also frequently used in protection magic to block all harm—physical, emotional, and spiritual.

Pau d'Arco

Pau d'arco is the common name of a genus of flowering trees called *Handroanthus*, which are native to the Antilles and Central and South America. The name *pau d'arco* is Portuguese for "bow wood," originating from the natives' use of its hard yet pliable wood to fashion their bows. In South America (especially among the Inca and the tribes of the Amazon), the inner bark of pau d'arco has been used for centuries as an herbal medicine for respiratory ailments, fungal infections, eczema, and even cancer. Modern research has found pau d'arco, however, to be slightly poisonous, and its modern usage in South America is now severely moderated and reserved for emergencies. Pregnant women are advised to avoid it altogether as it can act as an abortifacient and cause miscarriages. Energetically, it has abortive properties due to its abilities to abruptly eliminate diseases and cause spontaneous abortions. In spellwork, it is most commonly used in healing magic wherein the per-

---

60. Rain Noe, "Lignum Vitae: Wood So Bad-Ass, It's Used to Make Shaft Bearings for Nuclear Submarines (and More)," Core77. http://www.core77.com/blog/materials/lignum_vitae_wood_so_bad-ass_its_used_to_make_shaft_bearings_for_nuclear_submarines_and_more_25224.asp (accessed May 7, 2015).

son is in critical condition. It is also generally used to undo and abort magic spells that have gone wrong or whose manifestations are realized to be harmful.

Peach

Peaches have a long history as a magical tool in East Asia. In ancient China, peaches were used for exorcisms in a ritual wherein the removal of the pit symbolized the removal of demonic spirits within an otherwise sweet individual. The ancient Chinese also believed peaches to be the fruit of immortality due to the tree's nature to sprout flower blossoms before sprouting leaves. Energetically, peaches have "wise man" properties due to their pits resembling an elderly man's wrinkled scrotum or testicles. Because of this, peaches have a masculine flair to them and have been commonly used in spellwork for wisdom as well as protection when strategy and cunning are desired over direct confrontation. Due to the fruit's "sweet masculinity," it was used as a symbol for gay men in ancient China where homosexuality was often alluded to with peach euphemisms, making peach applicable for gay male love magic.

Peppermint

Native to Europe, this flavorful herb is commonly associated with Christmas and is a common flavor found in many candies, chewing gums, toothpastes, and mouthwashes. Use of peppermint as an herbal medicine dates back to around ten thousand years ago, and in modern medicine, peppermint (particularly peppermint tea) is used to treat a variety of throat and stomach ailments. The scent of this herb has also been found to enhance both memory and alertness. Energetically, peppermint has communicative properties due to its strong association with the mouth and throat as well as its effect on the mind to receive and retain information given by others. In spellwork, peppermint is often used by students to aid memorization for tests as well as by lawyers to stay mentally sharp during a court case. It is also commonly used to quell disagreements, arguments, and spats among friends, lovers, and coworkers by allowing each party to express themselves clearly and understand everyone else's points of view.

Plum

Plums are the feminine equivalent of peaches, being similarly shaped yet smaller, softer, and more delicate. In particular, their pits are noticeably much smaller and have a resemblance to the genitalia of an elderly woman. Because of this, plums energetically have "wise woman" properties and a feminine flair to them. In practical terms, dried plums (prunes) are well-known for their strong ability as a laxative to flush out blockages and expedite the elimination of waste, an act that has been often correlated to the feminine flushing of menstruation and the feminine yin attributes in the Taoist yin-yang. In spellwork, plums are used primarily in healing magic where we are blocking and impeding our own recovery. Similarly, plums can also be used to overcome any blockages that we may have in other areas of our lives, such as career, love, finances, and so on.

Pomegranate

Pomegranates have a strong association with both the underworld and femininity. In ancient Greece, the pomegranate was the fruit eaten by the goddess Persephone, ultimately giving her dominion over death and granting her the title of Queen of the Underworld. The fruit's physical appearance, when cut open, has been said to resemble a woman's ovaries, and its individual seeds are encased in a liquid sac symbolically similar to the embryonic fluid that encases a fetus in the womb. Despite this similarity to the feminine reproductive system, the seeds of pomegranates have been known to act as abortifacients, effectively terminating a pregnancy, an ability of the fruit much coveted by women of ancient times.[61] Energetically, pomegranates have "dark lady" properties, making the fruit popular among devotees of La Santa Muerte, who revere her as their personal dark lady. In spellwork, pomegranate is used

---

61. John Riddle, *Contraception and Abortion from the Ancient World to the Renaissance* (Cambridge, MA: Harvard University Press, 1994).

frequently in healing magic, especially for blood and feminine ailments. It has also been used in spells to increase fertility and prosperity due to the numerous seeds found within each fruit. Moreover, it is used by women to tap into the "dark lady" within them to bring out their own power, strength, and independent ambitions, as opposed to placing others before themselves in the traditional roles of mother and wife.

Rose

Roses are the premier flowers of love. In Greek mythology, the plant is sacred to both Aphrodite and her son Eros (renamed Cupid by the Romans). In the Catholic tradition, roses are symbolic of the Virgin Mary and in particular her apparition as Our Lady of Guadalupe, who performed a miracle of manifesting roses not native to Mexico. Energetically, roses have love properties, and while all roses are used in love spells, the color of the rose denotes the type of love one is trying to manifest. Red roses are used for erotic love. Pink roses are used for romantic love. White roses are used for "pure" platonic love, such as between family and friends, as well as self-love. Yellow roses are used for love of life. Devotees of La Santa Muerte hold the rose particularly sacred, partly because of its established association with Our Lady of Guadalupe and partly because, although beautiful and feminine, it has sharp thorns and will draw blood. Only those willing to risk getting hurt can ever appreciate the beauty of a rose.

Tobacco

Tobacco is an example of a misunderstood plant. Originally, its leaves were smoked by the natives of North America, including Mexico, but to them it was considered sacred and reserved for spiritual purposes. The arrival of the Spanish in the New World subsequently introduced the smoking of tobacco to the Old World where it was commercialized and not respected as sacred. This improper use of tobacco became a cause of disease and ill health, thus creating a reactionary movement that vilified the plant as evil. The plant, however, is not evil nor is it good. It simply is, and depending on how it is used, it causes spiritual ecstasy and communion with the Divine or disease and death. These aspects of duality, misunderstanding, and loss of respect often make the plant sacred to La Santa Muerte in the eyes of her devotees. Energetically, tobacco has "dark gentleman" properties due to its use by tribal chiefs to promote peaceful negotiations instead of war, as well as its modern vilification by humanity. In spellwork, tobacco is used by men to tap into the "dark gentleman" within them to bring out their own power, strength, and confidence, all for the good of others as opposed to solely pursuing their own interests in careers and sexual conquests.

Vanilla

Vanilla is a very sensual plant native to the hot and humid tropics. It is technically a vine and thus has no strong roots of its own, relying on its tendrils to coil around other plants and objects in order to support itself. This tangling of roots and vines has often been symbolic to the human entangling act of sex. Energetically, vanilla has sensual properties due to its constant caressing of other plants and its warm, inviting scent. In spellwork, vanilla is frequently used in lust magic, especially for non-penetrational sex such as foreplay, oral sex, or fetishes.

Wine

Grapes have been held sacred for thousands of years, most notably in religions native to the Mediterranean region, and primarily in the form of wine. In ancient Greece, grapes and wine were the symbols of the ecstatic god Dionysus and his devotional female followers, the Maenads, who were said to be wild and frenzied women that no man could tame. The Bible mentions wine as the premier beverage of Jewish feast days; in the Gospels, Jesus refers to the communal wine at the Last Supper as his blood, and the creation of wine was his first public miracle. Energetically, grapes have liberating properties due to the effects of wine causing people to liberate themselves from self-imposed pretenses and social constraints. In spellwork, grapes and more specifically wine are used in divination magic and the development of psychic abilities. Their deep purple color corresponds to the third-eye chakra, which is responsible for vision, both physical and spiritual, to see the truth beyond illusions and behind all things. When used in excess, wine can lead to false visions and create illusions, so even in magic, it should be used in moderation.

Yerba Mate

Yerba mate is a shrub related to holly and native to South America. It grows exclusively in the tri-border region of Argentina, Paraguay, and Brazil, and all attempts (thus far) to grow it commercially outside this region have proven unsuccessful. Originally, it was drunk as a tea by the Guaraní people native to that region to energize them. Similar to the coca leaf and coffee, yerba mate has caffeine-like xanthines: theobromine and theophylline. However, unlike the coca leaf and coffee, yerba mate helps to focus the mind and relax the muscles without the jittery and crash-like effects of caffeine.[62] In modern times, it is the national drink of Argentina, Paraguay, and Uruguay, and it is symbolic of community, owing to its traditional use among gauchos, where it is communally shared. Energetically, yerba mate has grounding properties due to its stubbornness in refusing to grow outside its native region and because of the grounding clarity and natural calm that it grants when drunk as a tea. In spellwork, yerba mate is used for protection spells requiring us to hold our ground and not back down. It is also commonly used in spells for mental clarity and self-confidence. In some witchcraft traditions, yerba mate is considered sacred to Ares, the god of war, and is used in spells to increase ambition, assertiveness, and bring out the warrior within.

This list of plants may seem lengthy, but this is because plant tools form the basic building blocks of all other tool sets. Many specialized candles, incense, crystals, and charms all have their roots based in the plant kingdom, whether it be through their scent, flavor, composition, or name. Even all around us in everyday life, the plant world is a common denomi-

---

62. Dr. Dave B. Mowrey, *Herbal Tonic Therapies* (Chicago: Keats Publishing, 1998).

nator for the senses and can be found in shampoos, perfumes, body lotions, sodas, hand soap, laundry or dishwasher detergent, air fresheners, distilled spirits, toothpaste, mouthwash, candies, gum, and more.

In a magical system that values thrift and practicality, these everyday items can be used in a pinch. Want to do a love spell, but you don't have access to fresh roses? That's fine, just spray some of your rose-scented air freshener in its place. Be creative, and know that through the Law of Correspondence all things of the same type are energetically connected, no matter their form.

Tool Set IV: Minerals

Minerals (which include rocks, metals, gems, and certain resins) are usually associated with the New Age community, and their use as tools in the Santa Muerte tradition does, indeed, come as a result of a cultural import from New Age practitioners who have become devotees of La Santa Muerte. Because true minerals can be expensive, they are not often seen among the majority of devotees, but their power and efficacy in spellwork is undeniable.

As a sign of respect (and for the efficacy of our spells), it is necessary to commune with the minerals beforehand and ask if they would be willing to assist us in our magic. If so, they should be properly blessed with the desired intention and instructions for how we would like them to help us. Unlike all the other tool sets mentioned so far, minerals are unique in that they don't disappear after being used. Candles and incense both burn away, and herbs and plants are consumed, used in a charm, or simply wither away. Minerals remain. That is why, after the manifestation of a spell, minerals should always be unblessed.

Amethyst

Amethyst is a purple semiprecious quartz whose name comes from the ancient Greek for "not drunk." An influential sixteenth century French poem, "L'Amethyste, ou les Amours de Bacchus et d'Amethyste," tells how Dionysus, god of wine and ecstasy, killed a maiden named Amethyste who, unbeknownst to him, was a lover of Artemis, goddess of the wild, animals, and women. Although she could not save her lover, Artemis transformed her into a crystal, and as a sign of regret and sorrow, Dionysus poured his wine onto the crystal as an offering, thus giving it a purple hue and its name. Energetically, amethyst has sobering properties and corresponds to the third-eye chakra. It is most often used to heal addictions, illusions, self-delusions, and unhealthy escapes from real-world issues. Amethyst is also sometimes used in lesbian love magic.

Citrine

Citrine is a semiprecious quartz with a color spectrum ranging from faint yellow to brown. Its name is similar to "citrus," and it carries many of the same properties as the citrus fruits already mentioned. Energetically, citrine has light properties and corresponds to the solar plexus chakra. In spellwork, it is most often used to heal self-image and self-esteem as well as combat depression. Because of its yellow color and similarity to the sun, it can also be used to attract success and wealth.

Copper

Copper is an auburn metal commonly found in many everyday objects. It has high thermal and electrical conductivity as well as a high resistance to corrosion, making it ideal for electrical wiring and distant communication materials. In ancient times, it was associated with Aphrodite, goddess of love, due to its unique ability to turn green (a symbolic color of Aphrodite) upon oxidization. Energetically, copper has attraction properties due to its historical use as a main component in compasses as well its modern use in connecting people via communication technologies. In spellwork, copper is used most often in love magic and prosperity magic, where the end goal is to attract a lover or sums of money.

Diamond

Diamonds are synonymous with wealth and luxury. The name comes from the ancient Greek for "unbreakable," and diamonds remain one of the hardest known substances on earth. They are also commonly associated with weddings due to their durability making them last "forever." Energetically, diamonds have enduring energy, owing to their durable nature and to the fact that their creation is the result of coal that withstood years of high heat and high pressure. They correspond to the crown chakra, and in spellwork, they are used in protection magic, especially for times of high stress and high pressure from the outside world.

Emerald

Emeralds are a form of green beryl often associated with love and beauty. Both of these associations are most notably found in being a stone sacred to Aphrodite, goddess of love. Energetically, emeralds have loving properties and correspond with the heart chakra. In spellwork, emerald is predominately used for love magic, both self-love and romantic love, as well as healing from wounds of love.

Gold

The most famous and valued of all minerals, gold gets its value from its rarity and unique beauty. Throughout human history, gold has been used in currency, jewelry, and chemistry where it is considered the most noble of noble metals. Energetically, gold has sun properties and is associated with the solar plexus chakra. Besides its obvious use in money magic, gold is often used in healing magic for self-confidence and letting our inner individuality shine.

Jade

Jade is an ornamental green stone most often associated with China and East Asia. In Chinese mysticism, jade was symbolic of the balance of female and male, dark and light, yin and yang energies. Energetically, jade has harmonizing properties and is used in love and relationship magic. In healing magic, it is often used for STDs and other ailments of the sexual organs as well as to balance our sexual desires.

Jet

Technically, jet is not a true mineral since it is derived from decayed wood that has been pressurized, but its deep black color has made it common in ornamental jewelry and art. Its profound darkness is where the descriptive term "jet black" originates, meaning totally and completely black. Jet was often worn by Queen Victoria as part of her signature black mourning ensemble, and her use made it the premier jewelry associated with funerals and grieving. Energetically, jet has somber properties, and because of that, it is beloved by the Santa Muerte community. In spellwork, it is used in protection magic, usually from spirits, harmful magic, and the supernatural. It is also popularly used in healing magic for the grieving process and the experience of loss. Because of its association with death and its composition of decaying wood, it is the premier stone used in necromancy.

Lapis Lazuli

Lapis lazuli is a deep-blue stone, often with golden speckles of pyrite. During the Renaissance, pigment made from lapis lazuli was frequently reserved for the clothing of the Virgin Mary in artwork. The stone's vivid color is where the word "azure" comes from. Energetically, lapis lazuli has communicative properties arising from the symbolism of clear water and the clear sky. It is associated with the throat chakra and is often used in healing magic for mouth, throat, hearing, and speech ailments. It has also been used to heal the communication between friends, lovers, and co-workers as well as promoting clear communication between one's own mind, body, and spirit. Because of its association with the Virgin Mary, devotees have also used lapis lazuli to get in touch with the divine feminine within.

Obsidian

Technically not a true mineral, obsidian is a volcanic glass that is hard and brittle. When fractured, it reveals extremely sharp edges, a trait that made obsidian a valuable additive to the clubs of Aztec warriors and the scalpels of modern surgeons. Polished obsidian was also used in the ancient world as a dark mirror. Energetically, obsidian has reflective properties. In spell-work, it is used in healing magic to heal emotional ailments and look at our own darkness in order to defeat our inner demons. Because of its well-known ability to cut, obsidian is also used in protection magic to "cut away" and end unhealthy relationships with people and things.

Opal

Opal is an amorphous mineraloid famous for its multicolored appearance. Its ability to diffract light allows it to appear as any color in the visible spectrum, often many different colors at once. Because of this rainbow effect, opals are believed to have the magical properties of all other mineral energies within them. Energetically, opals have heavenly energy and are often associated with the crown chakra. In spellwork, they are used as an all-purpose healing tool for when the specific ailment is unknown or there are multiple ailments occurring simultaneously. Their optical rainbow phenomenon often associates them with the LGBT community, being used in LGBT magic such as same-sex love, sexual identity transformation, and the healing of HIV/AIDS.

Pearl

Pearls are precious gemstones with a milky color that are produced within the soft tissue of a living shelled mollusk. They have been valued around the world since ancient times for their unique luster and iridescent appearance, and they have come to be a metaphor for something that is rare and valuable. Energetically, pearls have emphasizing properties that are used to amplify the potency of a spell. When worn as a charm, pearls are notorious for emphasizing one's current mood, thus making joyous moments even more joyous, and upsetting moments even more upsetting. Because of their smooth texture, milky color, and spherical shape, pearls have also been associated with mothers and are used in healing magic for children and for pregnancy ailments.

Pyrite

Pyrite is more commonly known by its nickname "fool's gold" due to its superficial similarity to actual gold. Its name comes from the Greek *pyrites* meaning "of fire," and in the sixteenth and seventeenth centuries, it was used as a source of ignition for firearms. In modern times, pyrite is commonly used to make both sulfuric acid and inexpensive jewelry that looks expensive. Energetically, pyrite has illusionary properties due to it commonly being mistaken for the more expensive and valuable mineral. In spellwork, it is used to heal psychosomatic diseases. It is also commonly used to check the ego and heal the mind from delusions of how we see ourselves, others, and world around us.

Quartz

Quartz is a crystalline mineral that comes in an array of colors, and like roses, each color denotes a different type of energy. Clear quartz has an association with the crown chakra and can be used to replace any other mineral in healing magic (much like a white candle). Rose quartz has an association with the heart chakra and is used much like a pink rose in love magic. Smokey quartz is associated with the root chakra and is used for grounding when we need to center ourselves and remain firm.

Ruby

Rubies are red gemstones, the most valued of which have a deep, blood-red color. Ruby is often associated with adventure and exoticism due to its history of being almost exclusively imported from the Far East. In India and China, rubies were symbolic of nobility and were often laid beneath a building's foundation to manifest good fortune. Energetically, rubies have intense energies due to their fiery red color and blood associations. In healing magic, rubies are primarily reserved for the most severe and critical cases. In general spellwork, they are used to add passion to spells for love, career, and vitality.

Silver

Silver is often thought of as a valuable yet "second-place" metal. In the Olympics, it denotes second place, and because of its associations with femininity, it is subconsciously given a second-place status in a patriarchal society that values masculinity (gold being the mineral of masculinity). For most of the ancient world, silver was the main metal used for currency, as gold was too rare and too valuable to be used for everyday exchange. In fact, in many modern Spanish and French dialects, the word for silver (*plata/argent*) is often used as the de facto word for money owing to Europe's influx of silver from the New World and use as colonial currency. Energetically, silver has moon properties, making it ideal for healing magic involving emotional and psychological ailments. Silver is also commonly used for dreamwork as well as to increase levels of intuition. Because of its history, silver is also often used in money magic for everyday exchanges.

Tiger's-Eye

Tiger's-eye is a type of quartz named for its curved stripes and amber color, resembling the eye of a tiger. Energetically, it has perceptive qualities and is often associated with the solar plexus chakra and the belly chakra. In spellwork, tiger's-eye is used in healing magic for vision ailments as well as to see and understand the root cause of an ailment. When used as a charm, tiger's-eye is notorious for instilling predatory qualities such as ambition, assertiveness, strength, endurance, and the ability to read other people's body language more effectively.

Tourmaline

Tourmaline is a semiprecious stone that comes in an array of colors. In Santa Muerte magic, black tourmaline is the color most commonly used. Energetically, black tourmaline has negating properties and is most frequently used in protection magic, especially from unforeseen danger and being at the wrong place at the wrong time. It is also used to negate a spell if its manifestation turns out to be harmful to ourselves and/or others.

Turquoise

Turquoise is a blue-green stone strongly associated with the natives of the southwest United States. In cultures all over the world, it has been highly prized as an ornamental stone as well as a holy stone. In many of the Islamic world's most decorative mosques, turquoise can be found as the prime material for aesthetic beauty. Energetically, turquoise has peaceful properties due to its resemblance to a clear sky and calm waters, and it is associated with the throat and heart chakras. In spellwork, turquoise is an all-purpose healing mineral used to calm the body, mind, and soul. Turquoise is also the premier mineral for friendship used in spells to promote understanding between two individuals. According to legend, it is considered bad luck to purchase your own turquoise, as it must be given as a gift for its magic to work.

———

All in all, there is magic in everything, and everything can be used as a magical tool. With an understanding of the Law of Correspondence, the Synchronicity of Colors, and sympathetic magic, you can become a master of any tool set you choose. As a devotee of La Santa Muerte, the more you focus on the philosophies and role of Death in our world, the more you can tailor each tool to be used in her magical tradition. Ultimately, tools are just tools. They can't and won't do the work for you, but they can and will help you. Experiment, have fun, and don't take things too seriously or be afraid to make mistakes. Laugh at it, laugh at yourself, and try again. After all, if death is loss, and we learn best from losing, then Death can be one of the best teachers you will ever have.

7
The Veneration of Death

*"You only live twice. Once when you are born
and once when you look death in the face."*
— IAN FLEMING, *YOU ONLY LIVE TWICE*

Up to this point, you have been learning various aspects of La Santa Muerte, her devotion, and her magic only in the context of separate pieces of information. But nothing in the world exists in a vacuum. Everything in life interacts with everything else, whether or not humans are fully conscious of it or understand it.

For most magical traditions around the world, everything comes together within the sacred space of a ritual. But for the Santa Muerte tradition, this is not the case. There are no grand rituals, no grand ceremonies, and no grand anything that puts all the pieces together in one uniting act for the purposes of veneration and spellwork.

Why are there no grand rituals or ceremonies? Well, it's because Santa Muerte magic is, essentially, practical magic. With a large number of devotees being among the working poor, most do not have the time to set aside and engage in a ritual nor the economic means for all the pomp and circumstance that goes along with ceremony. Moreover, an even larger number of devotees are the outcasts and unwanted who live on the margins of society. To these people, the participation in ritual and ceremony brings to mind too many bad memories and negative associations of both high society and the religious traditions that have shunned and ostracized them.

In general, devotees of the mystery school of La Santa Muerte try not to draw much attention to their faith. For most nondevotees, the devotion to Death is misunderstood and seen in a negative light. Death, by and large, scares people, and it is far easier to just keep that part of our life a secret known only to a trusted few rather than convince the world that the veneration of Death and necromantic spellwork can be a positive and self-empowering experience. To those few devotees who openly practice their faith, I have the utmost respect and admiration. In a world trying to conform you, being yourself is a supreme act of rebellion, and only through example will the world learn the benevolent magic of La Santa Muerte.

ALTARS

The most common form of ritual in the Santa Muerte tradition is the altar. Most magical practitioners have altars dedicated to their patron deity or deities, and even followers of more traditional faiths have similar altars, such as those dedicated to the Virgin Mary or Our Lady of Guadalupe. However, the altar of a magical practitioner doubles as a workbench for spellwork while such Marian altars are purely devotional.

When it comes to the specifics of altars, there really aren't any. Each altar varies from person to person in style, purpose, and aesthetic. They can be as large or as small as you like, and they can be made from materials and objects ranging from a specially crafted table to the top of a chest of drawers to just a space on the floor. The rule is "use what you can," and so long as you make an altar with respect and love, it becomes a sacred space no matter what or where it is.

But while personalization is encouraged, there are three unwritten rules for creating an altar that all devotees follow. First, the altar must be *only* dedicated to La Santa Muerte and her magic. Never is her altar to be shared with any other deities or magical traditions. If you have multiple patron deities, La Santa Muerte must remain separate and have her own altar.

Second, the altar should have some form of covering over the base material. The material of the covering does not matter (embroidered lace, blanket, sheets of paper towels, etc.) so long as it's clean. While using a separating surface doesn't actually have an effect upon the efficacy of spellwork, it is done as a sign of respect to La Santa Muerte. Much like the chivalrous act of a gentleman placing his coat over a puddle so that his lady may stay clean and dry, the same intention is behind the use of a separator on top of the altar.

Lastly, an image of La Santa Muerte must be present on the altar at all times. Most people prefer to use a statue or a statuette of her and place it in the back center of the altar, but this is only preference. I have seen altars where devotees have simply printed out a picture from the Internet and used that, and I've also seen altars where concert T-shirts depicting the skeleton-themed album cover of a heavy metal band were used as the main depiction. The black and white aspects are generally the most common ones, but really, any color aspect of her is perfectly acceptable.

All other altar adornments are purely optional. Flowers, candles, and photos of loved ones are common things found on an altar, but usually the decorations of an altar are materials left over from spellwork.

OFFERINGS

Offerings, in broad strokes, are essentially gifts to La Santa Muerte that are apart from both spellwork and decoration. Depending on whom you ask, you'll hear various rules about what is and is not acceptable as an offering to Death, but the truth is that there really are no rules on what constitutes an appropriate offering or even how to correctly offer it. So long as the offering is given out of respect and love, it is acceptable. Most people tend just to say a silent prayer and place the offering on their altar, but ultimately, like all gifts, it is the intention behind the act of giving that is more important than the presentation or gift itself.

With that said, when offering a gift to La Santa Muerte, the question a devotee must ask him- or herself is, "Would *I* like to receive this as a gift?" This means that if we are giving her something simply because we don't know what else to do with it, because we want to get rid of it, or because we are "re-gifting" it, then it is better not to give her the gift at all. Remember, her magic is co-creational magic, and we must establish a relationship with her in order to be able to work together. After all, if you had a friend who only gave you things as an excuse to get rid of stuff or as a pretense for other motives, is that person *really* your friend?

The most common examples of offerings among modern practicing devotees of La Santa Muerte are cigarettes, alcohol, and flowers. Cigarettes are the most common, and they are given in one of two ways: lit and left to burn in an ashtray or exhaling the smoke into her face on a statue or in a photograph. This gift is seen as communal because this same offering would be given to any other friend of the devotee through the lending of a cigarette. The gift giver and La Santa Muerte are, essentially, sharing a smoke together. To outside observers, the blowing of smoke into her face can come across as extremely rude, but within the magical community, this is a common practice. Since she obviously cannot physically inhale the cigarette, the devotee is assisting her and doing it for her. Needless to say, this offering is exclusive to smokers, since a person who is repulsed by cigarettes would never offer them to a friend, let alone their patron deity.

Alcohol is tied with cigarettes as the other most commonly offered gift. The gifting of alcohol is an age-old devotional, especially to the departed. As mentioned earlier, the French legend of the mineral amethyst tells of how it got its purple coloration when Dionysus poured out his wine as an offering to the deceased lover of Artemis. Even in modern times, this is a common practice, often seen in urban environments where a can or bottle of alcohol is poured onto the street or sidewalk in honor of a deceased loved one.

The selection of which type of alcohol to offer is usually based on the deceased's drink of choice while alive. On Santa Muerte altars, we most often see tequila, rum, and beer. However, this is more of a cultur-ally preferential selection due to the devotional community's Latino (and specifically Mexican) majority. When offering alcohol to La Santa Muerte, the standard amount to pour is usually no more than necessary to fill a shot glass. As with cigarettes, though, devotees who are adverse to alcohol consumption should not offer alcohol to their patron deity because, outside of magic, they would never offer a drink to their own friends.

Though not as common as cigarettes and alcohol, flowers are a pop-ular choice that all devotees can agree upon as an appropriate offering. As discussed in the previous chapter, each plant has its own energy and magic, but these properties and correspondences should not factor into whether a certain plant would make an acceptable gift. Aesthetic is the only quality you should consider for flowers given as an offering. If you think a flower is beautiful or if it has some special significance to you, it is a perfect flower for an offering. Some devotees like to fill a vase, oth-ers like to leave a single flower, but regardless of preference, the offering has the same value.

Unique to the Santa Muerte tradition, devotees will often offer wilted and dried flowers to symbolize death. This is perfectly acceptable given Santa Muerte's domain, and even if a fresh flower is given, it can remain on the altar as an offering long after it has faded. Nevertheless, be mindful to eventually remove the flowers once they have been there "long enough" to avoid being negligent and using the altar as a place to discard things.

But still, why do we give offerings to La Santa Muerte? We know that her supreme neutrality prevents us from being able to curry favor from her, and we also know that offerings are separate from spellwork. So why do we do it? It's not like Death *needs* these things. The answer is simple: we do it because she is our friend. Gift-giving is a natural part of a friend-ship. It helps strengthen and maintain the relationship. If we look at our own relationships with our friends, we can see that those with whom we have the closest bonds are the ones with whom we exchange gifts more often. The Santa Muerte tradition is all about making the Spirit of Death a friend and companion in our everyday life. Regarding her as some nebulous, mysterious, and unapproachable force placed on a pedestal simply prevents us from developing a relationship with her.

In the end, the types of offerings and the frequency with which offerings are given are entirely dependent upon the preference of the devotee. Expensive and ornate gifts are not needed to develop a relationship with La Santa Muerte. The price of a gift does not equate how much you appreciate the other person. If all we can afford is a single flower growing out of the sidewalk that we picked ourselves, then so long as it is given with love, it is a wonderful gift. Often, personalized gifts are the most treasured, but even so, do not feel obliged to give a gift if finances are tight. If forced to make the choice between paying the rent and keeping your Santa Muerte altar filled with fresh roses, by all means, skip out on the roses and pay the rent. Remember, self-denial is not a virtue, and though we may work magic on the spiritual level, we still live on the earthly level.

As with anything else, be mindful of your offering. Leaving lit cigarettes and glasses of alcohol in the presence of pets, children, and people trying to free themselves from addiction is never a good idea, and even with plants, make sure they are not toxic if accidentally consumed or touched by a pet or child. Disregarding safety and the needs of others automatically makes any offering to La Santa Muerte superficial, selfish, and vain.

COMMUNAL DEATH

Because these altars to the devotion of Death are almost always located in the home, they are designed for solitary practice of magic in the Santa Muerte community. Due to the stigma modern society places on death, magic, and anything not well understood by mainstream culture, most devotees are solitary practitioners. Nevertheless, there is a growing movement for a more communal approach to the devotion of Death.

In part I, we discussed the two most well-known groups: the ISCAT Mex-U.S.A, and Doña Queta's informal gatherings in Mexico City. But if we look in any region of the world that has a large Mexican immigrant population, we will find surreptitious ceremonies dedicated to the Spirit of Death. Usually, such a ceremony is called a "Mass," and, as the name suggests, is similar to the Catholic Mass held in churches on Sundays. For the most part, these Masses are informal, like those of Doña Queta, and because of the lack of dogma and a unified theology, each Mass is performed differently depending who is leading it.

Regardless of the leader, though, the essence of the Santa Muerte Mass revolves around communal prayer. The oldest and/or most experienced devotee leads the group in prayers, and sometimes this leader of the Mass gives a small anecdotal talk about Santa Muerte's ability to work miracles to bolster the faith of those present. To those familiar with Roman Catholicism, the Santa Muerte Masses are very similar to Catholic Masses, except without a holy text and without the transubstantiation of the Eucharist. The reason for the heavy Catholic influence in these Masses, again, originates from the community's predominately Mexican (and more specifically Catholic) cultural roots. With the mystery school's lack of a formulated group devotion ceremony or ritual, these devotees used what they knew and adapted it for their own religious purposes.

In larger cities, there are public temples and churches dedicated to the devotion of La Santa Muerte. These temples are usually Santa Muerte–specific esoteric stores and information centers that double as places of worship through weekly Masses held at night, though daytime Masses are starting to become more popular to accommodate the growing number of devotees' schedules. Because the community is largely made up of Spanish-speaking people, the Masses are almost always in Spanish.

I highly suggest attending at least one Mass if possible. Even if you don't speak Spanish, the atmosphere and communal energy will be apparent, electrifying, and different from any communal gathering you have experienced. Newer initiates will usually feel intimidated and even a bit scared, but this is normal, and the regular attendees will understand this. At the back of the book, I list a few of the more well-known Santa Muerte temples and shops in the United States so you can check them out for yourself. But even if you live in an area where there are no temples or the thought of going to a Mass reeks of unwanted Catholicism in your belief system, that is perfectly fine, too. Attendance of the Mass is not necessary, and only a small minority of devotees participate in them. As with many practices in the mystery school of La Santa Muerte, the Mass is just one way of expressing devotion to Death, but never is it the only way.

Be warned, though—like all organized institutions, some temples and churches dedicated to La Santa Muerte may be more dogmatic and closed to outsiders than others. Different ones will have different rules and protocol, and some may even have a hierarchy of clergy ingrained into the establishment. One memorable example of such differences occurred when I went out to the various Santa Muerte temples and churches in Los Angeles to do additional research for this book. My friend (who first dared me to walk into a Santa Muerte church) and I initially went to a very well-known temple in Hollywood, only to be met by a grungy looking man in a stained tank top and very revealing red boxer shorts. This man had an ego like no one's business and referred to himself in the third person as the "High Father/Priest" of the temple. After he attempted to play mind games and threatened to hex my friend and me, the two of us left, realizing he was probably not the best person from whom to receive objective information.

Nevertheless, a few blocks away in downtown L.A., another Santa Muerte church was very welcoming toward us. Noticing that my friend and I were not regular members of this particular church, a few priestesses showed us around, gave us a tour of the grounds, and offered to answer any questions we might have had. They were particularly excited when we told them that we were doing some additional research for an English-language Santa Muerte book, telling us that they would greatly welcome any new church members who felt called to the veneration of the Most Holy Death. Their kindness and helpfulness was a total 180 degrees from the temple in Hollywood that we had just visited, and if it wasn't for all the Santa Muerte statues, candles, and artwork in both locations, their contrasting actions could have easily been confused for completely different faiths.

MEETING DEATH

Now, before I end this chapter and begin part III, where you will manifest specific spells based on all you have learned thus far, one more exercise is necessary. As you've already read countless times, it is mandatory to establish a relationship with La Santa Muerte before being able to co-create magic with her. So far, you have learned many things, but you have yet to meet her.

This might sound morbid, but in reality, one does not need to die to meet Death. The exercise below is a meditation on meeting Death. Once you have met her, you may go on to part III and begin to co-create magic, but if you skip this step, the magic you attempt to co-create will ultimately be in vain, or worse, horridly backfire in ways unimaginable.

First, a brief note on meditation. Meditation is not necessarily a practice that entails hours of silent focus on attaining enlightenment. It most certainly can be, but it doesn't have to be. In its simplest sense, meditation is an act of clearing the mind. Spiritually, one could say that it is "listening" to God, the universe, the Tao. Scientifically, one could say that it is the conscious change of brainwave cycles, measured in cycles per second, or hertz (Hz).

In our wakeful state, our brains are usually in a beta state (13–30 Hz). A bit slower and we enter alpha state (8–13 Hz), the level of brain activity associated with daydreaming or those times when we are "spacing out" between the physical world and our mental world. Even more slow is the theta state (4–8 Hz), where we feel drowsy or are in a very light sleep. The slowest level is known as delta state (0–4 Hz), and this is the state where we experience deep sleep, rapid eye movements (REM), and dreams.[63]

Through meditation, we attempt to consciously control our brainwave cycles and, thus, enter into different levels of consciousness. To put it more poetically, we are wakefully creating a "dream state" wherein our subconscious and the universe speak to us and we can remember all that

---

63. Nigel F. Huddleston, "Brain Wave States and How To Access Them," Synthesis Learning. http://synthesislearning.com/article/brwav.htm (accessed May 7, 2015).

was said. As mentioned earlier, the Divine speaks to us through our subconscious, and by meditating, we are consciously tuning our brains to a frequency where we can hear the Divine.

That, in a general sense, is the essence of meditation. The slower you can get your brainwave cycles to be, the more vivid your meditational experience will be. Naturally, this will take time and practice, but not as long as you might think. Fifteen to twenty minutes a day is as much meditation as I would recommend for a new devotee and those unfamiliar with meditation. Within a week, one's level of profundity will increase.

So take time now to perform this meditational exercise. I know the urge to begin co-creating magic and starting to do spellwork is very strong, but unless you have met La Santa Muerte, you will never get the results you are looking for. Keep doing this meditation daily (preferably around the same time) until you have had a vivid experience in meeting her. Trust me, you will know when you have met her, and if you are ever unsure, then you probably haven't. An encounter with Death is undeniable. And for those who are frightened to have such an encounter, then the magic of La Santa Muerte is not for them.

In your meditation, talk with Death, listen to her, and most importantly ask for her blessing to be able to co-create magic with her. This blessing will be the most powerful aid you could ever have in all your magical workings. Be prepared for the unexpected, and I will see you again in part III after you have had your encounter with Death herself.

EXERCISE 2: MEDITATION TO MEET DEATH

1. Find a comfortable place free of distractions where you can be alone.

2. Sit in a comfortable position with your back straight.

3. Relax your body and close your eyes. Try to look at the center of your brow (third-eye chakra) without putting strain on your eyeballs.

4. Following the rhythm of your heartbeat, count down from 10 to 1, lowering your visual consciousness after each number. Imagine your conscious center (eyes, ears, nose, mouth, brain) is descending into your body from your head toward your heart with each heartbeat, like how an elevator slowly descends from floor to floor.

5. When you feel as if your conscious center is at heart level, imagine a door that leads into your heart. On the other side of this door, there is an empty void where everything is possible.

6. Open the door, and step inside.

7. Focus on the void. Various thoughts will come into your mind, but do not focus on them. Simply allow them to come and go like clouds floating on the breeze. Eventually, they will disappear of their own accord, and the void will be all that is left upon which to focus.

8. From this void, ask that Death appear in a form recognizable to you. She may come as La Santa Muerte, she may come as another deity of death, or she may even come in an appearance that only makes sense to you. Be open to anything. You will know her when you meet her.

9. If she does not appear to you, take it as a sign that you may require more meditational practice and end the meditation.

10. If she does appear, speak with her and ask for her blessing to co-create magic in her tradition. But most of all, listen to her. Listen to her wisdom, warnings, and advice. Keep the conversation simple and light. As with any first encounter with a new friend, the deeper and more profound questions are usually left unsaid and saved for when closer bonds have been forged. When she leaves, thank her for the encounter.

11. In the void, turn around and imagine seeing that same door through which you entered. Open it, and see yourself back at heart level in your body.

12. With each heartbeat, count up from 1 to 10, rising back up from your heart to your head with each number.

13. Slowly open your eyes and stand up. Do something that grounds you back to normal waking consciousness (having a bite to eat, taking a sip of something to drink, light shaking, etc.).

14. When you feel you are ready, superficially wipe your body down three times from the top of your head to your groin and then outward as if you are brushing dust off of yourself in three long strokes. On the first stroke, wipe your front, saying, "I am in balance with myself." On the second stroke, simultaneously wipe each side with each hand, saying, "I am in balance with the universe (the Tao, the Divine, etc.)." Lastly, wipe your backside, saying, "I wipe away all that does not serve my highest good." This is important since in a deep meditational state, unwanted energy may have entered your "lowered" consciousness.

Note: This meditation is a combined adaptation of meditational techniques as taught by the ancient/alternative Christianity philosopher B. Dave Walters, the Cabot Kent Hermetic Temple and its students, as well as my own personal style. The exercise as written above comes from my own practice of getting into a meditative state of consciousness. As you become more proficient in meditation, feel free to deviate from the specifics of this exercise and make it your own. If you are already an experienced practitioner of meditation, feel free to use whichever technique you are accustomed to using. The technique is not so important as the end result of meeting Death.

Part III

8

The Anatomy of Santa Muerte Spellwork

"Death and life are in the power of the tongue;
those who choose one shall eat its fruit."
~PROVERBS 18:21, NEW AMERICAN BIBLE REVISED EDITION

Congratulations! You've finally made it to the most-anticipated section of this book on La Santa Muerte and her magic: the section on spellwork. If you've read the table of contents (or skipped ahead), then you know that each of the subsequent chapters will deal with a specific category of spells such as money, love, lust, and so on. Before I give out any step-by-step instructions on how to go about doing these specific spells, though, it is important to understand exactly what a spell *is* and what it is *not*. This chapter will serve as a general explanation of spellwork and how it is both an art and a science. By breaking down the anatomy of a spell to its basic components, you will be better able to understand spellwork as a whole. Once you've become more experienced, you will be able to create your own spells and tailor existing spells to your needs.

When it comes down to it, Santa Muerte spellwork is not one of creation but of destruction. In magic, the manifestation of something can come about in two ways: either we forcefully attract it toward us or we get rid of any obstacles that prevent it naturally coming to us. While most people's idea of magic is the former, the magic of La Santa Muerte focuses on the latter. Both serve the same ends but go about it in different ways. It's like the difference between manifesting health and eliminating sickness. One creates, the other destroys, and yet the result is the same.

To work with La Santa Muerte is not to create new things, but rather to destroy the old things that are preventing the new. Partnering with Death involves specifying a desire and then further specifying what is preventing that desire from having already manifested. Be aware, though, that the most common obstacle to manifestation is often ourselves and our own thoughts and actions.

We must learn, understand, and accept that our thoughts have power. A belief is nothing more than a thought that we think over and over again until it becomes imbedded in our subconscious and then becomes the "default" or "autopilot" setting of our consciousness. Magic can only occur when we truly believe that the spellwork we are doing *will* manifest without a shadow of a doubt. Such strong faith in ourselves comes from a belief in our own power, which is nothing more than thinking that we have the power to work miracles over and over again until it becomes our default setting—our magical mindset.

If we go into spellwork with the thought that it might not work or that we are testing to see if magic is real or not, the spell will not manifest, or worse, it will manifest in an unintended, negative way. Full faith is necessary. This is why so many people claim magic is fake or a ruse. People who dabble halfheartedly in some magic spells they found somewhere often fail to manifest anything due to their own doubts and reservations (consciously or subconsciously). Then, after a few failed spells, they claim magic to be a lie and a hoax, never realizing that their own mind was the saboteur of their success.

If you are a new practitioner of magic, do not be upset or deterred by spells that fail to manifest. Until a magical mindset is honed, the manifestations of spellwork will be inconsistent. My suggestion is to start small. Perform little spells that you truly believe could manifest in daily life. A popular one is to manifest a cup of coffee within seven days—not out of thin air, but rather, that a cup of coffee is presented to you at some point. Or you could manifest a small, specific sum of unexpected money to manifest in your possession within a certain time frame. By building upon the successes of these little spells, you can build up your faith in your own magical ability.

It is important to reiterate the fact that *there is no such thing as coincidence*. Oftentimes, people will dismiss the belief in magic as a self-delusion because of the frequently stated argument, "It would've happened anyway, and the spell was incidental." So, how do we know if our magic is actually the cause of a manifestation that seems coincidental? Well, the truth is that no one knows. No one can empirically prove that our spells forcibly caused an event to occur in our physical reality. Like I said before regarding what happens to us after we die, no one knows. People have strong beliefs in what will happen in the afterlife and whether magic is real or not, but a belief (even a very strong belief) is not the same as knowing.

Thus the main hurdle to spellwork presents itself: the magical paradox of how 100 percent certainty in one's own magical abilities is necessary for the physical manifestation of a spell, yet no one can ever know with 100 percent certainty that spellwork is the cause of a physical manifestation. There is no simple answer to this, but the one most commonly used (and the one I, personally, use) is that it's a matter of faith. Most of our modern world insists that seeing is believing, but when it comes to magic, we must believe in order to see.

There is really only one question that we must ask ourselves whenever we are countered by nonbelievers in magic, and that is: *Does it really matter?* If we perform a spell to receive enough money to pay our overdue rent, and money manifests, does it really matter if magic or coincidence is the cause? No. We got what we wished for. If we say a prayer to cure an ailment, and within a few days, we are fully healed, does it matter if our recovery is due to the prayer or the illness taking its natural course? No. We got what we wished for. This might seem "anti- magical," but it is a practical truth, and if nothing else, the mystery school of La Santa Muerte is one of practicality.

So then, how can I say there are no coincidences and yet also say it doesn't matter if magic is responsible for seeming coincidences? I say it because it is the truth. In the world of magic and energy manipulation, there are many seemingly contradictory facts that are, paradoxically, both true. The important thing to remember is that faith in your own magical abilities—whether or not they are responsible for the final outcome—is paramount. As you begin to work more with magic and energy manipulation, you will begin to see too many "coincidences" in life that statistically could not be coincidental, and you just have to take it on faith that *you* are the agent responsible for these "coincidences."

Most people on earth live their entire lives with faith in one thing or another. Many have faith in the existence of a certain deity, many others have faith in a friend or a loved one, and many more have faith that when they go to sleep they will wake up to see the next day. So why can't we have faith in ourselves, and live our lives believing that our thoughts (conscious and subconscious) are ultimately responsible for our reality?

This brings up another common question: what are the limits of magic? If our thoughts create our reality, then are we technically able to do whatever we want? While theoretically this is true, it is almost never possible. But why? Why can't we fly through the air, walk on water, and cure disease in an instant? The answer is *us*. Deep down, we don't *truly* believe that we can do these things. We live in the physical world, and it is very, very difficult to separate the laws of physics from our human experience. In our heart of hearts, we don't believe that it is possible. Once in a long while, an ascended master will walk the earth and be able to perform these miraculous feats (Jesus, Buddha, Mohammad, Moses, and many more whose lives were never recorded). Their faith and knowledge of energy manipulation are so strong that they can transcend the laws of physics. So, while very much possible, it is highly improbable to be able to perform such magic ourselves.

In fact, magic manifests in the seemingly most innocent and natural of ways. Like water, it takes the path of least resistance. The energy of the universe has a natural flow to it, and it is much more likely that a spell will manifest in accordance with the energetic flow of the universe rather than suddenly produce an anomaly in space and time. In more practical terms, this means that if you perform a spell to have enough money to go to college, the spell will be much more likely to manifest in being approved for student loans than suddenly seeing your checking account with a few extra figures before the decimal point. Likewise, a love spell to find your significant other will be much more likely to manifest in someone messaging you on a dating website than in making your cheating ex-boyfriend or girlfriend suddenly have a change of heart. Remember, magic often manifests in ways that are "coincidental," not in ways that drastically defy the natural order of the universe.

The Building Blocks of a Spell

With that said, let us explore the fundamental building blocks of a spell (regardless of magical tradition). First, I will explain in generalities, and then I will take those generalities and apply them to the Santa Muerte tradition in particular.

In his book *Instant Magik*, Christopher Penczak explains that all spellwork can be boiled down to three essential building blocks: altering consciousness, focusing will, and directing energy. All spells have these three necessary factors, and everything else (including the style of these three factors) is a matter of tradition and preference. If a spell is missing any one of these three things, the spell will not manifest. In my experience with Santa Muerte magic, and magic in general, I can wholeheartedly say that this is true.

I: Altering Consciousness

The first component is altering consciousness. This has been previously explained as getting into a magical mindset and aligning the conscious and subconscious minds. Because the universe communicates with us on a subconscious level (often through symbolism), we must first be able to access that level in order to speak with the universe and petition a magical outcome. Scientifically, this involves changing brain frequencies from our waking beta level of consciousness to more dreamlike levels of consciousness—the alpha, theta, and delta levels.

Meditation is often the most common and the most preferred way to change one's brain frequency. Another popular method is through chanting, the repetition of certain words and phrases over and over again. The Catholic rosary (with its repetition of the "Hail Mary" and "Our Father" prayers) is a popular chanting technique, as are certain mantras used by Buddhist sects.

Magical tools are also a great way to get into a magical mindset. Lighting incense and candles, or even wearing a specific article of clothing reserved only for spellwork can quickly change our consciousness. There is no "official" way to alter one's consciousness and align the two minds, so we are free to be creative. Until you are more experienced, though, try to stick with only one method. In this way, the commencement of your chosen method will immediately signal to your subconscious "we are about to perform magic, so get ready." The more of a habit it becomes, the faster you will be able to transcend into (and out of) the magical mindset.

II: Focusing Will

The second component is focusing will. This is essentially the act of clarifying and making as specific as possible your desired manifestation. It is absolutely necessary to get *very* specific. The more specific we are, the more effective our manifestational outcome will be. To do this, we must look at our spell from every possible angle and ask ourselves the tough questions: Is it necessary? Can I obtain this by simpler means than magic? Is this for my highest good? How could not having this possibly benefit me? How could having this possibly harm me? This is the time when magical ethics come into the picture (which will be discussed in detail later on).

A good example of this is the age-old desire to find our significant other. All too often, people will use spellwork with the end goal of finding their true love, but when that person comes into their life, the person who initiated the spell will eventually drive them away through their personal issues and baggage that they bring from old relationships into this new one. While technically the spell *did* work, it didn't manifest exactly how the person thought it would. They didn't realize that what had been preventing them from finding their true love this whole time was their own issues and baggage from the past. They could have met Mr. or Ms. Right hundreds of times over, but because of their own unresolved issues, they kept preventing compatible partners from wanting to approach them in the first place. The real spellwork they should have done was for self-love and resolving past issues, which would then have paved the way for Mr. or Ms. Right to come into their lives and *stay* in their lives.

Such realization takes a lot of introspection and self-psychoanalysis. Most people don't do this. They believe magic is a "cure-all," wherein if they can just find the right spell they can solve all of their problems. But magic doesn't work that way. The world doesn't work that way. The universe doesn't work that way. We communicate with the world through our subconscious, and no matter how many love spells we perform, if our subconscious has the autopilot thought of "men/women always leave me," then men/women will always leave us. Thus, it is necessary to focus your will and get specific on the root issues of what you really want.

III: Directing Energy

The third component is directing energy. This is the most lively and most fun part of magic. Once we have attained a magical mindset and have focused our will to be very clear on what we *really* want, we can now manipulate the energy to bring about the intended manifestation.

Traditions all over the world have various ways of directing energy. Hindu traditions are famous for poses, such as those found in yoga, where the holding of certain bodily positions can manipulate energy. Many witchcraft traditions direct energy through the creation of a potion, poppet, or charm, wherein the symbolism put into their creation speaks to the universe and manipulates energy. Judeo-Christian traditions direct their energy through prayer and the lighting of candles. The Santa Muerte tradition is eclectic in that it uses any and all methods from other traditions to manipulate energy. In fact, the blessing of each tool used in your spellwork (discussed earlier) serves this purpose. Communicating with and charging the tool with the feeling and energy of having obtained what you want is a form of directing energy into your spells.

But if you would like to further enhance your energy, my suggestion is to do something you naturally love to do. By forcing yourself to do something you find uncomfortable or awkward, you'll just be effectively working against yourself. Personally, I enjoy dancing to manipulate energy. I absolutely love it. Through dance, I let go of control of my body and let my soul and subconscious mind take over. Specifically, I play music that corresponds with the end goal of my spell. If it's a lust spell, I will play a song that makes me feel sexy and then dance to its rhythm. If it's a money spell, I will play a song that sings about luxury or being wealthy. If it's a health spell, I'll play something that makes me joyous and carefree. By feeling the song, I'm directing my spiritual energy and subconscious into the belief that I already have what I want.

This is very important, and it is the ultimate aim of directing energy. You have to feel as if you already have what you want in order for it to manifest. This is due to the Hermetic Law of Vibration, which essentially states that like attracts like. On a physical level, opposites attract, but on a spiritual level, attraction is based on similarity. In a nutshell, everything is essentially made of vibrations; things that vibrate on the same frequency tend to attract each other. Thus if we can manipulate our mind to vibrate at the same frequency as what we want, then we will attract what we want into our physical reality. If we do a money spell, but we can't escape from poverty consciousness, then we never completed this directing-energy step of spellwork because our energy is still stuck in feeling poor, which will ultimately attract more poverty. Similarly, if we do a love spell, but we feel as if we are unlovable, then our energy is still stuck in feeling unlovable, which will ultimately attract a lack of love.

Just be creative and do whatever gives you the feeling of what it would be like to have your spell manifested. If you are musical, play a song on your instrument that gives you that feeling. If you are artistic, paint a picture. If you are poetic or literary, write a poem or a short story of a day in the life when the spell has already manifested. You know yourself best. Be creative, and get into that feeling place through whatever way best suits you.

Many traditions throughout the world often end the directing-energy portion of spellwork with the statement of an affirmation. This is a simple phrase that professes belief in the manifestation of the spell. In Christian traditions, they say the word "amen," which best translates to "I believe," thus subconsciously reinforcing their belief in God answering their prayer or petition. Wiccans often say "so mote it be," which equates to "it is so," thus stating that they believe the spell is already manifested into their reality. Most devotees of La Santa Muerte use the affirmation of "amen," but this is, once again, due to the majority's background in Catholicism. Find a word or phrase that you can say with meaning and conviction that asserts to yourself the efficacy of your magical abilities.

IV: Letting Go

In addition to these three building blocks, I would like to present a fourth essential step in spellwork: letting go. This is often the hardest step, and a common reason most spells never manifest. Oftentimes, magical practitioners feel empowered and enlivened while casting a spell, and immediately afterward, they still feel unstoppable in manifesting miracles. As time goes on, however, these same people begin to doubt and question their own abilities. Their internal fire fades away. Magic is rarely ever instantaneous, and so the waiting period leaves people feeling as if nothing happened and as if nothing is going to happen.

This line of thinking directly contradicts the "feeling as if you already have it" necessity of magic. Remember, we have to believe in order to see, not the other way around. The lack of instantaneous evidence can slowly eat away at a person psychologically and will ultimately self-sabotage the manifestation of a spell that just needed more time.

Ideally, devotees of La Santa Muerte would want to get into the feeling place of already having the end goal of our spellwork, and we would want to do this as often as possible. The more we can do this, the more energy we add to our magic after the spell. However, if we start to think "it's not coming," or "why hasn't it manifested yet?" or any other negative feeling about the efficacy of our magic, we need to stop thinking about it altogether. Once the spellwork is done, it's done. The manifestation is ours to lose if we self-sabotage it by over-thinking.

This is why letting go is so important, especially for new initiates into the mystery school of La Santa Muerte. Unless you are ultra-confident in your magical prowess, just let it go and get it out of your mind after completing the spellwork. Forget about it if you have to. By doing this, we effectively get out of our own way to allow the magic to manifest on its own.

A good analogy for this would be ordering something online. Once you've purchased an item on the Internet, everything is done. The rest of the work will be handled by outside forces, and all you have to do is wait for your order to come. And it will come when it comes. If you check the mail every day wondering why it hasn't arrived yet, you'll start to feel anxious, and doubt will race through your mind—perhaps a problem has occurred. If the doubt grows large enough, you may be convinced that it'll never come and subsequently cancel your online order. In truth, there was nothing wrong, and all you had to do was be patient and wait a little longer.

A similar analogy can be given in the example of gardening. When you plant a seed, the rest of the work is up to the seed. You can help it a little bit by watering it and giving it fertilizer, but in the end, it'll grow when it grows. If you keep wondering why it hasn't sprouted yet, you may become anxious that nothing is happening and dig up the seed to check its progress. But by digging up the seed, you disrupt its ability to grow and thus self-sabotage your own garden. If you had left the seed alone, it would have grown of its own accord. So unless you have something positive to add to the seed / spell, it's better to just leave it alone and let it go. It will let you know when it blooms / manifests.

Why a Spell Doesn't Manifest

Now that we know the essential building blocks of a spell, let us explore the main reasons why a spell doesn't manifest. In the Santa Muerte tradition, we devotees are in a unique position of having spells *always* manifest. As discussed earlier in this book, the supreme neutrality of Death removes the safety measure of preventing the manifestation of spells that will ultimately come to do us harm or are not for our greater good. This safety measure is a common reason why spells from other magical traditions seem not to work. In spellwork, our partner force (God, the universe, a patron deity) ultimately has our greater good in mind. As human beings, our foresight is often limited, and what seems like a good idea from our point of view may, in fact, be very harmful to ourselves or others. For our own safety, these kinds of spells are ultimately negated by our partner force and never manifest.

If our partner force is La Santa Muerte, this safety measure is not applicable. The spell will manifest regardless of whether it will be to our benefit or detriment. This is why Santa Muerte magic requires extreme self-discipline and knowledge of one's self. It is important to keep in mind that this lack of safety is not exclusive to the person performing the spell. That person's family and friends can become entangled in magical harm as well.

The most frequently told example of this is with the ever-popular spells for money magic. Without forethought or stipulations, a devotee does spellwork to receive a large windfall of unexpected income. Later that week, this devotee receives news that their parents have died, and in their will, they left all their financial assets to the devotee. Now, technically, the spell manifested, but there was no safety measure that would have prevented the manifestation from occurring if it would have done harm to a loved one. This is an extreme example, but it illustrates the necessity not to engage in Santa Muerte magic for frivolous reasons.

Still, the absence of the inherent "greater good" clause of Santa Muerte magic does not mean that a spell will always manifest. La Santa Muerte will always see to it that the magic manifests, but, like mentioned earlier, the onus of failure is on *us*. Below, I list the most common ways in which magical practitioners self-sabotage their spells. By avoiding these common pitfalls, you can manifest miracles much more effectively—to your benefit or to your detriment.

Not Letting Go

As I mentioned, the inability to let go is the most common reason a spell doesn't manifest in the Santa Muerte tradition. Spells manifest *with* the natural flow of energy in the universe, not against it. A successful spell will realize itself in the physical world in a way that often can be mistaken for coincidence, and rarely does it miraculously appear instantaneously or "out of thin air" as Hollywood would like us to believe. For the purposes of spellwork, patience truly is a virtue, and by letting go, you are effectively saying that you trust La Santa Muerte to help you. Conversely, through doubt and the inability to let go, you are saying that you don't trust La Santa Muerte to help you, and so you have to keep on worrying whether the spell will manifest. As the ancient/alternative Christianity philosopher B. Dave Walters says, "You can either worry or have faith, but not both."

Lack of Clarity

This is another common pitfall that I alluded to earlier in discussing the lack of Santa Muerte magic's "greater good" safety clause. A spell can manifest, but unless we have a very clear and specific intent, it may come about in a way that is displeasing or even unnoticeable to us. On a benign level, this could happen by doing love magic to find a spouse. Within a week, you meet the perfect person who is funny, kind, attractive, and stable. However, this person is also an ardent supporter of your opposing political party and wants significantly more children than you would like. Did the spell work? Absolutely. The problem is that you were not specific enough, and so, in appearance, it seems as if your spell didn't work since these fundamental differences will prevent a harmonious marriage. This is why clarity is so important. Know *exactly* what you want before engaging in any spellwork.

Never "Felt" It

Many people attempt to do spellwork but go into it halfheartedly. They go through the motions of saying all the right prayers, lighting a candle, buying a statue, and anything else that a spell requires … but they never actually *feel* it. They skipped the building block of directing energy. Getting into the feeling place of already having our spell manifested is the most important part of spellwork. The rituals, the prayers, the incantations, the tools, and everything else are all there to help us get into that feeling place and communicate it to our subconscious and the universe at large. Just robotically going step-by-step through a spell never works. Find whatever artistic outlet works best for you to get into that psychological state of believing. You have to *feel* it, or the spell will not manifest.

Oppositional Thinking

Oppositional thinking is often a subtle detriment to the efficacy of our magic. We may be saying and doing one thing, but our thoughts are on the exact opposite thing. A good example of this is spellwork for healing. We perform spellwork to heal ourselves of a certain ailment, but while our words and actions are focused on healing, our mind is focused on not being sick. Notice that in such cases, the majority of our thinking is focused on the sickness. And since we are obsessing more about the sickness than about wellness, we are not giving enough energy to our healing for wellness to manifest. This also commonly happens in money magic and love magic. For money magic, we may do a spell for wealth, but we do it from a feeling place and psychological mindset of not wanting to be poor anymore. Because our mind and feelings are essentially focused on being poor, we cannot manifest wealth. And for love magic, we may do a spell for finding a lover, but because we do it from a feeling place and psychological mindset of being lonely and/or unlovable, how could we ever manifest companionship and love—the exact opposite of where we are directing our energy? Remember, the Hermetic Law of Vibration dictates that like attracts like, and since we communicate with the universe through our subconscious, whatever is dominant in our subconscious is what we will ultimately manifest in our lives.

Not Meeting La Santa Muerte Halfway

Santa Muerte magic is, at its core, co-creational magic. The power of manifestation is not 100 percent our power and not 100 percent hers either. We must meet her halfway since she will not do all the work for us. To do this, we must take real-world action. Now, this may seem contradictory to letting go, but in actuality, it is not. Letting go involves getting out of our own way psychologically and allowing La Santa Muerte to do her part. Taking real-world action involves physically allowing ourselves to receive the spell's manifestation once La Santa Muerte has done her part. We cannot sit around all day expecting things to materialize out of thin air and into our laps. Again, magic often manifests as a coincidence, and so we must put ourselves into situations where coincidence is likely to occur, thus putting us in the natural flow of universal energy. If we perform a love spell for a new romantic partner, we need to do our part and create an online account on a dating website or frequent dating locales, for example, so as to "coincidentally" meet that person. More specifically, if we clarified our intention for that romantic partner to be fit and in shape, we should start frequenting a local gym. If we want that person to be a comic book aficionado, we should frequent comic book stores and conventions. If we want that person to be a certain ethnicity, we should frequent bars or clubs whose clientele is primarily of that ethnicity. The examples are endless, but the essential thing to remember is to meet La Santa Muerte halfway and put yourself into situations of "coincidence."

PRAYERS, MEDITATIONS, AND SPELLS: WHAT'S THE DIFFERENCE?

The Santa Muerte tradition of magic is highly eclectic. It absorbs the mystical elements of a multitude of sources and unites them through the philosophic outlook of Death. As the number of initiates continues to exponentially grow, the more diverse the backgrounds of devotees will become. For this reason, there are multiple avenues within the tradition in which to engage in magic.

By far, the most common avenue is through prayer. Currently, the vast majority of Santa Muerte devotees come from a Roman Catholic background, in which prayer is the only sponsored and acceptable way to commune with the Divine. While the Catholic tradition has a host of pre-made prayers on hand to recite for any given intention, the Santa Muerte tradition does not. The lack of a central theology and councils to officiate which prayers are acceptable and which ones aren't allows for more creativity and diversity in prayers.

Interestingly, though, it is not uncommon to come across prayers to God and Jesus within the Santa Muerte tradition. Since the mystery school of La Santa Muerte is not a religion unto itself, its philosophical framework often gets placed on top of a devotee's original faith landscape. Since most devotees' religious landscape is Roman Catholicism, it makes sense that some of them would still see the God of the Bible and Jesus as the primary miracle workers. The role Santa Muerte plays in such religious eclecticism is as the primary intercessor with God and Jesus, who advocates on behalf of those who seek her aid. Such devotees will often profess that Death is the most powerful force in the world, second only to the Holy Trinity of God, Jesus, and the Holy Spirit. For traditional Catholics, the Virgin Mary often plays this exact same role as motherly intercessor.

At its core, a prayer is a petition to the Divine. It can be as poetic or as straightforward as we like, but it always involves speaking (out loud or mentally) to the Divine. A prayer does not require a specific posture or a specific ritual. So long as our focus is on speaking directly to the Divine, we are engaged in prayer.

The best kinds of prayers in the Santa Muerte tradition are those that are spontaneous and from the heart. Reciting an already written prayer authored by another person often comes across as robotic or inauthentic. The beauty of spellwork is in speaking from the heart. By not having a prepared script to follow, our petition is more honest, and by "talking it out" with the Divine, we can more easily specify, clarify, and see the greater point of view of what we are asking for.

For this reason, I have limited the amount of prayers included in this book. Words that are not your own, even if they are for the same end goal, are never as effective as words spoken from the heart. One sentence that is spontaneous, sincere, and from a place of love is far, far more powerful than verbatim recitation of the most grandiose and poetic prayer ever written. If truly heartfelt, prayer is one of the most powerful avenues of magic we have.

Prayer, however, often gets confused with meditation. The idea that they are essentially the same thing, just from different faiths, is a common mistake. Meditation is more receptive than prayer. It is much more quiet and much less active. If prayer can be considered as *speaking* to the Divine, then meditation can be considered as *listening* to the Divine.

Listening is often the hardest part of communication, and in magic, it is no different. It's easy to state what we do and do not want, but it is much more difficult to listen to why we should not have it or what we have to do to get it. The hardest part about meditation is being able to accept whatever the Divine communicates to us. As humans, we often don't like to be told no, and if no is the answer we receive in meditation, we must be able to accept that. Yes, we can absolutely override this through Santa Muerte spellwork, but doing so will ultimately not be in our best interest. The goal of meditation is to awaken and see the truth of the world, our desires, and ourselves. By doing this, we can make more disciplined and educated choices in magic and in life. But if we go into it hoping only for self-validation, then we don't really want to know the truth and could very well cause great harm to ourselves.

Because prayer and meditation are common aspects of many of the world's more accepted and major religions, they may not feel very magical even though they are. Spells are often thought of as being the most magical aspect of the Santa Muerte tradition. But, again, this is due to society's common misuse of the word "magic" as being relegated to phenomena that humans don't fully understand. Since many people (including many devotees of La Santa Muerte) don't fully understand spellwork, it fits this societal definition of being "magical."

Most of part II of this book was dedicated to explaining this phenomenon of spellwork. At its most basic, a spell can be defined as a symbolic communication to the Divine from the union of our conscious and subconscious minds through the use of symbolism and tools. Because it is more involved than either prayer or meditation and contains a lot more artistic freedom, spellwork is often presumed to be more efficacious. In reality, though, it is just a different avenue of magic. But because it is more involved and dynamic (as well as less understood), there is a much higher learning curve in being able to perform spellwork successfully.

Essentially, prayer is direct communication that is spontaneous and subjective. Spellwork is indirect communication that is thought out and symbolic. Meditation is receptive communication that is neutral and objective. Devotees of Death can use any of these ways to communicate with her, including all three. The mystery school of La Santa Muerte is eclectic and is the lens through which we view any and all religious landscapes of our world. It deals in mysticism, not theology. And though the theological differences of our time divide the world's religions, their mystical similarities eternally unite them into speaking the same Truth.

ETHICS AND CONSEQUENCES OF WORKING WITH DEATH

When it comes to doing magic, there are innumerable deities with whom we can partner for spellwork. Most of the time, people seek the aid of La Santa Muerte because of her nonjudgment of them and because of the efficacy of her miracle workings. This combination has great potential to be extremely dangerous. Knowing they will not be judged by Death, people sometimes partner with her to manifest a petition that they, in their heart, know is malicious and harmful. Additionally, knowing that Death will not be adverse to such petitions and will not prevent them from manifesting (as other deities are wont to do) adds a higher level of danger to such spellwork.

So, then, if malicious and harmful magic is permitted in working with La Santa Muerte (though not condoned), what's to stop somebody from causing a rampage of evil? Well, the hard and fast answer is "nothing." But the more nuanced and detailed answer is twofold: cosmic reciprocity and the Law of Equivalent Exchange.

Cosmic reciprocity is a topic we have already discussed earlier in this book. It is more commonly known as "karma," or reaping what you sow. This phenomenon affects all things, and so if we, humans, do good things, then good things will come to us. If we do harmful things, then harmful things will come to us. Such tit-for-tat results, however, can vary in their immediacy. Actions can come back quickly and in little ways, but actions can also accumulate, build up, and come back in a massive way. This is because reciprocity is always equal in its severity. So if we do harmful magic, its severity will determine how severely the reciprocation will affect us. This reality is often more than enough for people to think twice about performing malicious and harmful magic.

The other preventive phenomenon is closely aligned with cosmic reciprocity: the Law of Equivalent Exchange. Unlike karma, which is more passive and whose effects are incidental to magic, the Law of Equivalent Exchange is a conscious, direct choice necessary for manifestation. According to universal law, in order to receive a thing, something of equal value must be given in exchange. Through this phenomenon, the universe keeps itself in balance. For those in the mystery school of La Santa Muerte, this is something we must consider greatly before beginning any spellwork.

If our desire is to manifest possession of a luxury car, are we willing to give up something of equal value? It is important to note that the term "value" is in reference to energy and not price. Thus, this does not mean that we must give up an equivalently expensive car or that we must give up something (or things) whose monetary value is equivalent to that of the new car. It just means that the amount of energy that we believe the car is worth must be given up in some way. And the ways to accumulate the equivalent energy value are endless. We could help others, donate to charities, pay it forward with random acts of kindness, and so on. In the end, we must somehow remain in energetic equilibrium with the universe.

Does the Law of Equivalent Exchange apply to more abstract manifestations such as health and love? Absolutely. Again, value corresponds with energy. Most commonly, in terms of health magic and love magic, the most powerful thing of equal value that we can give up is our old habits. Are we willing to give up our unhealthy eating habits in order to receive the manifestation of wellness? Are we willing to give up our promiscuity in order to receive a true love? The answers are ultimately up to each one of us. Fortunately, the equivalent sacrifice does not have to precede manifestation. Healing magic can miraculously manifest wellness, but if we don't live up to our end of the exchange, we will relapse and the sickness will return. Similarly, we can encounter our true love before giving up equivalent lifestyle habits. But if we don't live up to our end of the exchange, the relationship will be strained and a breakup is inevitable.

So how does this all pertain to being a deterrent to malicious and harmful magic? Well, think about it. If you are performing a spell with an ill intention toward someone (a hex), then in order for them to receive the harm, what goodness are you giving up that is of equal value? Spells to cause sickness often require the spellcaster to give up his or her own health. Spells to cause a couple to break up often require the destruction of an equivalent relationship in the spellcaster's own life. Spells for the acquittal of a guilty person often requires the imprisonment of something just as valuable to the spellcaster. The examples are endless.

For those spellcasters who are so fueled by hate that they are willing to sacrifice themselves for the sake of seeing others suffer, a word of caution must be given: the Law of Equivalent Exchange is not exclusive to the spellcaster. This means that goodness, happiness, or health could very well be taken away from a loved one in exchange for the target of our hate receiving the brunt of our magic. Remember, something of equal value must be given, and if seeing a loved one suffer is just as painful as the pain we manifest on others, that is an equivalent exchange.

Usually, to figure out what can be given (or will be given in the case of receiving the manifestation first), meditation can be done. Before you engage in spellwork, speak with La Santa Muerte to understand what the price will be. The price will never be up to you; it is always dictated by La Santa Muerte herself.

While cosmic reciprocity cannot be intentionally forced (since doing a good thing solely to receive a good thing ultimately negates the "goodness" of the first thing), the Law of Equivalent Exchange *can* be intentionally forced and, in fact, *must* be intentionally forced. To successfully manifest a spell when working with La Santa Muerte, we *must* be aware that something of equal value will be given in order for our spell to manifest.

All in all, when it comes down to it, working with Death is not something that should be taken lightly. La Santa Muerte is not a deity with whom we should partner if our desires are frivolous or not necessary to our well-being. If we can live well without having our petition manifest, then asking for Death's help is probably not a good idea. Are most people in the mystery school of La Santa Muerte disciplined enough only to call upon her aid for things that are necessary for survival? Not at all. Most practitioners call upon Death to help them with everything from finding lost keys and getting discounts on purchases to hexing ex-lovers and causing an annoying coworker to miss work.

Although effective, working with La Santa Muerte is ultimately not worth it nor advised in the long run unless our petition is absolutely dire and necessary to our well-being. This takes a lot of introspection because we might think that we "can't live without" a specific lover, a specific item, or even a specific event or experience, but the truth is that we very well can, we just don't *want* to. Differentiating between our wants and our needs is paramount in working with Death. And even if our petition is necessary, are we truly willing to give up something of equal value?

Now that you have been thoroughly informed and warned, you are ready to begin co-creating magic with La Santa Muerte. In the following chapters, you will be given step-by-step guidelines for specific spells with a specific manifestational intention. Included will be a description of *why* the spell works as well as all necessary and suggested tools to be used in the spell. If a tool is necessary, the spell cannot be performed without it. If a tool is merely suggested, however, the spell can be successfully done without it, but having it blessed and on your altar can add extra energy to the spell and help align your conscious and subconscious minds. Unless stated otherwise, all tools utilized should remain on your Santa Muerte altar (or designated spellcrafting workbench) until you have begun to see evidence of your spell's manifestation.

Don't allow these to be your only spells, though. Remember, the most effective spells are the ones that we make up ourselves since they have the strongest resonance with our subconscious. But for now, until you become confident in your magical prowess, let these spells be your introduction into Santa Muerte magic.

9
Money Magic

"Man cannot possess anything as long as he fears death.
But to him who does not fear it, everything belongs.
If there was no suffering, man would not know his limits,
would not know himself."

~LEO TOLSTOY, *WAR AND PEACE*

Money magic is by far one of the most common types of spellwork done by devotees of La Santa Muerte. In very general terms, her devotion is strongest among the poor and working classes of society. For them, the accumulation of money is more about survival than luxury. Yes, money magic is often the most frivolous kind of magic, but the value of a specific amount of money is relative. One hundred dollars is valued much differently by someone making minimum wage than it is by someone who makes a six-figure salary.

Oddly, there are many people who refrain from money magic because of the misconception that money is somehow "evil." But money is not evil. Money does not change people. Money (like alcohol) simply removes our inhibitions to reveal who we truly are without self-imposed restrictions. If we know that we *can* do something (because we can afford it or afford to pay off the consequences), then nothing is really there to stop us from doing it. Money is just a tool, and it can be used for great good just as it can be used for great harm. If it were truly evil, churches would not ask for it every Sunday. Moreover, if it's immoral to be wealthy, just imagine how much good you can do for charity organizations and scientific research without having a disposable income. The morality of money is fully dependent upon how we utilize it.

ENCHANTED CASH

The most effective kind of spell we can do to bring about wealth is one to eliminate poverty consciousness. Because one of the building blocks of a successful spell is to be able to feel as if the manifestation has already occurred, money magic requires the feeling place of already having the desired amount of money. However, the only people who know what it's like to feel wealthy are people who were born into it or have at some point in their lives been wealthy. For a person living paycheck to paycheck and drowning in debt, it's very hard to feel wealthy.

This is especially difficult when born into poverty, because all we truly know is poverty, and we carry that mentality of poverty with us in our subconscious for the rest of our lives. This is why most lottery winners often quickly end up right back where they originally were; their subconscious was still on the frequency of poverty, and so (according to the Law of Vibration) they attracted poverty back into their lives.

Enchanted Cash is a simple yet effective spell to eliminate poverty consciousness from your mind and get into the feeling place of wealth.

Suggested Tools:
Color/Aspect: Gold
Herbs/Scents: Berry, cinnamon
Minerals: Citrine, copper

1. Go to your bank and withdraw the largest denomination bill that you can. Whatever you can afford ($100 bill, $20 bill, etc.) is fine so long as you feel that it is a lot.

2. Get into a meditative state and place any of the above-suggested tools on top of the single bill.

3. Visualize the bill far in front of you, near a golden door, and imagine an elastic cord coming from your mid-back that is attached to poverty (however you imagine it).

4. You cannot fully see the poverty that you are attached to, but you know it is there, and every time you try and move toward the bill, the cord retracts and pulls you back toward poverty.

5. You see La Santa Muerte appear before you. Ask her to sever the cord that is attaching you to poverty.

6. Imagine her scythe swinging downward behind you, severing the cord.

7. Feel resistance slacken and walk confidently toward the bill to obtain it.

8. Without opening your eyes, grasp the actual bill and feel it in your hands.

9. Imagine folding the bill into a key and using it to open the golden door.

10. Behind the golden door is a vault of endless cash of the same denomination of bills as the key.

11. Open your eyes and reflect on the bill being your key to wealth, and thank La Santa Muerte for severing your attachment to poverty.

Now that you have properly blessed this bill, place it in your wallet/ purse, knowing that it is your key to wealth. Because it is your key, you never want to give it away by spending it. If you lose your key, you lose access to the wealth behind the door.

On an energetic level, this piece of currency will attract wealth to it equal to the value seen in the vault during spellwork. On a psychological level, having a large denomination bill in your possession at all times will eradicate the poverty consciousness credo of "I can't afford that." Everywhere you go, you will know that you have, in your possession at that very moment, enough money to buy those clothes in the store window, the most expensive thing on the menu, and so on. Knowing you can afford all of your daily wants will allow you to feel wealthy on a daily basis. Just be sure not to spend that bill—doing so will show La Santa Muerte that you are not serious about getting rid of your poverty consciousness and not meeting her halfway. Perform this spell too many times because you spent the cash, and La Santa Muerte will no longer be willing to help you in this spell.

Melting Away Debt

Wealth is not just about having large amounts of money. It is equally about being able to maintain large amounts of money consistently. The amount of disposable income is the determinate of wealth.[64] Thus, besides attracting money, the elimination of debt is essential to achieving financial wealth.

Necessary Tools:
Gold or yellow candle
Knife (or other carving utensil)
Lighter or matches

Suggested Tools:
Herbs/Scents: Lemon, lime, myrrh
Minerals: Obsidian
Paperwork of money owed

1. Assemble all of your tools and get into a meditative state.
2. Grab your knife and etch into the candle's wax the total amount of debt owed.
3. Hold the etched candle and imagine all the negative feeling of debt within you transfer into the candle.
4. When you feel all the negative energy is transferred from you into the candle, light the candle and let it burn completely.

---

64. The formula to calculate disposable income is: monthly income − (monthly living expenses + monthly payments of debt owed) = disposable income.

5. If you wish, place the candle on top of invoices of money owed by you to help absorb more of the negative energy.

6. Watch the etched candle wax melt away, and as it does so, imagine and know that your debt owed is melting away, too. Feel more and more relief as the candle of debt gets smaller and smaller until it disappears completely.

7. When the candle is completely melted, thank La Santa Muerte for helping to eliminate your debt, and know that everything will be all right.

This spell will help set into motion universal energies to help you overcome your financial debt, but it will not suddenly eradicate the debt. Instead, you will find circumstances and opportunities "coincidentally" appear that will help you more easily pay off the amount of debt owed, such as lower interest rates or more manageable payment plans. Just know that after this spell is finished, La Santa Muerte is working behind the scenes to help you overcome your debt.

SECURITY PRAYER

The greatest blessing that money offers is a sense of security. Whether it's the security of knowing that you can afford to buy the latest and greatest gadgets or the security of knowing that in case of an emergency (medical, natural disaster, legal matters), you can afford to take care of the situation. The more wealth we have, the more securely we can live our lives. The less we have, the more often we have to worry and stress over something going wrong and being forced into bankruptcy.

We can never attract true prosperity by living in a constant state of fear of bad things happening. So since we have to believe in order to receive, we must first find a way to feel secure in life before we can experience financial security. To do so, we have to trust that the Divine (however we conceive of it) will be there to help us when we fall on hard times.

This prayer is a simple way to affirm trust in La Santa Muerte, that no matter what misfortune befalls you, she will be there like a loving mother to protect you, support you, and nurture you back into well-being. Remember, a prayer that is said spontaneously from the heart is the most powerful kind of prayer, but until you feel more comfortable making your own prayers, you can use this one.

Suggested Tools:

Colors / Aspects: Brown, rainbow, white

Herbs / Scents: Agave, chrysanthemum, licorice, nag champa, palo santo

Minerals: Diamond, opal, tourmaline

Original Prayer

Oh, Santísima Muerte, mi compañera siempre presente en la vida, gracias por estar siempre a mi lado. Que tu presencia me recuerde que cada día es precioso y que preocuparme por las cosas que están por venir no sirve más que para perder preciosos minutos, de mi limitado tiempo en la tierra.

Ayúdame a saber que el futuro desconocido no está destinado a ser malo. Lo desconocido puede contener alegrías futuras y experiencias maravillosas que sólo puedo imaginar. Y si la desgracia está destinada a ocurrir, por favor guía mis pensamientos para ser capaz de cambiar lo que no puedo aceptar y de aceptar lo que no puedo cambiar.

Eres una madre para mí. Yo sé que estás presente en todo. Estoy rodeado por tu apoyo y tu protección en todo momento. Todo va bien. Estoy bien. El futuro será bueno.

Gracias.

English Translation

Oh, Santísima Muerte, my ever-present companion in life, thank you for always being by my side. May your presence remind me that every day is precious and that worrying about things yet to come only serves to waste precious minutes in my finite time here on earth.

Help me to know that the unknown future is not destined to be bad. The unknown contains future joys and wonderful experiences I can only imagine. And if misfortune is destined to occur, guide my thoughts to allow me to be able to change what I cannot accept and accept what I cannot change.

You are a mother to me. I know that you are present in all things. I am surrounded by your support and protection at all times. All is well. I am well. The future will be well.

Thank you.

Devotion to La Santa Muerte takes many forms. Here are some photos illustrating her manifestations and offerings, taken at two temples dedicated to La Santa Muerte in Southern California by photographer Anthony Louis of Twenty-Deux.

10
Love Magic

"'Tis better to have loved and lost / Than never to have loved at all."
~ALFRED, LORD TENNYSON, FROM "IN MEMORIAM A.H.H."

Love magic is, next to money magic, the absolute most common type of spellwork done by devotees of La Santa Muerte. Most Latin American esoteric shops are well stocked with prepackaged love concoctions and statuettes of the red aspect of La Santa Muerte. Love magic paraphernalia is by far the best selling of all the mystery school's merchandise.

This comes as no surprise. Love is universal. While people may have different preferences and wants in regard to financial wealth, *everyone* wants to be loved. Our modern word "love" falls short in describing the full spectrum of loves that we can encounter in life; it is not just a romantic bond between spouses. In Greek, however, they have three distinct words for love: *agape, philos,* and *eros.*

Agape is a divine love. It is the kind of love most identified when the phrase "true love" is used. It is a love that transcends time and space and unites multiple souls into one.

Philos is best described as "brotherly love." It is a nonromantic love between people resulting from respect, admiration, and solidarity. The love between best friends, relatives, mentors, and strangers working toward a common goal is the ideal of philos.

Eros (named for the Greek god of erotic love, later renamed Cupid by the Romans) is sexual, erotic love. It is a powerful, sacred, and divine instinct. This kind of desire is a love of the corporal human form and a satiation of basic instincts.

The best kind of love is a combination of all three loves: a person with whom we can work together toward a common goal, who uplifts our spirits and our soul toward the heavens, and with whom we can share sexual experiences. While each person may vary on specific traits (physical and behavioral) that are desired in a lover, deep down, we all want to be loved in the same way. We want to feel special, supported, respected, heard, attractive, and important to at least one other person in this world. To love one another is the most basic tenet of all religious and spiritual traditions throughout time. It is the most simple and natural thing we can do, and yet, due to our wants, desires, and emotional baggage from the past, it is commonly the hardest thing for many of us to do.

The spells in this chapter will focus on both the agape and philos definitions of love. The next chapter will focus on the more erotic and sensual definition of love, eros. Contrary to the opinion of Hollywood, eros does not go hand in hand with the other types of love. It is very possible to have sex with someone we don't love, and it is very possible to love someone with whom we don't have sex. For now, though, let us focus on the more romantic and companionship-oriented sides of love.

Natural Soulmate Spell

When it comes to love, a "soulmate" is the first thing most people think of. Because of this, there are numerous love spells specifically designed to attract a soulmate. Because we are working with La Santa Muerte, our magic will focus on the destruction of all obstacles or barriers that are preventing us from being with our soulmate. Before I give you one of the most efficacious love spells in the mystery school of La Santa Muerte, it is imperative that you understand two essential rules in the realm of love magic, concerning free will and specific lovers.

Magic (regardless of tradition), can never supersede a person's free will. We cannot *force* someone to love us who does not love us. Remember, magic works *with* the natural flow of the universe, not against it. By all means, magic can help create "coincidences" wherein a person has the opportunity to woo us or reconnect with us, but if they don't *want* to, they won't.

Love spells toward specific people are highly discouraged. To do a love spell for a specific person is like telling La Santa Muerte (the Divine, the universe, the Tao), "I know what's best for me, and this person is the best." But how can we possibly know that? We may *feel* like that, but we cannot *know* that objectively. The best kind of love spell we can do is one where we don't name specific people and, instead, trust that La Santa Muerte knows what is best for us in her wisdom that transcends human limitations.

Necessary Tools:
Apple (for heterosexuals), apricot (for transsexuals), peach (for gay males), plum (for lesbians)
Thorn of a pink rose (or other carving utensil)

Suggested Tools:
Color/Aspect: Red
Herbs/Scents: Agave, dragon's blood, hyacinth (for gay males), patchouli (for lesbians), a pink rose, sugarcane
Minerals: Copper, emerald, rose quartz

1. Assemble all of your tools and get into a meditative state.

2. Using your rose thorn, carve into the fruit all of the characteristics (physical and behavioral) that you would like your soulmate to have. Write as legibly as you can; geometric block letters tend to be easiest. Because there is not much room to write, carve only the desired characteristics that are the most important to you.

3. When finished, pour over the fruit any corresponding tools that you wish your relationship to possess—for example, agave or sugarcane for sweetness, dragon's blood for passion, etc.

4. Hide the fruit in a place out in nature where it can decompose naturally without being found or thrown away.

5. When the fruit fully decays, your soulmate will present him or herself in a distinguishable way.

6. Never return to look for the fruit again. If you are impatient and check to see how far along the fruit's decomposition is, the spell will be undone.

For those people desiring polyamorous relationships, use as many fruits as you would like partners and hide them all together.

After the spell is completed, remember to meet La Santa Muerte halfway by actively putting yourself in places and situations where your soulmate can meet you. If you don't exert any effort beyond the spell, don't expect La Santa Muerte to pick up your slack. You do not have to frequent bars, clubs, or other singles locations, but do start going to public places or online dating sites where you can meet like-minded people and/or people who have the characteristics that you carved into the fruit.

HEALING A BROKEN RELATIONSHIP

After a relationship is attained, it takes effort to maintain it. Like any living thing, it needs to be nurtured, cared for, and supported, or else it will die. The most difficult thing about a broken relationship is knowing when to salvage it or when to let it go. Remember, the Santa Muerte Mysteries teach that nothing lasts forever, and in time, all things pass. Sometimes people come into our lives as lessons or as a support system, and after having done their spiritual task, they part ways with us.

No relationship will ever be perfect. Perfection does not exist. When a lover, friend, or relative makes a mistake, that does not necessarily mean we must expel them from our lives. Each instance requires that we look inward to determine whether or not having this person in our lives is benefitting us more than it is hurting us.

Like La Santa Muerte's scales, if the positive outweighs the negative, then it is our duty to attempt to heal the relationship. But if the negative outweighs the positive, then it is our duty to let this person go. However, if we find ourselves repeating this spell over and over, it is *time* to let them go, because we are blinding ourselves to the actual balance of the scales, seeing the person how we want them to be as opposed to how they actually are.

Necessary Tools:
Blue candle
Pen with blue ink
Paper

Suggested Tools:
Color / Aspect: Blue
Herbs / Scents: Aloe vera, beans, peppermint, sandalwood, tobacco
Minerals: Emerald, lapis lazuli, rose quartz, turquoise

1. Assemble your tools in a room where you plan on having a serious talk with the intended person. Get into a meditative state.

2. On a sheet of paper, write down all of the characteristics that made you fall in love with them or made you want them to be your friend.

3. Place the candle on top of the sheet of paper.

4. Light the candle, and as it burns, reminisce on all the good times you had together.

5. Think of all the times you have been the cause of their hurt, and all the times they have forgiven you.

6. Think of all the things the Divine (the universe, the Tao) has forgiven you for. And think of all the near-death experiences you've had when La Santa Muerte chose not to take you into the afterlife.

7. When the candle has burned completely, know that it has infused the air with the spirit of communication.

8. Within the next seven days, bring the intended person into that room, and openly have a discussion about what is happening to the relationship.

9. Do not blame, accuse, or talk about the past. Talk only about how you feel in the present moment and how you want to continue the relationship for the future.

10. If the person is *willing* to work on maintaining the relationship, keep the paper and read it every day for three months upon waking up and before going to sleep. If the person is *unwilling* to work on maintaining the relationship, burn the paper (in a safe container) and know that this relationship no longer serves your greater good.

In this spell, it is important to be honest and express ourselves. Oftentimes, we never let our lover, friend, or relative know that something they are doing is hurting us. We expect them to somehow know what we are thinking and feeling at all times, but this is an unrealistic expectation. If we do not express ourselves, we should not assume they know how we feel. Communication is key to maintaining a healthy relationship, and it is paramount in healing a broken one.

Amulet to Banish a Toxic Relationship

Just because something feels good doesn't mean that it is good for us. A lot of times, we get into relationships to escape from something, most commonly loneliness. Being on the margins of society makes many of us feel disconnected from other people. We want so desperately to belong and to be accepted by other people that we latch on to the first person who gives us the time of day. This attention is often confused for love, and in our hearts, we know the truth, but we convince our mind to believe the lie.

Frequently, the people who put up with those of us so desperate to be loved are toxic people. Anyone who *truly* loves him or herself will never settle for a lover who is only escaping their own loneliness. Those who do settle are either using their desperate partner (as a backup sexual partner, as an ATM machine, as an enabler for their own addictions, etc.) or are trying to escape loneliness themselves. But there is a difference between being lonely and being alone. If we love ourselves, we are always in good company. If we don't, we will need the "love" of others to not feel alone. But sharing loneliness is never better than being alone.

This spell will help repel such people who are using us or who are not for our greater good (even if we have convinced ourselves that they are). The effects may be slow or sudden, but if we love ourselves enough to do this spell and wear the amulet every day, the truth will eventually be revealed.

Necessary Tools:
Piece of cloth (any material or fabric that can be used to form a
    small sachet, preferably black, green, pink, or white)
Herbs/Scents: Belladonna, cactus, jasmine, lily, nettle
Minerals: Amethyst, emerald, jet, pyrite

1. Assemble your tools. Use a mixture of as many herbs/scents and minerals as you have. It is not necessary to have them all. Get into a meditative state and reflect upon the relationship.

2. Bless each tool, holding it and feeling its protective properties. Commune with the tools to specify how you would like them to help you repel all relationships that are toxic to your soul and not for your greater good.

3. Mix everything together on the open piece of cloth. Break larger items up into smaller pieces or grind them into a powder.

4. Tie the corners of the cloth together to form a small sachet, making sure that none of the small pieces inside will fall out or that the tie will come undone.

5. Keep the sachet with you at all times (except when sleeping or showering). Have it in your pocket or in your purse, and let no one touch it or see it. It is your secret amulet.

The manifestation of this spell will be very uncomfortable. Essentially, we are asking La Santa Muerte to help free us from being addicted to a toxic person, and like any addiction recovery process, we will have to go through a stage of detox. This means that things will feel much worse before they feel better, but it is all part of the healing process. The detox stage can manifest in a number of ways, including the intended person revealing themselves as a user/player/cheater or being harshly and suddenly dumped. Just know that whatever happens is ultimately for your greater good.

This spell can work for broken relationships that cannot or should not be healed. So long as we wear the amulet and trust La Santa Muerte, toxic people will start disappearing from our lives. Without their poison, we can then become free to truly love and be loved in return.

11
Lust Magic

"Sex and death. They're different but the same. To reach that final moment,
that climax, you gotta give up control of your body, of your soul."
~AUGUSTUS HILL, *OZ*

Lust magic is often assumed to go hand in hand with love magic, but this is a common misconception. The assumption that love and sex are somehow bound together is a truism passed down from generation to generation in almost every culture. This form of thinking often leads to unfulfilled and unrealistic expectations, which inevitably become sources of much unhappiness. The assertion that sex must involve love or that love always involves sex sounds nice in theory, but in our biological world, neither of these is always true.

Sex and love are two separate things. When combined together, they form an immense and beautiful power that allows us to more easily see the divine here on earth. Thinking that they *have to* or that they *should always* be found together is a recipe for misery.

Think about it for a moment. Is it possible to have sex with someone whom you don't like, let alone love? Absolutely! Is it also possible to love someone dearly but not in an erotic or sexual way? Absolutely! In terms of neurological gender wiring (speaking in generalities, not absolutes), the former is a trait more common in men, while the latter is a trait more common in women. Regardless of gender, though, in this dichotomy, often the biggest mistake we make is when we make love with someone who is just having sex.

Once we can reconcile that sex and love are separate energies, we immediately gain ownership over their powers. For millennia, countless rules and laws have been applied to sex because of its power. Sex is powerful. It is one of the most liberating acts of divine communion that we can experience. So, to control the populace, control over sex was mandated by the powers that be. Thus shame and guilt became common symptoms of having dared experience the sacred liberation of sex. Being devotees of La Santa Muerte, we rid ourselves of such self-inflicted negative thoughts and take part in this carnal sacrament.

Nevertheless, self-control is always advised because, energetically, the only thing casual about sex is one's attitude toward it. Spiritually, the act of sex is always a communal affair in that we exchange energy with whomever our partner is, forever linking us together energetically, so be selective when choosing your partners. Ask yourself if this person deserves you or if their energy is something you would like to forever mix with yours. If the answer is yes, then, by all means, enjoy.

Glamour Bath

Any kind of lust magic is always a little controversial. In particular, spells that entice the erotic attraction of another person are often demonized as "immoral" since they seem to try and manipulate a person's free will. As discussed earlier, we already know that magic cannot override a person's free will. But more than that, isn't it ironic that the people who denounce lust spells often have no qualms about wearing makeup, perfume, jewelry, and clothing that shows off their natural assets when going out on a date or to social settings? Aren't those all devices we use to enhance our erotic appeal to attract a mate? Yet they are not considered manipulative.

This spell works in just the same way. Historically, a "glamour" was a spell used to change one's appearance as perceived by other people. It does not physically change you, but it changes how others see you. From this magical practice, we have our modern definition of glamour: the state of enhancing one's appearance through the use of clothing, cosmetics, and jewelry. After having a glamour bath, you will temporarily possess an otherworldly erotic appearance to anyone who sees you.

Necessary Tools:
Bathtub filled with warm water
Towel
Herbs / Scents: Aloe vera

Suggested Tools:
Color / Aspect: Red
Herbs / Scents: Avocado, aloe vera, dragon's blood, honeysuckle, jasmine, a red rose, vanilla
Minerals: Copper, opal, pearl, ruby

1. Assemble your tools and draw a warm bath.

2. Light any incense you may have. After dipping them in the water, place any suggested tools that could harm your drainage system along the rim of the bath. If you have avocado, feel free to wear its pulp on your skin as an impromptu facial mask, but do not use the aloe vera just yet. Keep it aside.

3. Relax in the warm bath water and get into a meditative state (be careful not to fall asleep).

4. Imagine yourself as the most sexually attractive person in the world. See yourself walking into your date or social function and having all heads turn, captivated by your beauty and magnetism. Really *feel* the desire in your date's or the crowd's eyes.

5. Once you have visualized to the point of feeling supernaturally sexy, step out of the bath water, clean off any materials used in the bath, and drain the water. Dab off any excess water on your body with a towel.

6. Use the aloe vera all over your body (or at least the parts of your body where skin will be exposed) to seal in the essence of the magical bath water.

Traditionally, you have until sunrise the next day before the glamour spell wears off. In my experience, however, the spell will last as long as you feel sexy. Normally, after waking up in the morning, we lose all sense of feeling sexy, and so the superstition arose out of this universal behavior. But if you plan to be out well past sunrise, don't worry. Just know that although you may feel that nothing has changed, people will be seeing the glamourized you that you envisioned during the spell.

ENCHANTED ATTRACTION CHARM

Because we are working with the energy of La Santa Muerte, this charm works by disarming the inhibitions of those in our proximity. By this, I mean that the charm will make it harder for people who are attracted to you not to engage in conversation or approach you. The little excuses people tell themselves in order not to approach someone they are attracted to will become weakened when that someone is us with our charm.

It is worth noting, though, that this charm does *not* hypnotize people into becoming attracted to you, nor does it make you immune from being turned down or being told no. If a person is naturally not attracted to you (due to your physicality, your behavior, or their sexual orientation), they will not suddenly develop an attraction toward you. Also, just because a person is more likely to approach and get to know you does not mean you can't still be rejected. This charm just makes those who are naturally already attracted to you more receptive to get to know you and see if there is sexual chemistry.

Necessary Tools:

Piece of cloth (any material or fabric that can be used to form a small sachet, preferably black or red)

Cherries with stems intact (one for you and one for each sexual partner you would like to have at one time)

Suggested Tools:

Color/Aspect: Black, red

Herbs/Scents: Chocolate, cinnamon, hyacinth (for attracting gay men), patchouli (for attracting lesbian women), a red rose, vanilla, yerba mate

Minerals: Gold (if you identify as male), ruby, silver (if you identify as female)

1. Assemble your tools and get into a meditative state.

2. Bless each tool, feeling its power in breaking down the walls that we erect around ourselves that keeps us from going after someone that we find attractive.

3. Take the cherries and twist or tie all the stems together, symbolically representing the carnal entanglement of sex.

4. Keeping the cherries tangled together, mix any additional suggested tools together on the open piece of cloth. If some things are larger, break them up into smaller pieces or grind them into a powder (except the cherries).

5. Tie the corners of the cloth together to form a small sachet, making sure that none of the small pieces inside will fall out or that the tie will come undone.

6. Keep the sachet with you whenever you are out on the town looking for a sexual encounter. Have it in your pocket or in your purse, and let no one touch it or see it. It is your secret charm.

Because the charm is on your person, its powers affect you, too. Remember, you have to meet La Santa Muerte halfway. She will help destroy the barriers of self-imposed inhibitions, but it's up to you to approach someone or be receptive to someone else's approach. Don't expect the other person to do all the work involved in the dance to the bedroom. Courtship goes both ways, and all parties involved must participate in the dance for it to be a success.

Fidelity / Fertility / Virility Candle Magic

Fidelity, fertility, and virility spells were the original lust magic repertoire of the ancients. While fertility and virility spells are still seen as good magic, fidelity spells have gained a relatively recent reputation as being malicious magic. It makes sense, since forcing an adulterous lover to become more chaste seems to go directly against a person's free will. But put yourself in the shoes of the women of the past who perfected chastity magic. They lived in a time where women were essentially property. They had no legal recourse or avenue of divorce or separation if their husband was a lecher. If their husband left them for someone younger or more subservient, their entire financial security disappeared, forever after being harshly equated to undesirable used merchandise. To them, fidelity magic was about survival. This continues to go on in many parts of our world today. Nowadays, it is much wiser for a person to leave an adulterous lover rather than perform a fidelity spell (especially in light of the Law of Equivalent Exchange), but regardless, here is a candle spell that can be used for chastity, fertility, or virility, depending on your particular needs.

Necessary Tools:
Red candle
Knife (or other carving utensil)

Suggested Tools:
Color/Aspect: Red
Fidelity Herbs/Scents: Cactus, chili pepper
Fertility Herbs/Scents: Beans, berry, myrrh
Virility Herbs/Scents: Avocado, frankincense, yerba mate
Minerals: Obsidian (fidelity), pearl (fertility), ruby (virility)

1. Assemble your tools and get into a meditative state.
2. Hold the red candle firmly in your hands, and visualize the manifestation of that which you desire (the fidelity of a lover, becoming pregnant or impregnating a spouse, erectile ease).

3. When you reach the feeling place of already experiencing the manifestation of the spell, release all of that energy into the candle so that it is overflowing with the energy.

4. Anoint the candle with any tools that you desire and etch the name of the person in question into the wax, even if it is your own name.

5. Light the candle, and as it burns, know that your spell is being sent out into the universe.

Unique to candle magic involving love spells, Santa Muerte devotees will often use specially crafted red candles that are in the shape of an erect penis. Remember, the universe converses with you on a subconscious level where signs and symbols speak more loudly than words. Burning down a phallus-shaped candle helps to evoke the penile powers involved in fidelity, fertility, and virility magic. In fact, the efficacy of these candles is so profound that they are one of the highest-selling pieces of Santa Muerte merchandise in many botánicas.

In terms of fidelity spells, as with any spell, a person's free will cannot be overridden by magic. The casting of a fidelity spell on someone only facilitates their chances not to be adulterous (such as seeing or thinking of their kids as they take out their wallet to buy their conquest a drink or even being asked if they are in a relationship by their conquest), but it will not stop or prevent them from going through with it. If you know your lover is cheating and you live in a place where you have the freedom to leave them, then I highly suggest not wasting your time in trying to hinder their natural appetites. Your time could be much better spent getting to know someone who doesn't need to be hexed with a fidelity spell in the first place.

12
Healing Magic

"Millions long for immortality who don't know what to do
with themselves on a rainy Sunday afternoon."
~SUSAN ERTZ, *FIRE IN THE SKY*

Although it is not the most popular magic in the Santa Muerte tradition, I'd argue that healing magic is the most important kind of magic, in any tradition. Without our health, we are incapable of enjoying any other facet of life. While these spells are helpful in manipulating the energies of health in your favor, they *are not* a substitute for advanced Western medicine. Healing spellwork is best used as a supplement to more modern healing practices and procedures. In fact, oftentimes healing magic will manifest by "coincidentally" creating a situation where you can be exposed to a medical professional and/or medicines. To someone not familiar with Western medicine, these pills and procedures might seem magical in restoring health, but because you and I are accustomed to them, we no longer consider them to be magical at all. Truly they are magical, though. In the endeavor to get well, do not shut out magical avenues of healing just because they come in the form of a prescription.

WATER TRANSFERENCE SPELL

The most important kind of healing work we can do is prevention. The cures of a disease are often much more costly and dramatic than daily preventive maintenance such as a healthy diet and exercise. Moreover, it is much easier to do a preventive healing spell while still in good health than to do a curative healing spell while in the throes of debilitating sickness.

For devotees of La Santa Muerte, in particular, there is a strange disconnect when it comes to our own bodies and the Divine. When we give offerings to Death on our altars, the offerings are usually of the highest affordable quality and the altar is usually kept clean. But when it comes to our own selves, we settle for offering our bodies unhealthy foods and allow ourselves to be stagnant, gather dust, and not exercise. Such devotees forget that we, too, are divine, and by caring for our bodies we are showing thanks and appreciation for the vessels that the Divine has given us in order to experience the wonders of this world. This spell will help energetically cement in our subconscious the link between our physical bodies and the Divine.

Necessary Tools:
Water in a transparent glass

Suggested Tools:
Color/Aspect: Rainbow, white
Herbs/Scents: Camphor, chrysanthemum, coca leaves, licorice, nag champa, palo santo, yerba mate
Minerals: Diamond, opal, pearl

1. Assemble your tools in front of your altar and get into a meditative state.

2. Surround your glass of water with a circle of any suggested tools you desire to add to the spell. Meditate on each tool, and feel their energy being absorbed by the water.

3. Feel the presence of La Santa Muerte, commune with her, and ask her to bless the water to be a conduit of her energies.

4. Drink the water.

5. Feel the water being absorbed in your body. Feel it spread and immerse itself into every cell. Know that the water and all the energies within it are now a physical part of your body.

6. Leave the empty glass on the altar as a reminder to yourself of the emptiness of the altar now that La Santa Muerte resides in you.

After this spell, devotees generally begin treating their body differently. They realize that everything they eat is an offering to La Santa Muerte. They realize that to be lazy and not exercise is to allow the foundations of La Santa Muerte's new temple to fall into disrepair. And she will let you know it, too. By being more conscious of housing divine energy, we will begin to treat our physical bodies with much more respect, love, and honor, and our reward will be good health and youthfulness at all stages of life.

Breaking Addictions Amulet

Within the Santa Muerte community, there is no more widespread impediment to health than addiction. In general terms, addictions often result as a means to escape or avoid a troubling issue. Usually stemming from a traumatic incident or a self-perceived lack of something (like love and affection), we find comfort in addictions as a way to numb the pain rather than go through the arduous and uncomfortable task of uprooting and confronting the impetus of our addiction.

Since most devotees of La Santa Muerte are marginalized by society and by their own families, there is a higher than average tendency to utilize the numbing comfort of addictions to keep the psychological pains away. Addictions take many forms other than the use of mind-altering substances and can include addictions to things (hoarding), addictions to people (toxic relationships), addictions to work (workaholics), and addictions to food (obesity or body dysmorphia). Any comforting diversion used to prevent ourselves from dealing with uncomfortable issues can become an addiction. This spell will create an amulet to help destroy the psychological barriers that prevent us from dealing with the root impetus of addictions in order to overcome them.

Necessary Tools:
Piece of cloth (any material or fabric that can be used to form a small sachet, preferably purple)
Black string
Scissors

Suggested Tools:
Color/Aspect: Purple
Herbs/Scents: Coffee bean, dandelion, grape, jasmine, licorice
Minerals: Amethyst, obsidian, pyrite

1. Assemble your tools (a mixture of any and all of the suggested tools) and get into a meditative state.

2. Bless each tool, holding it and feeling its protective properties. Commune with the tools to specify how you would like them to help you repel all addictions that are toxic to your soul and not for your greater good.

3. Take the string, tie it around your arm or finger, and imagine transferring all the darkness of your addiction into this string that is binding you.

4. Grab your scissors. They are symbolic of La Santa Muerte's scythe. Ask that she help you cut this addiction out of your life.

5. Cut the string off your body, and then continue to cut it into smaller and smaller segments.

6. Place the bits of string among the other tools in your open sachet.

7. Tie the corners of the cloth together to form a small sachet, making sure that none of the small pieces inside will fall out or that the tie will come undone.

8. Keep the sachet with you at all times (except when sleeping or showering). Have it in your pocket or in your purse, and let no one touch it or see it. It is your secret amulet.

With the addiction cut into smaller pieces and being kept in check by the other tools in the sachet, it is now time to dig deep within and face your inner demons. This amulet will not make your addiction disappear. No magic can do that. Rather, this amulet will help tear down the obstacles that are preventing true healing. This would be a great time to seek counseling and / or medical help, and working together with the amulet, know that you are on your way to overcoming addiction.

Self-Healing Prayer

Within our minds, we have the power to heal ourselves. Unless we truly believe this, we will be incapable of facilitating our own healing through magic. Everything in life begins with a thought, including illness. The simplest way to heal, therefore, is to stay away from negative and harmful thoughts. As humans, though, this can be very difficult to do, and so we will each become sick time and again throughout our lives. The type, severity, and duration of our illness, however, are entirely up to us. Remember, there are no coincidences.

Suggested Tools:
Color / Aspect: Purple
Herbs / Scents: Belladonna, jasmine, lemon, lime, palo santo, pau
  d'arco, a white rose, sandalwood
Minerals: Amethyst, quartz

Original Prayer

Oh, Santísima Muerte, te pido ayuda para alcanzar el bienestar. Yo sé que tengo el poder de lograrlo. Sé que, con mi mente, tengo el poder tanto de destruir como crear. Ayúdame a ver y cambiar mis propios pensamientos negativos y destructivos. Ayúdame a ver lo positivo en cada situación, evento, persona y cosa en mi vida para crear una vida mejor.

Sé que no existen las coincidencias. Sé que habrá gente en mi vida que me enfadará, me molestará, y me causará tanto dolor, ayúdame a recordar siempre que estas personas son mis maestros y yo soy su estudiante. Ellos me enseñarán cómo no debo ser. Cuando aprenda su enseñanza, sé que su negatividad va a desaparecer de mi vida, y que, últimamente, serán dignos de lástima y no de desdén.

Ayúdame a apreciar la ayuda que reciba y a saber que la enfermedad es la forma en que mi cuerpo se comunica conmigo, que me dice que alguna forma de mi pensar necesita de un cambio. Ayúdame a aceptar este cambio y ponerlo en práctica, para que pueda continuar teniendo una buena salud y disfrutar de cada día como si fuera el último.

Gracias.

English Translation

Oh, Santísima Muerte, I ask for help in attaining wellness. I know that I have the power. I know that, with my mind, I have the power to both destroy and heal. Help me to guard against my own negative and harmful thoughts. Help me to see the positive in every situation, event, person, and thing in my life.

I know that there are no coincidences. People will come into my life who will anger me, upset me, and cause me much pain. Help me to always remember that these people are my teachers. They teach me how not to be. When I learn their teaching, I know that their negativity will disappear from my life, and that ultimately, they are to be pitied rather than scorned.

Help me to appreciate help and know that sickness is the way my body communicates to me that some way of thinking needs to change. Help me to accept this change and implement it into my life so that I can continue to experience good health and enjoy each day as if it was my last.

Thank you.

13
Protection Magic

"Cowards die many times before their deaths;
the valiant never taste of death but once."
~WILLIAM SHAKESPEARE, *JULIUS CAESAR*

Protection magic is possibly the most publicized type of Santa Muerte spellwork in the media today. Sensationalist stories of how devotees use "black" magic to evade the law and carry out wicked deeds without consequence abound in the general public's image of what this perceived "Mexican death cult" is all about. Having read this far, you know that this is not true, but because sensationalist stories tend to attract more attention than realistic stories, the public's perception will always be shaped in whatever way brings in the most financial profit to the media.

While it is true that cartel members and assassins use protection magic to hide from capture or legal consequences, this is true of extremists in any faith whose personal desires outweigh the fundamental teachings of that faith. On a more common basis, protection magic in the Santa Muerte tradition is one of necessity. Rather than the end goal being to protect ourselves from the consequences of knowingly doing harm, the *real* end goal of protection magic is to be able to live a joyous and peaceful life without negative forces interrupting. This chapter will share three main spells to cover the three main aspects of protecting ourselves through magic.

CLOAK OF INVISIBILITY

The Cloak of Invisibility is a type of spell common to any tradition that venerates a dark deity. It works by making us invisible to harm. While we don't literally become invisible, we do go "off radar" to people who are out looking for trouble. Think of this as a type of glamour spell, except instead of gaining attention, the object is to detract attention. Oftentimes, though, the best way to protect ourselves is by avoiding a situation that would endanger us in the first place.

Suggested Tools:
Color/Aspect: Black
Herbs/Scents: Cactus, frankincense, nettle
Minerals: Jet, tourmaline

1. Assemble any tools and get into a meditative state.

2. Visualize yourself standing before La Santa Muerte. You see her enshrouded in her long, flowing, black cloak. Her demeanor is strong, yet loving, like an iron fist wrapped in a velvet glove.

3. Commune with her, and ask that she protect you on your journey.

4. Listen to any advice she may have about where you are about to go. Are there warnings? Are there signs of things to stay away from? You may not fully understand now, but when you do come across them in the physical world, remember to take caution.

5. Envision her wrapping her black cloak around you, and as you come out of your meditation, know that you are protected.

A common mistake that a lot of devotees make when performing this spell is overusing it. This is not a spell to be used all day every day. This spell makes us "invisible" by not having us stand out in any discernible way to any onlooker. Thus, people looking for trouble will not target you to be their victim because you "aren't there" to them. But if we are driving our cars, at our place of work, or interacting with friends and family, we *need* to be visible and present. This spell is best used when we go out for a walk alone or have to be in a bad area where our chances of being targeted as victims are high. The best thing to do is to avoid such places, but this spell is a good second choice if that's not possible.

NEUTRALIZING SPHERE

The only way to avoid conflict in the world is to avoid the world. The reality of life is that it has its ups and downs, and throughout our lives, we will come face to face with conflict and with people who intentionally wish us harm. Fortunately, the people who knowingly send out negative energy to harm us (also known as "psychic attacks") are few and far between. It is *much* more likely that we will be harmed by accidental psychic attacks in the form of collateral damage from people who are so upset and unhappy in life that they can't help but radiate negative energy out to everyone. Such negative energy wasn't *intended* to harm us, but it did all the same. This spell will help combat these psychic attacks (intentional and accidental) through the use of a neutralizing sphere.

Suggested Tools:
Color/Aspect: Black, white
Herbs/Scents: Burdock, frankincense, palo santo, tobacco
Minerals: Diamond, obsidian, jet, tourmaline

1. Assemble any tools and get into a meditative state.
2. In your heart space, imagine a sphere emanating around you from within you.
3. Imagine it expanding away from your body to one and a half times the length of your arm.
4. As you visualize this, feel your physical body reacting. Feel the air around you move differently, as if it is contained inside something, along with you.
5. Commune with La Santa Muerte and ask her to bless this sphere with her touch of death, making it so that all negative energy

dies upon coming into contact with the sphere, but that any act of love or kindness can pass through to you unharmed.

6. Thank La Santa Muerte. As you come out of your meditation, know that you are in that sphere until you dismantle it in another meditation.

This spell, unlike the Cloak of Invisibility, has no effect on the way people visually perceive you. They cannot sense the sphere around you, and, to them, nothing about you has changed. If any psychic attacks (intentional or accidental) come toward you, they will be immediately neutralized by the sphere around you.

The sphere itself can be personalized in any way most suitable to you. I prefer to imagine an opaque, geometric crystal sphere around me wherein the psychic attacks are neutralized and safely refract toward the ground. Another popular choice is a sphere of dense smoke that confuses the energy, ultimately leaving it lost and neutralized in the smokescreen. However you visualize this neutralizing sphere is entirely up to you.

Two words of warning with this spell, though. First, never visualize a mirror sphere. Mirrors have the ability to reflect energy, which sends it right back to where it came from—or toward an innocent bystander. While the "avenger" in us would love to give people a taste of their own medicine, the karmic consequences would ultimately come back at us, making it not worth it. Besides, the vast majority of psychic attacks are accidental, and the last thing someone so entrenched in suffering needs is to feel even worse by being shot back with their own wayward energy. Such people are more to be pitied than scorned.

The second warning is not to overuse this spell. That sphere is essentially your own energy, and having it out and expanded all day every day is incredibly draining. My suggestion is to create a discreet signaling device to have it expand and retract at will so that when you sense negative energy being shot in your direction, you can efficiently neutralize it and go back to normal. My personal signaling device is to hold my thumb, index, and middle finger together. It is discreet enough to be done in any social setting, yet distinct enough to only have my fingers in that position if I intend to expand the sphere. A common one among devotees is crossing the index and middle finger, and some clench their nondominant hand into a fist. The choice of the signaling device is yours, but be sure that you develop one so as to be efficient with your energy.

Slashing Self-Sabotage

We are our own worst enemy. Nothing sabotages our hopes, dreams, ambitions, and future more than ourselves. Advanced devotees in the Santa Muerte Mysteries understand that they are ultimately responsible for everything in their lives—all good things and all bad things. While common human tendency makes us want to credit ourselves only for our successes and blame our failures on other people or circumstances, true magical practitioners know that all that occurs in our lives does so because of what we choose to do and not do. These choices are the result of the beliefs, knowledge, and thinking centered in our minds. Thus, if we can control our minds, we can control our destinies.

The way you can begin to take control of your mind is to become aware of it. How many times have you said or done things that you later regretted, simply because you were on mental autopilot or giving a knee-jerk reaction? And how many more times have you been negative or abusive in your thinking, knowing you could get away with such insults because no one can hear them? As magical practitioners, we know that our thoughts are energy that always goes out to the universe and creates our reality, whether intentional or not. This spell will help you take control over those negative thoughts so you can better train your mind to naturally be more positive, thus effortlessly creating a positive reality for you.

Necessary Tools:
Energy signaling device (the same one described in the previous
   Neutralizing Sphere spell)

Suggested Tools:

Color/Aspect: Black, white

Herbs/Scents: Grape, jasmine, licorice, peppermint, sandalwood, yerba mate

Minerals: Amethyst, pyrite, obsidian, tourmaline

1. Assemble any tools and get into a meditative state.

2. Visualize the energy in your heart space traveling up your chest, down your arm, and into your hand.

3. Feel the energy pool in your hand, gaining more and more energy.

4. Imagine a target in front of you not too far away.

5. Enact your signaling device (the same you use to summon your neutralizing sphere), and as you do, imagine the scythe of La Santa Muerte descending from the shadows and slashing the target.

6. Ask that La Santa Muerte bless this routine to become your mechanism for destroying your own negative thoughts.

The objective of this spell is twofold: to become aware of how frequently you think negative, self-sabotaging thoughts and to neutralize those thoughts before they completely merge with the universe and become your reality.

You'll be amazed how often you will use this spell throughout the first week; I know I was. Every time you make a mean or insulting comment about something, someone else, or yourself, use the spell to quickly visualize the thought and slash it out of existence. Every time you doubt yourself, give an excuse, or pity yourself, use the spell. Any negative thought whatsoever is reason to use the spell. In time, the need to neutralize your own thoughts will lessen as you become more self-aware of your own mind and its autopilot instinct is trained to be more positive.

14

Hexes

"Then Jesus said to him, 'Put your sword back into its sheath,
for all who take the sword will perish by the sword.'"
~MATTHEW 26:52, NEW AMERICAN BIBLE REVISED EDITION

Aside from finding a nonjudging place to belong, many people delve into the magic of La Santa Muerte to hex people. Simply put, a hex is a magical spell done with the intention of harming another person. While a curse is verbal (hence the origin of "curse words"), hexes encompass all forms of malicious magic.

Being marginalized by society, there is a deep temptation within many devotees to take revenge on those who make us feel like outcasts or who manipulate the system to keep us oppressed. The temptation is further augmented by our knowledge that La Santa Muerte is a deity who is not against assisting us in harmful magic. For this reason, Santa Muerte magic is dangerous and requires strict discipline. Give anyone with a grudge who has been constantly put down by society the power and means to inflict harm on other people, and the results can be tragic.

For this reason, I am not going to outline any method to hex someone. By giving another person the means to harm, I am responsible for harming that victim regardless of whether I was only involved indirectly.

Moreover, any hex we do will ultimately come back and harm us more than our intended target. An ancient Buddhist treatise says that holding on to anger is like grasping a hot coal with the intent of throwing it at someone; you are the one who gets burned. The anger and hate we harbor within us affects us negatively. Even before releasing a hex and suffering the karmic consequences of doing so, anger and hate make us spiritually and physically sick. We think we are in control of our own hate, but when we allow ourselves to seethe over other people's actions, those people dominate our thoughts, which in turn dominate our actions and our reality. When hate is what we think, speak, and dream on a daily basis, then it is hate that actually has control over us.

While this is not a book on the magic of forgiveness, it is worth noting that he who controls your thoughts is he who masters you. If you cannot get the thought of being wronged by another out of your head, you have allowed that person to master your thoughts, all because of what they did or did not do. Without being the master of your own thoughts, you cannot manipulate energy effectively, and thus, you cannot successfully co-create magic with any deity.

Remember, we are all connected to one another in the web of life. If we purposely damage any single thread, we place our own stability and the stability of the ones we love in jeopardy. Keeping in mind the Law of Equivalent Exchange, there is nothing of equal value that we can give up in order to harm another person without suffering a lifetime of regret. Death reminds us that nothing lasts forever, and that includes our emotions. So be sure not to make a permanent decision based on a temporary emotion, whether it be anger, sadness, or revenge.

15

Legal Magic

"Many that live deserve death.
And some that die deserve life.
Can you give it to them?
Then do not be too eager to deal out death in judgment.
For even the very wise cannot see all ends."

~J. R. R. TOLKIEN, *THE FELLOWSHIP OF THE RING*

Legal magic is an interesting genre of spellwork. While many traditions have evolved their own blend of spells to aid them in the legal process, none have gone so far as to make legal magic a defining pillar of their own tradition as has the mystery school of La Santa Muerte.

Those critical of the devotion to La Santa Muerte would say that this is the natural result of having unrepentant criminals and societal undesirables make up a large portion of devotees. And the truth is, they're absolutely right, but not for the reasons they might expect.

Throughout history, those who were economically or socially disenfranchised were victimized by the powers that be, whose attack dogs were the courts and legal systems. Corruption and injustice within the justice system is still alive and well today, especially in the birthplace of the Santa Muerte tradition: Mexico. The same can be said about the modern justice system in relation to Mexican migrants who often have little to no power in the courts.

For such people, being able to use magic to swing a court ruling in their favor was often a matter of survival. This is evident when we look at how the majority of spells for legal magic are largely focused on helping the defense as opposed to the prosecution. Below are two of the most common spells in legal magic. Use these as a springboard to tailor your own for your legal needs.

Tipping the Scales of Justice

Suggested Tools:
Color/Aspect: Green
Herbs/Scents: Myrrh, peach, plum, peppermint
Minerals: Lapis lazuli, quartz, tiger's-eye, tourmaline

1. Assemble any tools and get into a meditative state.
2. Visualize yourself as a small person standing on one side of a pair of large, golden scales. On the other side stands the opposing party (the prosecution or defense).
3. Visualize that La Santa Muerte is holding the scales.
4. You and your opponent start out on even footing, but you slowly feel the scales tipping in your favor. Truth, justice, and purity are adding considerable weight to your side.
5. If you feel the other side tipping more strongly, ask that La Santa Muerte remove the weight of pretense, lies, and misdirectional truths from the opposing party, thus making their side lighter.
6. When you feel fully stable and convinced that your side is unequivocally heavier and that the scales of justice are overwhelmingly in your favor, end the meditation and carry that feeling within you during the course of the trial.

It is important to note that for this spell to work effectively, you *actually* have to be on the side of justice. If you know that you are guilty or if you are unaware that you are actually guilty, the spell will not work. Such failing will be due to the fact that truth, justice, and purity are not actually on your side to give you any additional weight. So, before performing this spell, have an honest discussion with yourself in that meditative state to know if you should waste any time and effort on a spell that is doomed to fail.

Expediting Jail Time

This is the most common spell in legal magic. It is also the number-one spell that converts people into lifelong devotees. While this spell should ideally be done by the person who is incarcerated, it can also be done by loved ones as a way in which the affected person can experience some "coincidences" that enable them to realize the error of their ways. Due to its preference of being performed while in prison, there are rarely any tools used in this spell.

Suggested Tools:
Color/Aspect: Green
Herbs/Scents: Grape, honeysuckle, licorice, lily, pau d'arco
Minerals: Amethyst, jade, jet, obsidian, pyrite

1. Assemble any tools (if possible) and get into a meditative state.

2. In your mind, replay the incident that led to your conviction.

3. Replay it from every angle of every person involved, including you, the victim, the onlookers, the police, God, etc.

4. Once you see the event from all angles, think of all the small decisions you made to create the event. Oftentimes, large actions are just the result of millions of tiny actions.

5. Imagine the event occurring differently. Replay it in your mind in such a way that would not have led to your incarceration. Replay as many scenarios as you can think of where your choices could have reshaped the history of the lives of everyone involved.

6. In your heart space, imagine the spirit of your victim, and talk to him or her. Ask for forgiveness, and express how you will make it up to them once released from prison.

220 | Legal Magic

7. After the meditation, the spirit of the victim—which is free from ego—will approach La Santa Muerte and advocate either for or against your expedited release.

This is a spell that often needs many repetitions. Most people who experiment with this spell do it as a "get out of jail free card," which inevitably fails. For the spell to work, three things are needed: sincere remorse, an authentic apology, and a solid plan for how to rebalance your karma after release. Without any one of these (or even with a weak one), the spell will not work. If the spell is being done for a loved one in prison, as with all spells for other people, the ultimate effectiveness will depend entirely on them and where their heart is.

Also, the spell does not end once you are released early from prison. If you don't take sincere action to balance your karma and fulfill your end of the deal to the spirit of the victim, La Santa Muerte will quickly create another "coincidence" where you find yourself once again in prison. This time you will have another strike on your record, a more severe sentence, and very little chance of successfully performing this spell again since it has been proven that your actions don't live up to your words, no matter how remorseful or sincere.

16
Create Your Own Magic

"Death is not the greatest loss in life.
The greatest loss is what dies inside us while we live."
~NORMAN COUSINS

Magic is at its strongest when we create our own spells. Because the universe communicates with us (and vice versa) through signs and symbols, our artistic subconscious is the key to all spellwork. A single symbol can elicit a number of emotions in a number of different people, but only we know how that symbol makes us feel.

If we rely on books and manuals to perform magic, the limits of our own power will forever be only as large as the imaginations of other people. And even then, mechanical step-by-step perfection of a spell will never produce a result unless the feeling place is there. For this reason, I encourage you to go beyond this book—and all books—and create your own magic spells. Use the information written here to understand the range of tools you can work with and to get a taste of how to go about performing spellwork. Once you begin to see the patterns of Santa Muerte magic, feel free to mimic these patterns and further expand upon them. Below are two creative spells that don't fall into any specific category. Take them as examples of how to think outside the box, or better yet, get rid of the box and create something all your own.

COMMUNION WITH THE DEAD

Suggested Tools:

Color/Aspect: Black, brown

Herbs/Scents: Camphor, chrysanthemum, licorice, lily

Minerals: Diamond, jet, obsidian

1. Assemble any tools and get into a meditative state.

2. In your heart space, ask that you be able to commune with the spirit of a person who has physically died.

3. The spirit will often take the form of how you know him or her best, whether or not you've actually met them or whether that is how they actually physically looked.

4. Once in their presence, thank them, and explain your reason for wanting to talk with them today. Depending on the spirit, the explanation of "just to talk" will not be sufficient.

5. If the spirit agrees, speak with them, and listen. As with any person, the more you speak with them, the more familiar their communication style will be to you and the more open they will be.

6. With spirits, especially if they are relatives or friends, petty questions regarding past drama and hurts are not desirable topics.

7. When the conversation begins to lag, do not try to revive it. Thank the spirit for their time, and end the meditation, knowing that you can always return to your heart space and talk with them again.

For this spell, I suggest beginning with someone close to you who has died. The familiarity with their spirit on earth will allow you to more easily understand how their spirit communicates in the afterlife. When you are more advanced, feel free to seek the wisdom of historical greats such as Joan of Arc, Lao Tzu, Aristotle, etc. The only rule is that you must be specific about whom you wish to speak with. Thus, nebulous identities such as "the person who did ___" will not suffice. Do your research and learn everything you can about the person before you contact them so as best to understand their spirit when they communicate with you.

ACADEMIC SUCCESS

Necessary Tools:
Textbook

Suggested Tools:
Color/Aspect: Blue
Herbs/Scents: Coca leaves, peach (men), plum (women), sandalwood, yerba mate
Minerals: Citrine, gold, lapis lazuli, quartz

1. Assemble your tools and get into a meditative state.

2. Read a section of your textbook, and then, in your heart space, see the spirit of your memory (however you envision it) and teach it the knowledge. Do not teach it verbatim, but rather, explain the information to your memory as if you were teaching a child. Break it down into simple, relatable ideas, giving symbolic examples if necessary.

3. Once you have instructed your memory to record the teaching session, thank it and ask it to save the information for test day.

4. On test day, return to your heart space and ask your memory to replay the lessons as you complete the exam.

This spell, though simple, has a profound effect in enhancing memory. Our subconscious understands signs and symbols better than direct statements of information. It is surprising how much better we can recall knowledge when described to our subconscious memory through the signs and symbols of analogies and "speaking our own language" rather than the long-winded jargon of academia. Of course, this spell relies quite heavily on the information you give to your subconscious. While you will see a markedly more profound ability to recall information, if that information was not correct to begin with, then being able to recall it won't suddenly make it correct.

17

The Beginning

"To the well-organized mind, death is but the next great adventure."
~J. K. ROWLING, *HARRY POTTER AND THE PHILOSOPHER'S STONE*

Beginnings are nothing more than endings, and endings are nothing more than beginnings. The beginning of your new magical life with Death could not be possible if this book didn't end. And the new adventures that await us in the great unknown of the afterlife could not be possible if our physical lives here on earth didn't end. That is the supreme lesson of Death: destruction is the necessary precursor to creation. Without the destruction of the egg and the caterpillar, how could the miracle of the baby chick or the glory of the butterfly even be possible?

This is why death, the mystery school of La Santa Muerte, and everything in this book is a philosophical study of *life*. It is said that the Buddha began his spiritual journey after his first encounter with a corpse, a sight that forced him to confront the impermanence of all life.

When we can truly see the world and everything in it as a temporary experience, we appreciate it more. The tourist sees and appreciates a location on a much more profound level than the local inhabitant. For the tourist, the sights and sounds of a city or the natural beauty of a landscape must be lived fully here and now and observed in detail because the tourist knows that his or her time there won't last forever. For the local, the sights and sounds of the city and the beauty of the landscape are taken for granted because he or she has "forever" to enjoy them. But that is the supreme irony; the locals never do enjoy it as much as the tourists. Did the city or the landscape change? No. It was only their perspective.

Our awareness of death is what makes life all the more enjoyable. We are all nothing more than tourists here on earth in these physical bodies. We won't be here forever, and neither will anything else. Next year will be different, next month will be different, next week, tomorrow, an hour from now, a minute from now, *now*. Even if it doesn't seem like it, everything is constantly changing, breaking down, and becoming something new.

Imagine filling a glass to the brim with water. If you take a look at it an hour later, it will still seem to be the same glass with the same amount of water. But it's not. At the most microscopic level, that water began to evaporate the moment you filled the glass. There is actually less water there now, and all those water molecules that left the glass are now in the air you are breathing, possibly already in your lungs, nourishing the cells of your body.

Those cells are also continuously being transformed. Our cells die and are replaced in a constant cycle. The bodies we have now are physiologically not the same bodies we had even a month ago. Every single cell we had a few years ago is dead, and our current cells are brand-new cells that didn't exist back then. Their deaths are what allows us to live. If these cells did not die and weren't replaced, our bodies as a whole would never make it to old age, a privilege that is denied to many. Then, of course, this process slows down, and, like everything, our life ends.

When looked at through the lens of the Santa Muerte Mysteries, this inspires us to take advantage of the here and now. I'm not talking about being reckless, because those who truly appreciate themselves, their bodies, and the world around them would never dare to be careless about these gifts. I'm talking about doing those things you've always wanted to do. Tomorrow is not guaranteed. So take that vacation, learn that skill, paint that painting, write that book, compose that song, and open up that bottle of champagne you've been saving for a special occasion. Today *is* special.

While you're at it, take the time to appreciate those around you. Their time here is also limited. No matter how expected a loved one's death may be, it's still surprising because we've convinced ourselves right until the end that "it could never happen." How many times have words gone unsaid, hugs not been given, and precious moments not experienced with a loved one because of their physical death? How many of these stolen moments were actually never stolen but rather withheld due to some argument, disagreement, or misunderstanding that let pride get in the way of a wonderful relationship? How important and serious they seemed to be while our loved one was still alive, and yet how trivial and unimportant they truly are now that the hindsight of a death has given us clearer vision.

Treat those you love with La Santa Muerte's teaching of impermanence always in the back of your thoughts. Keep the bigger picture in mind whenever an argument or spat manifests—and they *will* manifest because that is part of life. Do as much as you can with your loved ones while you still can. No one on their deathbed has ever said, "I wish I had spent more time in the office" or "I wish I had slept more and spent more time watching TV on the couch."

Nothing lasts forever. All good things and all bad things are only temporary. The time is going to pass no matter what we do or don't do. And I guarantee that you will be more regretful for the things you never did than the things you tried that just didn't work out.

Too many people never truly live their lives. They allow their dreams to slowly die within them rather than step out of their comfort zone and experience life at its fullest. With this book, you now have introductory knowledge into the mystery school of La Santa Muerte and you have the tools to manipulate the natural forces of energy to co-create miracles. You no longer have an excuse not to live the life you've always wanted. Just keep going and stay in motion. Remember, death is rigidity. Death is stagnation. Life is fluidity. Life is movement. A thing that is dead is hard, unbending, and unmoving. We see this in the withered leaves that fall to the ground, the overturned trees that refused to bend during a storm, and in the rigor mortis of a corpse. A thing that is alive is constantly growing, flexible, and always in movement. We see this in the softness of leaves still in their prime, the survival of the trees that were humble enough to bend during a storm, and the dynamic movement of our bodies in motion.

Those of us who are hard, inflexible, unbending, prideful, and unwilling to grow, learn, or change might as well already be dead. That is not life. To be truly alive is to be soft, flexible, willing to bend when necessary, humble, and always striving to grow, learn, and change. The moment we stop doing these things, we begin to die spiritually from the inside out.

Of course, death is inevitable, but as discussed before, that doesn't mean it is something to fear. For all we know, it could be more amazing and wonderful than anything we can imagine. No one can guarantee this, but no one can disprove this either. So why not focus on death being a positive experience? It seems too much of a "coincidence" that all people all around the world who briefly died on the operating table have described a similar story: a blinding, white, alluring light radiating peace. Even more "coincidental" is the fact that both the Tibetan Book of the Dead and the Egyptian Book of the Dead (two manuals of funerary rites and the afterlife) describe the same scenario, written thousands of years ago and apart from each other in very different cultures.

I will end this book with a brief story regarding death, passed down through the ages from the sages of ancient China to your hands right here and now. Before I do, I would like to welcome you to the beginning of your new magical life. You will never see the world the same way again, now that you've seen Death herself. Be confident, because you have gained a powerful friend. It's better to do so now, anyway, because we will all meet her sooner or later. *That* is the one thing I can absolutely promise you.

THE DISTANT KINGDOM

Once upon a time in ancient China, there was a youthful girl. She was one of the emperor's most beloved daughters. She lived in a beautiful palace, surrounded by beautiful gardens, talented entertainers, and lots of friends. As she grew older, she became jaded by the same flowers and entertainers, and some of her former friends were becoming too preoccupied in their own endeavors to spend time with her anymore. It was around this time that the emperor announced that he had arranged for her to be married to the prince of a faraway kingdom beyond the western borders of the empire.

The daughter was saddened by this. She spent her last weeks in the beautiful palace locked in her room. When the day came for her to leave, her handmaidens assisted in making her as beautiful as she could be for the prince. They put on her makeup, styled her hair, and dressed her in the finest silk robes.

"I don't want to go," the bride-to-be said as her handmaidens fussed about her.

"Why not?" asked the girl who was applying the makeup. "I hear he is very handsome. I'm sure you will be most pleased."

"But what if he's not?" the bride countered. "No one in the kingdom has ever seen him."

"I hear he is very rich," said the hairdresser. "I'm sure it'll be a comfortable life."

"But what if he is cruel?" the bride worried. "How can I be comfortable with a cruel man?"

"Don't worry," comforted the elderly seamstress, "for many generations your ancestors have gone to marry people in that faraway kingdom. You will not be alone there."

"But what if they are unhappy there? None of them have ever returned to tell us anything about that place."

They continued to talk, but then the moment came. The caravan was ready to take the bride away to the faraway kingdom, never to return. As she left the palace, she noticed how beautiful the gardens had suddenly become, how talented the entertainers were, and how sad she felt that she would be leaving her friends and family.

The journey was long, but it seemed to pass so quickly for the bride. When she arrived, the prince greeted her and helped her down from her sedan chair. She stood in awe of the faraway kingdom and instantly knew why none of her relatives ever returned to the empire.

Appendix

Santa Muerte Locales in the United States

Below is a list of some locales in the United States where you can find Santa Muerte temples, churches, stores, and shrines. Not all of the places on the list, however, are exclusively dedicated to La Santa Muerte. Many of them are general Latin American/Caribbean esoteric shops that happen to sell Santa Muerte paraphernalia (statues, candles, incense, etc.). Due to the exponentially growing numbers of Santa Muerte devotees in the U.S., it is becoming quite profitable for esoteric stores of all denominations and cultures to stock their shelves with Santa Muerte merchandise. So if no dedicatedly Santa Muerte stores are near you, try a local Vodou or Santería store and see if they have an item or two of the Most Holy Death.

Know that this is by no means an exhaustive list and that Santa Muerte materials can be found anywhere. In fact, while recently shopping at a secular thrift store in Bell Gardens, California, I noticed a number of black Santa Muerte candles being displayed right next to the more well-known religious candles of the Virgin Mary, Jesus, and the Catholic saints. But even if you live in the most rural of areas far from places with a concentrated population of Latinos, there is always the Internet. With a simple search online, you can easily find a digital merchant of Santa Muerte wares.

A final note on Santa Muerte–themed locales: they can be quite secretive and ephemeral. At the time of this writing, the veneration of La

Santa Muerte is still an underground mystery school, and many devotees are "on the down-low" with their faith while out in public. This is even true of many priests, priestesses, shopkeepers, and other personnel at many of these stores. Because of this, it is not uncommon for phone calls and e-mails to go unanswered, even if you speak fluent Spanish. Additionally, Santa Muerte centers of worship tend to shut down operations very frequently and relocate nearby under a different name (if at all). In fact, in the time between writing the first and last chapters of this book, three well-known locations that I wrote on my preliminary list had closed down: one in San Francisco, one in Lynwood, California (without notice), and one in Washington, D.C. So keep all this in mind when you go to any of these places and/or contact them. Remember, all things pass and nothing lasts forever.

Arizona
Yerberia La Santísima Muerte
3650 W. Camelback Rd.
Phoenix, AZ 85019
(602) 246-0281

California
Casa de Oración de La Santísima Muerte
808 S. Alvarado St.
Los Angeles, CA 90057
(213) 382-1438
casadeoracionsantamuerte@gmail.com
[Location of my encounter with the priestesses as mentioned in
    chapter 7]

Iglesia de La Santa Muerte
7848 Pacific Blvd.
Huntington Park, CA 90255
(323) 589-0648

Santuario Universal de La Santa Muerte
810 S. Alvarado St.
Los Angeles, CA 90057
(213) 382-1438 or (213) 471-9908
santuariouniversalsantamuerte@gmail.com

Templo Mayor de La Santa Muerte
7602 Pacific Blvd.
Huntington Park, CA 90255
(323) 328-3506 / (323) 583-2295
templomayorsantamuerte13@gmail.com

Templo Santa Muerte
4902 Melrose Ave.
Los Angeles, CA 90029
(323) 462-1134
www.santamuerte.org
[Location of my encounter with the "High Priest/Father" as
    mentioned in chapter 7]

Florida
Botánica Santa Barbara
16943 SW 145th Ave.
Miami, FL 33177
(305) 969-6261

Botánica Yemaya and Chango
6111 SW 8th St.
West Miami, FL 33144
(305) 267-7858

Illinois
Botánica Lucero
4644 N. Kedzie Ave.
Chicago, IL 60625
(773) 463-6840

Louisiana
The New Orleans Chapel of the Santísima Muerte
240 S. Olympia St.
New Orleans, LA 70119
www.santisimamuerteneworleans.org

Nevada
Santuario de La Santa Muerte
820 E. Sahara Ave.
Las Vegas, NV 89104
(702) 666-7752

New Mexico
Yerberia Santa Fe
1532 Cerrillos Rd.
Santa Fe, NM 87505
(505) 982-0487
www.yerberiasf.com
info@yerberiasf.com

New York
Botánica Floresteria Santa Rosa
545 W. 125th St.
New York, NY 10027
(212) 316-2181

Oregon

Botánica Brillante

600 SE 181st Ave.

Portland, OR 97233

(503) 669-2538

www.botanicabrillante.com

admin@botanicabrillante.com

Texas

Botánica La Santa Muerte

1706 NW 28th St.

Fort Worth, TX 76164

(817) 625-0668

Virginia

Botánica El Angel

5739 Hull Street Rd.

Richmond, VA 23224

(804) 276-1288

Bibliography

Allen, James P. *Middle Egyptian: An Introduction to the Language and Culture of Hieroglyphs*. New York: Cambridge University Press, 2000.

American Chemical Society. "'Gift of the Magi' Bears Anti-Cancer Agents, Researchers Suggest." ScienceDaily. http://www.sciencedaily.com/releases/2001/12/011205070038.htm (accessed May 7, 2015).

Araujo Peña, Sandra Alejandro; Barbosa Ramírez, Marisela; Galván Falcón, Susana; García Ortiz, Aurea & Uribe Ordaz, Carlos. "El culto a la Santa Muerte: un estudio descriptivo" [The cult of Santa Muerte: A descriptive study]. *Revista Psicologia*. Mexico City: Universidad de Londres. http://www.udlondres.com/revista_psicologia/articulos/stamuerte.htm.

Bayly, Susan. *Saints, Goddesses and Kings: Muslims and Christians in South Indian Society, 1700–1900*. New York: Cambridge University Press, 2004.

Bennett, Bradley C. "Doctrine of Signatures: An Explanation of Medicinal Plant Discovery or Dissemination of Knowledge?" *Economic Botany* 61, no. 3 (2007): 246–255.

Biggs, B.G. *An Encyclopaedia of New Zealand*, 1st ed., s.v. "Maori Myths and Traditions." Wellington: Government of New Zealand, 1966.

Bolaños, Claudia. "Dan 66 años de cárcel al líder de la Santa Muerte." ElUniversal.mx. http://www.eluniversal.com.mx/notas/853603.html (accessed May 7, 2015).

Booth, William. "Mexico's cult of the death saint." *Washington Post*, Dec. 5, 2009. http://www.washingtonpost.com/wp-dyn/content/article/2009/12/04/AR2009120402610.html.

Braybrook, Jean. *Rémy Belleau et l'art de guérir*. London: Versita/De Gruyter, 2013.

Charles, Dan, David Dickson, Roger Lewin, and Stephanie Pain. "On the scent of a better day at work." *New Scientist* 1758 (1991).

Chen, Yingli, Chunlan Zhou, Zhendan Ge, Yufa Liu, Yuming Liu, Weiyi Feng, Sen Li, Guoyou Chen, and Taiming Wei. "Composition and potential anticancer activities of essential oils obtained from myrrh and frankincense." National Center for Biotechnology Information. http://www.ncbi.nlm.nih.gov/pmc/articles/PMC3796379/ (accessed May 7, 2015).

Chesnut, Andrew R. *Devoted to Death: Santa Muerte, the Skeleton Saint*. New York: Oxford University Press, 2012.

Chesnut, Andrew R. "Vatican Official Denounces Santa Muerte as 'Sinister and Infernal'". *Huffington Post*, April 22, 2013, accessed May 7, 2015. http://www.huffingtonpost.com/r-andrew-chesnut/vatican-official-denounces-santa-muerte-as-sinister-and-infernal_b_3128619.html.

Cunningham, Scott. *Cunningham's Encyclopedia of Magical Herbs*. St. Paul, MN: Llewellyn, 1985.

Dallapiccola, Anna. *Dictionary of Hindu Lore and Legend*. New York: Thames & Hudson, 2002.

de Dreuille, Mayeul. *From East to West: A History of Monasticism*. Leominster, UK: Gracewing Publishing, 1998.

Deary, Susan. "The History and Tradition of 'Day of the Dead.'" Gomanzanillo. http://www.gomanzanillo.com/features/Day of the Dead/ (accessed May 7, 2015).

Didier, Boremanse. *Contes et mythologie des indiens lacandons: contribution à l'étude de la tradition orale maya*. Paris: L'Harmattan, 1986.

diGregorio, Sophia. *Grimoire of Santa Muerte: Spells and Rituals of Most Holy Death, the Unofficial Saint of Mexico*. n.p.: Winter Tempest Books, 2013.

Doughty, Caitlin. *Smoke Gets in Your Eyes and Other Lessons from the Crematory*. New York: W. W. Norton & Company, 2014.

Espinosa, Victor Adrian. "Santa Muerte: Doña Queta, guardiana del altar en Tepito." *El Universal DF*, July 13, 2011. http://www.eluniversaldf .mx/cuauhtemoc/nota29968.html.

Farmer, Steven D. *Earth Magic: Ancient Shamanic Wisdom for Healing Yourself, Others, and the Planet*. Carlsbad, CA: Hay House, 2009.

Fernández, Adela. *Dioses Prehispánicos de México*. Mexico City: Panorama Editorial, 2012.

Fleming, Fergus, and Alan Lothain. *The Way to Eternity: Egyptian Myth*. Amsterdam: Duncan Baird, 1997.

Foley, Helene P. *The Homeric "Hymn to Demeter."* Princeton, NJ: Princeton University Press, 1994.

Foster, Steven, and Rebecca L. Johnson. *Desk Reference to Nature's Medicine*. Washington, DC: National Geographic Society, 2006.

Freese, Kevin. "'The Death Cult of the Drug Lords Mexico's Patron Saint of Crime, Criminals, and the Dispossessed." Foreign Military Studies Office, September 2005. http://fmso.leavenworth.army.mil/ documents/Santa-Muerte/santa-muerte.htm.

Gazzani, Gabriella, Maria Daglia, and Adele Papetti. "Food components with anticaries activity." *Current Opinion in Biotechnology* 23, no. 2. (2012): 153–159. http://www.sciencedirect.com/science/article/ pii/S0958166911006781 (accessed May 7, 2015).

Gil Olmos, José. *La santa muerte: La virgen de los olvidados*. Mexico City: Penguin Random House Grupo Editorial México, 2012.

Gray, Steven. "Santa Muerte: The New God in Town." *Time*. Oct. 16, 2007, accessed May 7, 2015. http://content.time.com/time/nation/ article/0,8599,1671984,00.html).

Guillermoprieto, Alma. "Mexican Saints." *National Geographic*, May 2010. http://ngm.nationalgeographic.com/2010/05/mexico-saints/guillermoprieto-text/1.

Harder, Ben. *The Free Library*, s.v. "Evolving in their graves: early burials hold clues to human origins." *Science News*, 2001. http://www.thefreelibrary.com/Evolving+in+their+graves%3a+early+burials+hold+clues+to+human+origins.-a081827792 (accessed May 7, 2015).

Harrison, Regina. *Signs, Songs, and Memory in the Andes: Translating Quechua Language and Culture*. Austin: University of Texas Press, 1989.

Hay, Louise L. *You Can Heal Your Life*. Carlsbad, CA: Hay House, Inc., 1984.

Hough, Walter. *Censers and Incense of Mexico and Central America*. Washington, DC: Smithsonian Institution Press, 1912.

Huddleston, Nigel F. "Brain Wave States and How to Access Them." Synthesis Learning. http://www.synthesislearning.com (accessed May 7, 2015).

Johnston, Sarah Iles. *Ancient Religions*. Cambridge, MA: Belknap Press/Harvard University Press, 2007.

Jones, Mark David, and J. Jeff Kober. *Lead with Your Customer: Transform Culture and Brand into World-Class Excellence*. Alexandria, VA: American Society for Training and Development, 2010.

Kannappan, Ramaswamy, Subash Chandra Gupta, Ji Hye Kim, Simone Reuter, and Bharat Bushan Aggarwal. "Neuroprotection by Spice-Derived Nutraceuticals: You Are What You Eat!" *Molecular Neurobiology* 44, no. 2. (2011) 142–159. http://www.ncbi.nlm.nih.gov/pmc/articles/PMC3183139/pdf/nihms307525.pdf (accessed May 7, 2015).

Kojiki. *Crónicas de antiguos hechos de Japón*, 2nd ed. Trans. by Carlos Rubio and Rumi Tami Moratalla. Madrid: Trattora Editorial, 2012.

Kunz, George Frederick. *Magic of Jewels and Charms*. Philadelphia: Lippincott Company, 1915.

Kurz, Josh. "Getting to the Root of the Great Cilantro Divide." National Public Radio. http://www.npr.org/templates/story/story.php?storyId=98695984 (accessed May 7, 2015).

Langenheim, J. *Plant Resins: Chemistry, Evolution, Ecology, and Ethnobotany.* Portland, OR: Timber Press, 2003.

Lieberman, Philip. *Uniquely Human.* Cambridge, MA: Harvard University Press, 1991.

Lin, Derek. *Tao Te Ching: Annotated and Explained.* Woodstock, VT: SkyLight Paths, 2006.

———. *The Tao of Daily Life: The Mysteries of the Orient Revealed, The Joys of Inner Harmony Found, The Path to Enlightenment Illuminated.* New York: Tarcher/Penguin, 2007.

———. *The Tao of Success: The Five Ancient Rings of Destiny.* New York: Tarcher/Penguin, 2010.

Mab y Farwolaeth. "La Santisima Muerte: A Practitioner's Overview." The Witches' Voice. Oct. 16, 2007, accessed May 7, 2015. http://www.witchvox.com/va/dt_va.html?a=usla&c=words&id=15198.

May, Clifford D. "How Coca-Cola Obtains Its Coca." *New York Times,* July 1, 1988.

Mercier, Patricia. *The Chakra Bible.* London: Octopus Publishing Group, Ltd., 2007.

Morrow, John Andrew. *Encyclopedia of Islamic Herbal Medicine.* Jefferson, NC: McFarland, 2011.

Mowrey, Dave B. *Herbal Tonic Therapies.* Chicago: Keats Publishing, 1998.

Nicholson, Henry B. *Handbook of Middle American Indians.* Austin: University of Texas Press, 1971.

Nilsson, Martin P. *Greek Popular Religion.* New York: Columbia University Press, 1947.

Noe, Rain. "Lignum Vitae: Wood So Bad-Ass, It's Used to Make Shaft Bearings for Nuclear Submarines (and More)." Core77. http://

www.core77.com/blog/materials/lignum_vitae_wood_so_bad-ass_its_used_to_make_shaft_bearings_for_nuclear_submarines_and_more_25224.asp. (accessed May 7, 2015).

Oliver, N. *A History of Ancient Britain.* London: Phoenix/Orion Publishing Group, Ltd., 2012.

Osborn, Marijane. *Romancing the Goddess: Three Middle English Romances about Women.* Champaign: University of Illinois Press, 1998.

Palmer, Sharon. "Coffee Buzz – Trends and Possible Perks of America's Beloved Beverage." *Today's Dietitian* 11, no. 5 (2009): 26. http://www.todaysdietitian.com/newarchives/050409p26.shtml (accessed May 7, 2015).

Pardo, Gastón. "El culto mexicano de la Santa Muerte gana espacio en la Mara Salvatrucha." VoltaireNet, Aug. 12, 2005. http://www.voltairenet.org/article125582.html.

Pausanias. *Description de la Grèce.* Trans. by M. Clavier. Paris: Société Royale Académique des Sciences, 1821.

Penczak, Christopher. *Gay Witchcraft: Empowering the Tribe.* San Francisco: Red Wheel/Weiser, 2003.

———. *Instant Magick: Ancient Wisdom, Modern Spellcraft.* Woodbury, MN: Llewellyn, 2006.

———. *The Outer Temple of Witchcraft: Circles, Spells, and Rituals.* St. Paul, MN: Llewellyn, 2004.

———. *The Plant Spirit Familiar: Green Totems, Teachers, and Healers on the Path of the Witch.* Salem, NH: Copper Cauldron, 2011.

———. *Spirit Allies: Meet Your Team from the Other Side.* Boston: Weiser, 2002.

———. *The Witch's Coin: Prosperity and Money Magick.* Woodbury, MN: Llewellyn, 2009.

———. *The Witch's Heart: The Magick of Perfect Love and Perfect Trust.* Woodbury, MN: Llewellyn, 2011.

———. *The Witch's Shield: Protection Magick and Psychic Self-Defense.* Woodbury, MN: Llewellyn, 2004.

Powis, Terry G., W. Jeffrey Hurst, María del Carmen Rodríguez, Ortíz C. Ponciano, Michael Blake, David Cheetham, Michael D. Coe, and John G. Hodgson. "Oldest chocolate in the New World." *Antiquity* 81, no. 314 (2007). http://www.antiquity.ac.uk/projgall/powis/ (accessed May 7, 2015).

Prescott, William H. *History of the Conquest of Mexico and the Conquest of Peru.* New York: The Modern Library, 1948.

Proceso. "Dan 66 años de cárcel a líder de la Iglesia de la Santa Muerte." June 14, 2012. http://www.proceso.com.mx/?p=310895.

Randall, C., H. Randall, F. Dobbs, C. Hutton, and H. Sanders. "Randomized controlled trial of nettle sting for treatment of base-of-thumb pain." *Journal of the Royal Society of Medicine* 93, no. 6 (2000): 305–309. http://jrs.sagepub.com/content/93/6/305.full.pdf (accessed May 7, 2015).

Rapp, George Robert. *Archaeomineralogy.* New York: Springer, 2002.

Reader, Ian. *Simple Guides: Shinto.* London: Kuperard, 2008.

Riddle, John. *Contraception and Abortion from the Ancient World to the Renaissance.* Cambridge, MA: Harvard University Press, 1994.

Rudgley, Richard. *Lost Civilizations of the Stone Age.* New York: Free Press, 2000.

Sahagún, Bernardino de, and Carlos María de Bustamante. *Historia General de las Cosas de Nueva España.* Madrid: Alianza Editorial, 1988.

Schütz, Katrin, Reinhold Carle, and Andreas Schieber. "Taraxacum—A review on its phytochemical and pharmacological profile." *Journal of Ethnopharmacology* 107, no. 3 (2006): 313–472.

Shepherd, Rowen, and Rupert Shepherd. *1000 Symbols: What Shapes Mean in Art and Myth.* London: Thames & Hudson, 2002.

El Siglo de Torreón. "Modifican imagen de la Santa Muerte." Aug. 16, 2007. http://www.elsiglodetorreon.com.mx/noticia/291964.modifican-imagen-de-la-santa-muerte.html.

Smith, Henry G. *Gems and Precious Stones: With Descriptions of their Distinctive Properties; the Methods for Determining Them.* Sydney: Charles Potter Government Printer, 1896.

Spranz, Bodo. *Los Dioses en los Códices Mexicanos del Grupo Borgia: Una Investigación Iconográfica.* Mexico City: Fondo de Cultura Económica, 2006.

Sturlson, Snorri. *The Prose Edda.* Trans. Jesse Byock. New York: Penguin Books, 2006.

Tels de Jong, and Leontine Louise. *Sur quelques divinités romaines de la naissance et de la prophétie.* Amsterdam: A. M. Hakkert, 1960.

Tuckman, Jo. "Mexican 'Saint Death' cult members protest at destruction of shrines." *The Guardian,* April 10, 2009. http://www.theguardian.com/world/2009/apr/10/santa-muerte-cult-mexico.

Van Tuerenhout, Dirk R. *The Aztecs: New Perspectives (Understanding Ancient Civilizations).* Santa Barbara, CA: ABC-CLIO, 2005.

Velazquez, Oriana. *El libro de la Santa Muerte.* Mexico City: Editores Mexicanos Unidos, S.A., 2005.

Walters, B. Dave. *49 Secrets Of Peace, Love, and Money.* Seattle: CreateSpace Independent Publishing Platform, 2009.

Ward, Deborah. "Patchouli Uses." Nature's Garden. http://www.naturesgardencandles.com/blog/patchouli-uses/ (accessed May 7, 2015).

Wheeler, Brannon M., *Historical Dictionary of Prophets in Islam and Judaism.* Lanham, MD: Scarecrow Press, 2002.

Online Webpage Sources

40 Hadith Nawawi. http://40hadithnawawi.com

Bible Gateway. https://www.biblegateway.com/

BuddhaNet. http://www.buddhanet.net/

Central New Hampshire Wicca Page. http://www.nhwicca.org/Fingle/stone.html

Chinese Text Project. http://ctext.org

Couleur Nature. http://blog.couleurnature.com

Essential Apothecary. http://www.essentialapothecary.com/

Good Reads. http://www.goodreads.com

The Human Club. http://www.humanclub.org/golden_rule.htm

Internet Sacred Text Archive. http://www.sacred-texts.com/

Lady Winter Wolf's Haven. http://ladywinterwolf.fcpages.com/ haven.html

The Magickal Cat. http://www.themagickalcat.com

Most Holy Death. http://skeletonsaint.com/

National Center for Complementary and Integrative Health. https:// nccih.nih.gov/

Nothingistic. http://nothingistic.org/

Online Etymology Dictionary. http://www.etymonline.com

The Order of the Good Death. http://www.orderofthegooddeath .com/

Pagan Power. http://www.paganpower.com/

Rob's Magick Blog. https://robjo.wordpress.com/2010/03/22/. 16-common-incenses-and-their-uses/

Santuario Jardín de San La Muerte. http://www.sanlamuerte.net/

Soul Service Tumblr. http://soul-service.tumblr.com/ post/27568135062/santa-muerte-santa-muerte-is-a-sacred-figure

Theoi Greek Mythology. http://www.theoi.com/

University of Michigan-Dearborn Native American Ethnobotany. http://herb.umd.umich.edu

Wicca Spirituality. http://www.wicca-spirituality.com/

World Scripture: A Comparative Anthology of Sacred Texts. http:// www.unification.net/ws/theme015.htm

Index

To Write to the Author

If you wish to contact the author or would like more information about this book, please write to the author in care of Llewellyn Worldwide Ltd. and we will forward your request. Both the author and publisher appreciate hearing from you and learning of your enjoyment of this book and how it has helped you. Llewellyn Worldwide Ltd. cannot guarantee that every letter written to the author can be answered, but all will be forwarded. Please write to:

Tomás Prower
℅ Llewellyn Worldwide
2143 Wooddale Drive
Woodbury, MN 55125-2989

Please enclose a self-addressed stamped envelope for reply,
or $1.00 to cover costs. If outside the U.S.A., enclose
an international postal reply coupon.

Many of Llewellyn's authors have websites with additional information and resources. For more information, please visit our website at http://www.llewellyn.com.